Short Dictionary of BIBLE PERSONAL NAMES

Short Dictionary of
BIBLE
PERSONAL NAMES

H. H. Rowley

BASIC BOOKS, Inc., Publishers

New York

50971

PREFACE

This short dictionary aims to include every personal name mentioned in the Bible and to indicate as briefly as possible the biblical information about the bearer. The scope of the dictionary makes it impossible to give all the extra-biblical information about many of the persons named, or to enter into critical discussion of the significance of some of the biblical statements. All names are given in the form they have in RSV and the cross-references in bold type will enable the reader to supplement the information from other entries. It is hoped that the user of the dictionary will be enabled speedily to distinguish between the various persons who bore the same name and to trace the sometimes bewildering variety of names borne by the same person.

H. H. ROWLEY

ABBREVIATIONS

ASV	American Standard Version
AV	Authorized Version
EVV	English Versions
LXX	Septuagint (Greek) Version
NT	New Testament
OT	Old Testament
RSV	Revised Standard Version
RV	Revised Version
Vulg.	Vulgate (Latin) Version

Books of the Bible

OLD TESTAMENT

Gen.	Jg.	1 Chr.	Ps.	Lam.	Ob.	Hag.
Exod.	Ru.	2 Chr.	Prov.	Ezek.	Jon.	Zech.
Lev.	1 Sam.	Ezr.	Ec.	Dan.	Mic.	Mal.
Num.	2 Sam.	Neh.	Ca.	Hos.	Nah.	
Dt.	1 Kg.	Est.	Isa.	Jl	Hab.	
Jos.	2 Kg.	Job	Jer.	Am.	Zeph.	

APOCRYPHA

1 Esd.	Tob.	Ad. Est.	Sir.	S 3 Ch.	Bel	1 Mac.
2 Esd.	Jdt.	Wis.	Bar.	Sus.	Man.	2 Mac.
			Ep. Jer.			

NEW TESTAMENT

Mt.	Ac.	Gal.	1 Th.	Tit.	1 Pet.	3 Jn
Mk	Rom.	Eph.	2 Th.	Phm.	2 Pet.	Jude
Lk.	1 C.	Phil.	1 Tim.	Heb.	1 Jn	Rev.
Jn	2 C.	Col.	2 Tim.	Jas	2 Jn	

Short Dictionary of BIBLE PERSONAL NAMES

A

AARON: Brother of **Moses** (Exod. 6:20). He accompanied Moses when he went to Pharaoh (Exod. 5:1). In the battle against the Amalekites he and **Hur** (1) held up Moses' hands (Exod. 17:12), and he went up to Mt Sinai with Moses (Exod. 19:24), but later, while Moses was up the mountain, he made the Golden Calf (Exod. 32:4). Despite this, he and his sons were chosen to be priests (Exod. 28:1). He and his sister **Miriam** (1) complained of Moses' marriage to a Cushite woman (Num. 12:1), and later the people murmured against him and Moses (Num. 14:2, 16:41), but he was vindicated by God making his rod to sprout (Num. 17:8). His rod was preserved 'before the testimony' (Num. 17:10), and in the NT it is said to have been placed in the Ark (Heb. 9:4). He stopped a plague by offering incense (Num. 16:46ff.), but at Meribah he sinned by unbelief (Num. 20:12), and in consequence was debarred from entering the Promised Land (Num. 20:12). He died at Mt Hor (Num. 20:28), near Moserah (Dt. 10:6). **Elizabeth**, the mother of **John** (6) the Baptist, was descended from him (Lk. 1:5).

ABADDON: The angel of the bottomless pit (Rev. 9:11).

ABAGTHA: One of the seven eunuchs of **Ahasuerus** (1) (Est. 1:10).

ABDA: 1. Father of **Adoniram** (1 Kg. 4:6).
  2. A Levite of post-exilic days (Neh. 11:17); called **Obadiah** (5) in 1 Chr. 9:16.

ABDEEL: Father of **Shelemiah** (7) (Jer. 36:26).

ABDI: 1. Grandfather of **Ethan** (3) (1 Chr. 6:44).
  2. A Merarite Levite, father of **Kish** (4) (2 Chr. 29:12).
  3. One who married a foreign wife (Ezr. 10:26; 1 Esd. 9:27).

ABDIEL: Father of **Ahi** (1 Chr. 5:15).

ABDON: 1. A minor Judge, from Pirathon (Jg. 12:13ff.).
  2. A Benjaminite (1 Chr. 8:23).
  3. A Gibeonite (1 Chr. 8:30, 9:36).
  4. Son of **Micah** (5) and an officer of **Josiah** (1), sent to **Huldah** (2 Chr. 34:20); called **Achbor** (2) in 2 Kg. 22:12.

ABEDNEGO: One of the companions of **Daniel** (5) (Dan. 1:7). His Hebrew name was **Azariah** (25) (Dan. 1:6f., 11, 19). He was cast into the fire for refusing to worship the image of **Nebuchadnezzar** (Dan. 3:20ff.), and uttered a prayer (S 3 Ch. 2ff.) and praised God (S 3 Ch. 28ff.).

1

ABEL: Son of **Adam** (Gen. 4:2). He offered acceptable sacrifice to God (Gen. 4:4) and was murdered by **Cain** (Gen. 4:8). He is mentioned in the NT as the first martyr (Mt. 23:35; Lk. 11:51) and as a hero of faith (Heb. 11:4).

ABI: The mother of **Hezekiah** (1) (2 Kg. 18:2); called **Abijah** (8) in 2 Chr. 29:1.

ABIALBON: One of **David's** heroes (2 Sam. 23:31); called **Abiel** (2) in 1 Chr. 11:32.

ABIASAPH: A descendant of **Korah** (2) (Exod. 6:24); called **Ebiasaph** in 1 Chr. 6:23.

ABIATHAR: Son of **Ahimelech** (1) (1 Sam. 22:20) and descendant of Eli (1 Sam. 14:3). He escaped from Nob when the priests there were slain (1 Sam. 22:20), and was with **David** when **Saul** (1) pursued him (1 Sam. 30:7). When David reigned in Jerusalem he was priest there alongside **Zadok** (1) (2 Sam. 20:25), and when **Absalom** (1) rebelled he was loyal to David (2 Sam. 17:15ff.); but he mistakenly favoured **Adonijah** (1) (1 Kg. 1:7), and was consequently dismissed by **Solomon** (1 Kg. 2:26). In Mk 2:26 Abiathar is a mistake for Ahimelech (cf. 1 Sam. 21:20). He is called the father of Ahimelech instead of the son in 2 Sam. 8:17; 1 Chr. 18:16, 24:6.

ABIDA: Grandson of **Abraham** through **Keturah** (Gen. 25:4; 1 Chr. 1:33).

ABIDAN: Representative of Benjamin at the census in the wilderness (Num. 1:11) and on other occasions (Num. 2:22, 7:60, 65, 10:24).

ABIEL: 1. Grandfather of **Saul** (1) and father of **Kish** (1) (1 Sam. 9:1). In 1 Chr. 8:33, 9:39 the father of Kish is called **Ner**, while in 1 Sam. 14:51 Ner is said to be the son of Abiel.
    2. One of David's heroes (1 Chr. 11:32); called **Abialbon** in 2 Sam. 23:31.

ABIEZER: 1. A Manassite (Jos. 17:2), son of **Hammolecheth,** the sister of **Machir** (1) (1 Chr. 7:18); called **Iezer** in Num. 26:30. **Gideon** belonged to the clan of the Abiezrites, which dwelt at Ophrah (Jg. 6:11).
    2. One of David's heroes (2 Sam. 23:27; 1 Chr. 27:12).

ABIGAIL: 1. Wife of **Nabal** (1 Sam. 25:3). She averted **David's** revenge on her husband (1 Sam. 25:23ff.), and after Nabal's death married David (1 Sam. 25:39ff.). She was the mother of **Chileab** (2 Sam. 3:3).
    2. Mother of **Amasa** (1) and sister of **Zeruiah** (1 Chr. 2:16f.); called **Abigal** in 2 Sam. 17:25.

ABIGAL: *See* Abigail (2).

ABIHAIL: 1. A Levite, father of **Zuriel** (Num. 3:35).
    2. Wife of **Abishur,** a Jerahmeelite (1 Chr. 2:29).
    3. A Gadite, son of **Huri** (1 Chr. 5:14).

4. Daughter of David's brother, Eliab (3), and mother of Rehoboam's wife, Mahalath (2) (2 Chr. 11:18).

5. Uncle of Mordecai (2) and father of Esther (Est. 2:15, 9:29).

ABIHU: Son of Aaron (Exod. 6:23; 1 Chr. 6:3). He accompanied Moses and Aaron to the sacred mountain (Exod. 24:1, 9) and became a priest (Exod. 28:1), but offered unholy fire and was consumed by divine fire (Lev. 10:1f.; Num. 3:4, 26:61).

ABIHUD: Son of Bela (2), a Benjaminite (1 Chr. 8:3).

ABIJAH: 1. Son of Rehoboam (1 Chr. 3:10; 2 Chr. 11:20, 12:16). He succeeded his father and reigned for three years. He is called Abijam in 1 Kg. 14:31. He defeated Jeroboam (1) in battle (1 Chr. 13:2ff.).

2. Son of Samuel (1 Sam. 8:2).

3. Son of Jeroboam (1). He died while still a child (1 Kg. 14:1, 17).

4. A Benjaminite (1 Chr. 7:8).

5. A priest who gave his name to the eighth of the priestly courses (1 Chr. 24:10), to which Zechariah (34) belonged (Lk. 1:5).

6. A priest who sealed the covenant (Neh. 10:7).

7. A priest who returned with Zerubbabel (Neh. 12:4, 17).

8. Mother of Hezekiah (1) (1 Chr. 29:1); called Abi in 2 Kg. 18:2.

ABIJAM: *See* Abijah (1).

ABIMAEL: Son of Joktan (Gen. 10:28; 1 Chr. 1:22).

ABIMELECH: 1. King of Gerar (Gen. 20:2), who was warned in a dream that Sarah (1) was Abraham's wife (Gen. 20:3), and who made a covenant with Abraham (Gen. 21:22ff.). In Gen. 26:1ff. we read that Abimelech was saved from taking Rebekah into his harem.

2. Son of Gideon who made himself king at Shechem (Jg. 8:31, 9:1ff.), and who lost his life when attacking Thebez (Jg. 9:50ff.; 2 Sam. 11:21).

3. In Ps. 34 Heading Abimelech is for Achish (1) (cf. 1 Sam. 21:13).

ABINADAB: 1. A man of Kiriath-jearim, into whose house the Ark was taken (1 Sam. 7:1f.). It stayed there until it was brought to Jerusalem (2 Sam. 6:1ff.).

2. Son of Jesse (1 Sam. 16:8, 17:13).

3. Son of Saul (1) (1 Sam. 31:2).

ABINOAM: Father of Barak (Jg. 4:6, 12, 5:1, 12).

ABIRAM: 1. Son of Eliab (2). He conspired against Moses with Dathan (Num. 16:1, 26:9; Dt. 11:6), and was swallowed up (Num. 16:31; Ps. 106:17).

2. Son of Hiel. He lost his life when Jericho was rebuilt (1 Kg. 16:34).

ABISHAG: A Shunammite woman who nursed David when he was old (1 Kg. 1:3f., 15), and whose hand was sought by Adonijah (1) (1 Kg. 2:17ff.).

ABISHAI: Brother of Joab (1) and son of Zeruiah (1 Sam. 26:6). He saved

3

David's life (2 Sam. 21:17), and also slew three hundred foes (2 Sam. 23:18). He wanted David to kill **Saul** (1) (1 Sam. 26:8), and asked to be allowed to kill **Shimei** (2) (2 Sam. 16:9ff., 19:21). He conquered Edom (1 Chr. 18:12f.; cf. 2 Sam. 8:13f.) and commanded part of the army against the Ammonites (2 Sam. 10:10) and against **Absalom** (1) (2 Sam. 18:2) and **Sheba** (1) (2 Sam. 20:6ff.). He supported Joab in slaying Abner (2 Sam. 3:30).

ABISHALOM: Form of the name Absalom (1) found in 1 Kg. 15:2, 10.

ABISHUA: 1. A priest, son of **Phinehas** (1) and father of **Bukki** (2) (1 Chr. 6:4f.; Ezr. 7:4f.).
    2. A Benjaminite, son of **Bela** (2) (1 Chr. 8:4).

ABISHUR: Son of **Shammai** (1), a Jerahmeelite (1 Chr. 2:28).

ABITAL: Wife of **David** (2 Sam. 3:4; 1 Chr. 3:3).

ABITUB: A Benjaminite, son of **Shaharaim** by **Hushim** (3) (1 Chr. 8:11).

ABIUD: An ancestor of **Jesus** (1) (Mt. 1:13).

ABNER: Son of **Ner** (1 Sam. 14:50) and cousin of **Saul** (1) (1 Sam. 14:50). He was commander of Saul's army (1 Sam. 17:55, 26:5) and later of **Ishbosheth's** (2 Sam. 2:8ff.). He killed **Asahel** (1), the brother of **Joab** (1), in battle (2 Sam. 2:23), and was murdered by Joab in revenge (2 Sam. 3:30). In the meantime he had taken Saul's concubine, **Rizpah** (2 Sam. 3:7ff.), and incurred the anger of Ishbosheth. David attended Abner's funeral and composed an elegy over him (2 Sam. 3:31ff.).

ABRAHAM: The son of **Terah** and at first called **Abram** (Gen. 11:26). He was born in Ur (Gen. 11:28) and migrated with his father to Haran (Gen. 11:31). With Lot he left Haran (Gen. 12:3f.) for Canaan, at the call of God (Gen. 12:1ff.). He journeyed to Shechem (Gen. 12:6), to Egypt (Gen. 12:10), to Bethel (Gen. 13:3ff.), to Hebron (Gen. 13:18), to Gerar (Gen. 20:1), and to Beersheba (Gen. 21:33, 22:19). His name was changed to Abraham at the time of God's covenant with him (Gen. 17:4). He was the father of **Isaac** by **Sarah** (1) (Gen. 21:2f.), of **Ishmael** (1) by **Hagar** (Gen. 16:15), and of six sons by **Keturah** (Gen. 25:1ff.). He pursued and defeated the four kings and rescued Lot (Gen. 14) and gave tithes to **Melchizedek** (Gen. 14:20; Heb. 7:4). He interceded for Sodom (Gen. 18:22ff.) and was ready to sacrifice Isaac in the land of Moriah (Gen. 22). He passed Sarah off as his sister in Egypt (Gen. 12:11ff.) and in Gerar (Gen. 20:1ff.). He expelled Hagar and her son (Gen. 21:14) and sent his servant to Mesopotamia to find a wife for Isaac (Gen. 24). He is called the friend of God (Isa. 41:8) and is named among the heroes of faith (Heb. 11:8, 17).

ABRAM: *See* Abraham.

ABSALOM: 1. Son of **David** by **Maacah** (2) (2 Sam. 3:3). He caused his half-brother **Amnon** (1) to be murdered (2 Sam. 13:29) because he had raped **Tamar** (2) (2 Sam. 13:1ff.), and fled to Geshur (2 Sam. 13:37). When he returned (2 Sam. 14:23) he fomented disaffection against David (2 Sam. 15:1ff.) and finally rebelled at Hebron (2 Sam. 15:10). His army was defeated (2 Sam. 18:1ff.) and he was slain by **Joab** (1) (2 Sam. 18:4). He is called Abishalom in 1 Kg. 15:2, 10.

2. Father of **Mattathias** (2) (1 Mac. 11:70), and perhaps also of **Jonathan** (16) (1 Mac. 13:11).

3. An envoy (2 Mac. 11:17); perhaps the same as 2.

ABUBUS: Father of **Ptolemy** (9) (1 Mac. 16:16).

ACCOS: Grandfather of **Eupolemus** (1 Mac. 8:17). The Hebrew form of his name is Hakkoz.

ACHAICUS: A Corinthian Christian with **Paul** (1 C. 16:16) in Ephesus (1 C. 16:8).

ACHAN: A Judahite, son of **Carmi** (2) (Jos. 7:1), who kept some of the spoil of Jericho, and who paid the price with his life (Jos. 7:25); called **Achar** in 1 Chr. 2:7.

ACHAR: *See* Achan.

ACHBOR: 1. An Edomite, father of **Baalhanan** (1) (Gen. 36:38; 1 Chr. 1:49).

2. Son of Micaiah (2) and an officer under **Josiah** (1) (2 Kg. 22:12). He was the father of Elnathan (2) (Jer. 26:22). He is called **Abdon** (4), the son of Micah (5), in 2 Chr. 34:20.

ACHIM: An ancestor of **Jesus** (1) (Mt. 1:14).

ACHIOR: An Ammonite leader (Jdt. 5:5), who became a Jewish proselyte (Jdt. 14:10).

ACHISH: 1. King of Gath, to whom **David** fled (1 Sam. 21:10, 27:2). He put David in charge of Ziklag (1 Sam. 27:6). He took David and his men to Aphek to attack **Saul** (1) (1 Sam. 29:2), but the other Philistine leaders insisted on his being sent back (1 Sam. 29:4ff.). In Ps. 34 Heading he is called Abimelech (3) in error (cf. 1 Sam. 21:13).

2. King of Gath to whom the slaves of **Shimei** (2) fled (1 Kg. 2:39f.). He may be the same as 1, or his grandson.

ACHSAH: Daughter of **Caleb**, whose hand was promised to the captor of Kiriath-sepher, and who was accordingly given to **Othniel** (Jos. 15:16f.; Jg. 1:12f.). At Othniel's suggestion she asked Caleb to give her springs of water.

ADAH: 1. One of the wives of **Lamech** (1) (Gen. 4:19f.).

2. One of the wives of Esau (Gen. 36:2); called **Basemath** (1) in Gen. 26:34. She was the daughter of Elon (1), a Hittite.

ADAIAH: 1. Grandfather of **Josiah** (1) (2 Kg. 22:1).

2. A Levite (1 Chr. 6:41); called **Iddo** (2) in 1 Chr. 6:21.

5

3. A Benjaminite, son of **Shimei** (10) (1 Chr. 8:21).
4. A priest, son of **Jeroham** (4) (1 Chr. 9:12).
5. Father of **Maaseiah** (2) (2 Chr. 23:1).
6. One who married a foreign wife (Ezr. 10:29).
7. Another who married a foreign wife (Ezr. 10:39).
8. A Judahite (Neh. 11:5).
9. A priest (Neh. 11:12), perhaps to be identified with 4.

ADALIA: Son of **Haman**, slain by the Jews (Est. 9:8).

ADAM: The first man (Gen. 3:17), who was placed in the Garden of Eden (Gen. 2:8), but who disobeyed God (Gen. 2:17, 3:6) and was sent away from the Garden (Gen. 3:23). He was the father of **Cain** and Abel (Gen. 4:1f.) and of **Seth** (Gen. 4:25). His life is given as 930 years (Gen. 5:5).

ADBEEL: Son of **Ishmael** (1) (Gen. 25:13; 1 Chr. 1:29).

ADDAR: Grandson of **Benjamin** (1) (1 Chr. 8:3); called **Ard** in Gen. 46:21; Num. 26:40.

ADDI: 1. Ancestor of some who married foreign wives (1 Esd. 9:31).
2. An ancestor of **Jesus** (1) (Lk. 3:28).

ADDUS: Ancestor of some who returned with **Zerubbabel** (1 Esd. 5:34).

ADIEL: 1. A Simeonite (1 Chr. 4:36).
2. A priest (1 Chr. 9:12).
3. Father of David's treasurer, **Azmaveth** (3) (1 Chr. 27:25).

ADIN: 1. Ancestor of some who returned with **Zerubbabel** (Ezr. 2:15; Neh. 7:20; 1 Esd. 5:14) and with **Ezra** (1) (Ezr. 8:6; 1 Esd. 8:32).
2. One who sealed the covenant (Neh. 10:16).

ADINA: A Reubenite military leader in David's time (1 Chr. 11:42).

ADLAI: Father of **Shaphat** (5) (1 Chr. 27:29).

ADMATHA: One of the seven princes of **Ahasuerus** (1) (Est. 1:14).

ADMIN: An ancestor of **Jesus** (1) (Lk. 3:33).

ADNA: 1. One who married a foreign wife (Ezr. 10:30); perhaps the same as **Naathus** in 1 Esd. 9:31.
2. A priestly head (Neh. 12:15).

ADNAH: 1. A Manassite who deserted from **Saul** (1) to **David** (1 Chr. 12:20).
2. An officer of **Jehoshaphat** (4) (2 Chr. 17:14).

ADONI-BEZEK: King of Bezek, defeated and captured by the Simeonites and Judahites, who mutilated him (Jg. 1:5ff.).

ADONIJAH: 1. David's fourth son (2 Sam. 3:4), who was probably the oldest surviving son at the time of David's death. When David was failing (1 Kg. 1:1ff.), Adonijah counted too openly on the succession, with the support of **Abiathar** and **Joab** (1) (1 Kg. 1:5ff.). He was opposed by **Nathan** (2) and **Bathsheba**, who persuaded David to elevate **Solomon** to the throne before he died (1 Kg. 1:11ff.). Adonijah fled for sanctuary to the altar (1 Kg. 1:50) until Solomon promised not to harm him (1 Kg. 1:52). When Adonijah aspired to marry **Abishag**, Solomon interpreted this as a new bid for the throne (1 Kg. 2:13ff.) and promptly had him killed (1 Kg. 2:25).

2. A Levite in the time of **Jehoshaphat** (4) (2 Chr. 17:8).

3. One who sealed the covenant (Neh. 10:16).

ADONIKAM: Ancestor of some who returned with **Zerubbabel** (Ezr. 2:13; Neh. 7:18; 1 Esd. 5:14) and with **Ezra** (1) (Ezr. 8:13; 1 Esd. 8:39).

ADONIRAM: An official of Solomon's in charge of forced labour (1 Kg. 4:6, 5:14); called **Adoram** in 2 Sam. 20:24; 1 Kg. 12:18, and **Hadoram** (3) in 2 Chr. 10:18. Rehoboam sent him to quell the rebellion of the northern tribes, but he was stoned to death (1 Kg. 12:18; 2 Chr. 10:18).

ADONIZEDEK: King of Jerusalem in the time of **Joshua** (1) (Jos. 10:1). He headed a coalition against the Gibeonites, which Joshua defeated (Jos. 10:3ff.). Adonizedek was captured and killed (Jos. 10:26).

ADORAM: *See* **Adoniram**.

ADRAMMELECH: 1. A god of Sepharvaim (2 Kg. 17:31).

2. A son of **Sennacherib** who with his brother murdered their father (2 Kg. 19:17; Isa. 37:38).

ADRIEL: A Meholathite who married **Merab** (1 Sam. 18:19; 2 Sam. 21:8).

ADUEL: An ancestor of **Tobit** (Tob. 1:1).

AENEAS: A paralytic at Lydda, healed by **Peter** (Ac. 9:33f.).

AGABUS: A Jerusalem prophet who foretold a famine (Ac. 11:27), and who predicted **Paul's** imprisonment (Ac. 21:10f.).

AGAG: An Amalekite king, captured by **Saul** (1) (1 Sam. 15:8) and slain by **Samuel** (1 Sam. 15:33). The reference to the name in Num. 24:7 is obscure.

AGEE: Father of **Shammah** (3) (2 Sam. 23:11).

AGIA: Wife of **Jaddus** (1 Esd. 5:38).

AGRIPPA: Herod Agrippa II, mentioned in Ac. 25:13ff. (*see* **Herod** 7). Paul made his defence before him (Ac. 26). He was the son of Herod Agrippa I (*see* **Herod** 6).

AGUR: Son of **Jakeh** and author of Prov. 30.

AHAB: 1. Son of **Omri** (1) and king of Israel (1 Kg. 16:28). He married **Jezebel** (1) (1 Kg. 16:31), and allowed her to promote Baal worship and to suppress the prophets of the Lord (1 Kg. 18:4), and also to have **Naboth** unjustly killed (1 Kg. 21), thereby incurring the hostility of **Elijah** (1). He was frequently at war with the Syrians, but spared **Benhadad** (2) when he had him in his power (1 Kg. 20:34). His daughter **Athaliah** (1) married **Jehoram** (2) of Judah (2 Kg. 8:18). He was killed in the battle of Ramoth-gilead (1 Kg. 22).

2. A false prophet (Jer. 29:21ff.).

AHARAH: A Benjaminite (1 Chr. 8:1); called **Ahiram** in Num. 26:38.

AHARHEL: A Judahite (1 Chr. 4:8).

AHASBAI: Father of **Eliphelet** (2) (2 Sam. 23:34); corresponding to **Ur** in 1 Chr. 11:35.

AHASUERUS: 1. A Persian king, who reigned between **Darius** (1) and **Artaxerxes** (1) (Ezr. 4:6), and therefore identified with Xerxes. Probably the same king as the Ahasuerus of the book of Esther (Est. 1:1).

2. The father of **Darius** (3) (Dan. 9:1).

3. In Tob. 14:15 Ahasuerus is said to have destroyed Nineveh with **Nebuchadnezzar.** But it was Cyaxares the Mede who did this.

AHAZ: 1. Son and successor of **Jotham** (2) (2 Kg. 15:38) and father of **Hezekiah** (1) (2 Kg. 16:20). The kings of Syria and Israel attacked him (2 Kg. 16:5f.; Isa. 7:1ff.) and he appealed to Assyria for help (2 Kg. 16:7ff.), despite the assurances of **Isaiah** (Isa. 7:3ff.). Ahaz went to Damascus to meet the Assyrian king (1 Kg. 16:10) and modified the Temple arrangements to conform to what he saw there (1 Kg. 16:10ff.).

2. A great-great-grandson of **Saul** (1) (1 Chr. 8:35, 9:41).

AHAZIAH: 1. Son of **Ahab** (1) and king of Israel (1 Kg. 22:51). He fell from a window and injured himself, and as a result died after a short reign (2 Kg. 1).

2. Son of **Jehoram** (2) and king of Judah (2 Kg. 8:25). He was killed by **Jehu** (2) (2 Kg. 9:27); called **Jehoahaz** (3) in 2 Chr. 21:17.

AHBAN: A Jerahmeelite (1 Chr. 2:29).

AHER: A Benjaminite (1 Chr. 7:12).

AHI: A Gadite (1 Chr. 5:15).

AHIAH: One who sealed the covenant (Neh. 10:26).

AHIAM: One of **David's** heroes (2 Sam. 23:33; 1 Chr. 11:35).

AHIAN: A Manassite (1 Chr. 7:19).

AHIEZER: 1. Representative of the Danites at the census in the wilderness (Num. 1:12) and on other occasions (Num. 2:25, 7:66, 71, 10:25).

2. A Benjaminite who deserted from **Saul** (1) to **David** and came to Ziklag (1 Chr. 12:3).

AHIHUD: 1. An Asherite leader for the division of the land (Num. 34:27).
    2. A Benjaminite (1 Chr. 8:7).

AHIJAH: 1. A priest, son of **Ahitub** (1) and descended from Eli (1 Sam. 14:3). He consulted the oracle for **Saul** (1) on the field of Michmash (1 Sam. 14:18f.). Either the brother of **Ahimelech** (1) (1 Sam. 21:1, 22:9) or to be identified with him.
    2. A secretary of Solomon's (1 Kg. 4:3); brother of **Elihoreph**.
    3. A prophet from Shiloh who incited **Jeroboam** (1) to divide the kingdom (1 Kg. 11:29ff.), but afterwards turned against him (1 Kg. 14:2ff.).
    4. Father of **Baasha** (1 Kg. 15:27, 33).
    5. A Jerahmeelite (1 Chr. 2:25).
    6. A Benjaminite (1 Chr. 8:7); called **Ahoah** in 1 Chr. 8:4.
    7. One of David's heroes (1 Chr. 11:36).
    8. A Levite, treasurer of the Temple (1 Chr. 26:20).
    9. Father of **Ahitub** (3) and ancestor of **Ezra** (1) (2 Esd. 1:1f.).

AHIKAM: One of those sent by **Josiah** (1) to **Huldah** (2 Kg. 22:12, 14). He protected **Jeremiah** (1) (Jer. 26:24) and was the father of **Gedaliah** (1) (Jer. 39:14).

AHIKAR: **Tobit**'s nephew (Tob. 1:21f., 2:10, 11:18, 14:10f.).

AHILUD: 1. Father of **Jehoshaphat** (1) (2 Sam. 8:16, 20:24; 1 Kg. 4:3; 1 Chr. 18:15).
    2. Father of **Baana** (1) (1 Kg. 4:12).

AHIMAAZ: 1. Father-in-law of **Saul** (1) (1 Sam. 14:50).
    2. Son of **Zadok** (1) (2 Sam. 15:36). He waited at En-rogel for news to carry to **David** when **Absalom** (1) rebelled (2 Sam. 17:17), and carried news to David after Absalom's death (2 Sam. 18:19ff.).
    3. Son-in-law of Solomon and the king's officer in Naphtali (1 Kg. 4:15); possibly to be identified with 2.

AHIMAN: 1. Descendant of Anak (Num. 13:22), driven out from Hebron by **Caleb** (Jos. 15:14) or defeated by Judah (Jg. 1:10).
    2. A family of Levite gatekeepers of the Temple (1 Chr. 9:17f.).

AHIMELECH: 1. Son of **Ahitub** (1), who either succeeded **Ahijah** (1) or is to be identified with him (1 Sam. 21:1, 22:9). He gave **David** showbread (1 Sam. 21:6) and this cost him his life (1 Sam. 22:18). He was the father of **Abiathar** (1 Sam. 22:20). In 2 Sam. 8:17 Ahimelech is called the son of Abiathar, instead of his father (cf. 1 Chr. 18:16, 24:6).
    2. A Hittite who followed **David** (1 Sam. 26:6).

AHIMOTH: A Levite (1 Chr. 6:25).

AHINADAB: Officer of Solomon in Mahanaim (1 Kg. 4:14).

AHINOAM: 1. Daughter of **Ahimaaz** (1) and wife of **Saul** (1) (1 Sam. 14:50).
   2. Wife of **David** (1 Sam. 25:43) and mother of **Amnon** (1) (2 Sam. 3:2).

AHIO: 1. Son of **Abinadab** (1) and brother of **Uzzah** (2 Sam. 6:3), who preceded the Ark when it was taken to Jerusalem (2 Sam. 6:4).
   2. A Benjaminite (1 Chr. 8:14).
   3. Uncle of **Saul** (1) (1 Chr. 8:31, 9:37).

AHIRA: Representative of Naphtali at the census in the wilderness (Num. 1:15) and on other occasions (Num. 2:29, 7:78, 83, 10:27).

AHIRAM: A Benjaminite (Num. 26:38); called **Aharah** in 1 Chr. 8:1. Perhaps **Ehi** in Gen. 46:21 is for Ahiram.

AHISAMACH: A Danite craftsman (Exod. 31:6, 35:34, 38:23).

AHISHAHAR: A Benjaminite (1 Chr. 7:10).

AHISHAR: Officer in charge of **Solomon**'s household (1 Kg. 4:6).

AHITHOPHEL: A wise counsellor of **David** (2 Sam. 15:12, 16:23; 1 Chr. 27:33). He supported **Absalom** (1) in his rebellion (2 Sam. 15:12, 31). His advice (2 Sam. 17:1ff.) was countered by **Hushai** (2 Sam. 17:5ff.), and Ahithophel went and hanged himself (2 Sam. 17:23).

AHITUB: 1. Grandson of **Eli** and father of **Ahijah** (1) (1 Sam. 14:3, 22:9, 11f., 20).
   2. Father of **Zadok** (1), according to 2 Sam. 8:17; 1 Chr. 6:8, 18:16, but grandfather according to 1 Chr. 9:11; Neh. 11:11.
   3. Father of **Zadok** (6) (1 Chr. 6:11f.; cf. Ezr. 7:2; 1 Esd. 8:2; 2 Esd. 1:1).
   4. Ancestor of **Judith** (2) (Jdt. 8:1).

AHLAI: 1. Daughter of **Sheshan** (1 Chr. 2:31; cf. 2:34).
   2. Father of **Zabad** (3) (1 Chr. 11:41).

AHOAH: A Benjaminite (1 Chr. 8:4).

AHOHI: Father of **Dodo** (2) (2 Sam. 23:9). The parallel 1 Chr. 11:12 has 'the Ahohite'.

AHUMAI: A Judahite (1 Chr. 4:2).

AHUZZAM: A Judahite (1 Chr. 4:6).

AHUZZATH: Adviser of **Abimelech** (1) (Gen. 26:26).

AHZAI: A priest (Neh. 11:13); called **Jahzerah** in 1 Chr. 9:12.

AIAH: 1. A Horite (Gen. 36:24; 1 Chr. 1:40).
   2. Father of **Rizpah** (2 Sam. 3:7, 21:8, 10f.).

AKAN: A Horite (Gen. 36:27); called **Jaakan** in 1 Chr. 1:42.

AKKUB: 1. A descendant of **Solomon** (1 Chr. 3:24).
   2. A family of Levite gatekeepers of the Temple (1 Chr. 9:17; Ezr. 2:42; Neh. 7:45, 11:19, 12:25; 1 Esd. 5:28).

3. Ancestor of some Temple servants who returned with **Zerubbabel** (Ezr. 2:45; 1 Esd. 5:30).

4. A Levite who expounded the Law (Neh. 8:7; 1 Esd. 9:48).

ALCIMUS: A priest of the line of **Aaron** (1 Mac. 7:14). He collaborated with the enemies of the Jews, but strove to get himself appointed High Priest (1 Mac. 7:5, 21; 2 Mac. 14:3ff.). He was received by the Hasidaeans (1 Mac. 7:13ff.), whereupon he killed sixty of them (1 Mac. 7:16). **Judas** (1) resisted him (1 Mac. 7:21) and said he had done more harm than the Gentiles (1 Mac. 7:23). His death is recorded in 1 Mac. 9:54ff.

ALEMETH: 1. A Benjaminite (1 Chr. 7:8).

2. A descendant of **Saul** (1) (1 Chr. 8:36, 9:42).

ALEXANDER: 1. Alexander the Great, son of Philip of Macedon, who defeated **Darius** (2) (1 Mac. 1:1), and died after reigning twelve years (1 Mac. 1:7). He left valuable weapons in the temple of Elymais (1 Mac. 6:2). He is referred to, though not by name, in Dan. 8:5ff., 21, 11:3f.

2. Alexander Balas, the reputed son of **Antiochus** (4), who rose against **Demetrius** (1) and occupied Ptolemais, taking the title of Epiphanes (1 Mac. 10:1). He competed successfully with Demetrius for the support of **Jonathan** (3) (1 Mac. 10:3ff., 15ff., 22ff., 46f.), and appointed him High Priest (1 Mac. 10:20ff.), and confirmed him in this office (1 Mac. 10:59ff.) after he had defeated and killed Demetrius (1 Mac. 10:48ff.). Later he honoured Jonathan further (1 Mac. 10:88), but was later attacked by his father-in-law, **Ptolemy** (6) (1 Mac. 11:13ff.), and fled to Arabia, where he was murdered (1 Mac. 11:16f.).

3. Son of **Simon** (11) (Mk 15:21).

4. A member of the High Priest's family (Ac. 4:6).

5. A Jew who tried to speak for the Jews during the riot at Ephesus (Ac. 19:33f.).

6. One who abandoned the faith and was condemned by **Paul** (1 Tim. 1:19f.).

7. A coppersmith who did **Paul** great harm (2 Tim. 4:14). Some would identify him with **5**, but there is insufficient evidence to establish this.

ALIAH: An Edomite chief (1 Chr. 1:51); called Alvah in Gen. 36:40.

ALIAN: A Horite (1 Chr. 1:40); called Alvan in Gen. 36:23.

ALLON: A Simeonite (1 Chr. 4:37).

ALMODAD: Son of Joktan (Gen. 10:26; 1 Chr. 1:20).

ALPHAEUS: 1. Father of **James** (2) (Mt. 10:3; Mk 3:18; Lk. 6:15; Ac. 1:13).

2. Father of **Levi** (4) (Mk 2:14).

ALVAH: An Edomite (Gen. 36:40); called Aliah in 1 Chr. 1:51.

ALVAN: A Horite (Gen. 36:23); called **Alian** in 1 Chr. 1:40.

AMAL: An Asherite (1 Chr. 7:35).

AMALEK: Son of **Eliphaz** (1) by **Timna** (1) (Gen. 36:12, 16), and eponymous ancestor of the Amalekites.

AMARIAH: 1. Ancestor of **Zephaniah** (1) (Zeph. 1:1).
  2. Grandfather of **Zadok** (1) (1 Chr. 6:7, 52).
  3. Grandfather of **Zadok** (3) (1 Chr. 6:11; cf. Ezr. 7:3; 1 Esd. 8:2; 2 Esd. 1:2).
  4. A Levite (1 Chr. 23:19, 24:23).
  5. A priest in the reign of **Jehoshaphat** (4) (2 Chr. 19:11).
  6. A Levite who distributed portions (2 Chr. 31:15).
  7. One who sealed the covenant (Neh. 10:3).
  8. One who married a foreign wife (Ezr. 10:42; 1 Esd. 5:24).
  9. Ancestor of a Judahite who lived in Jerusalem (Neh. 11:4).
  10. A priest who returned with **Zerubbabel** (Neh. 12:2).
  11. Ancestor of a priest who lived in the days of **Joiakim** (Neh. 12:13); perhaps the same as 10.

AMASA: 1. Nephew of **David** (1 Chr. 2:17). He commanded the army of **Absalom** (1) (2 Sam. 17:25) and was defeated (2 Sam. 18:6ff.), but David appointed him commander-in-chief in place of **Joab** (1) (2 Sam. 19:13). Sent to suppress the rebellion of **Sheba** (1) (2 Sam. 20:4), he proved inefficient (2 Sam. 20:5) and was treacherously slain by Joab (2 Sam. 20:8ff.).
  2. An Ephraimite who opposed the bringing of Judahite prisoners into Samaria (2 Chr. 28:12f.).

AMASAI: 1. A Levite (1 Chr. 6:25).
  2. An officer of **David's** (1 Chr. 12:18).
  3. A priest (1 Chr. 15:24).

AMASHSAI: A priest (Neh. 11:3).

AMASIAH: A commander in the reign of **Jehoshaphat** (4) (2 Chr. 17:16).

AMAZIAH: 1. Son and successor of **Jehoash** (1) (2 Kg. 14:1). He did not put to death the children of his father's murderers (2 Kg. 14:6). He fought successfully against the Edomites (2 Kg. 14:7) and unsuccessfully against Israel (2 Kg. 14:8ff.; 2 Chr. 25:17ff.). After a reign of twenty-nine years (2 Kg. 14:1), he faced rebellion and fled to Lachish, where he was captured and slain (2 Kg. 14:20).
  2. Priest of Bethel in the time of **Amos** (Am. 7:10).
  3. A Simeonite (1 Chr. 4:34).
  4. A Levite (1 Chr. 6:45).

AMI: Ancestor of some of Solomon's servants who returned with **Zerubbabel** (Ezr. 2:57; 1 Esd. 5:34); called **Amon** (3) in Neh. 7:59.

AMITTAI: Father of **Jonah** (2 Kg. 14:25; Jon. 1:1).

AMMIEL: 1. A Danite, one of the twelve spies (Num. 13:12).

   2. Father of Machir (2) (2 Sam. 9:4f., 17:27).

   3. Father of Bathsheba (1 Chr. 3:5), who is here called Bathshua (2); he is called Eliam (1) in 2 Sam. 11:3.

   4. Son of Obed-edom (2), who shared in the care of the storehouse (1 Chr. 26:5, 15).

AMMIHUD: 1. Father of Elishama (1) (Num. 1:10, 2:18, 7:48, 53, 10:22), great-grandfather of Joshua (1) (1 Chr. 7:26).

   2. Father of Shemuel (1) (Num. 34:20).

   3. Father of Pedahel (Num. 34:28).

   4. Father of Talmai (2) (2 Sam. 13:37).

   5. Son of Omri (3) (1 Chr. 9:4).

AMMINADAB: 1. Father of Nahshon (Num. 1:7, 2:3, 7:12, 17, 10:14; Ru. 4:20; 1 Chr. 2:10), father-in-law of Aaron (Exod. 6:23). He was an ancestor of Jesus (1) (Mt. 1:4; Lk. 3:33).

   2. Son of Kohath (1 Chr. 6:22).

   3. A Levite, who helped in bringing the Ark to Jerusalem (1 Chr. 15:10f.).

AMMISHADDAI: A Danite, father of Ahiezer (1) (Num. 1:12, 2:25, 7:66, 71, 10:25).

AMMIZABAD: Son of Benaiah (1) (1 Chr. 27:6). He was one of David's commanders.

AMNON: 1. David's eldest son (2 Sam. 3:2). He violated his half-sister, Tamar (2) (2 Sam. 13:1ff.), for which Absalom (1) had him slain (2 Sam. 13:23ff.).

   2. A Judahite (1 Chr. 4:20).

AMOK: A priest who returned with Zerubbabel (Neh. 12:7) and ancestor of Eber (6) (Neh. 12:20).

AMON: 1. Son and successor of Manasseh (2) (2 Kg. 21:18), king of Judah. He reigned for two years and was then assassinated (2 Kg. 21:19ff.).

   2. Governor of Samaria in the time of Ahab (1) (1 Kg. 22:26).

   3. Ancestor of some of Solomon's servants who returned with Zerubbabel (Neh. 7:59); called Ami in Ezr. 2:57; 1 Esd. 5:34.

   4. Egyptian god, the centre of whose worship was at Thebes (Jer. 46:25).

AMOS: A prophet from Tekoa (Am. 1:1), who prophesied at Bethel (Am. 7:10ff.) in the time of Jeroboam (2).

AMOZ: Father of Isaiah (Isa. 1:1; 2 Kg. 19:2; 2 Chr. 26:22).

AMPLIATUS: A Roman Christian greeted by Paul (Rom. 16:8).

AMRAM: 1. A Levite, son of Kohath (Exod. 6:18; Num. 3:19, 26:58; 1 Chr. 6:2), who married Jochebed, the mother of Moses (Exod. 6:20; Num. 26:59).

   2. One who married a foreign wife (Ezr. 10:34; 1 Esd. 9:34).

AMRAPHEL: King of Shinar (Gen. 14:1), one of the kings defeated by Abraham (Gen. 14:15, 17). He has often been improbably equated with Hammurabi of Babylon.

AMZI: 1. A Levite (1 Chr. 6:46).
  2. A priest (Neh. 11:12).

ANAEL: Brother of Tobit and father of Ahikar (Tob. 1:21).

ANAH: 1. Son of Zibeon and father of Oholibamah (1) (Gen. 36:2, 14, 18, 25; 1 Chr. 1:40), who found hot springs in the wilderness (Gen. 36:24).
  2. A Horite, brother of Zibeon (Gen. 36:20, 29; 1 Chr. 1:38).

ANAIAH: 1. A Levite in the time of Ezra (1) (Neh. 8:4; 1 Esd. 9:43).
  2. One who sealed the covenant (Neh. 10:22).

ANAK: Name of a family of giants in southern Palestine (Num. 13:22; Dt. 1:28), driven from the Hebron district by Caleb (Jos. 15:14; Jg. 1:20), but remaining in Philistia (Jos. 11:22).

ANAMMELECH: A god of Sepharvaim (2 Kg. 17:31).

ANAN: One who sealed the covenant (Neh. 10:26).

ANANI: Son of Elioenai (1) (1 Chr. 3:24).

ANANIAH: Father of Maaseiah (10) (Neh. 3:23).

ANANIAS: 1. A Jerusalem Christian who lied to the Apostles and fell down dead (Ac. 5:1ff.).
  2. A Damascus Christian who baptized Paul (Ac. 9:10ff., 22:12ff.).
  3. A High Priest who presided at Paul's trial before the Council (Ac. 23:2) and who went to Caesarea to accuse Paul (Ac. 24:1).
  4. A relative of Tobit's, with whose son the angel Raphael identified himself (Tob. 5:12).
  5. An ancestor of Judith (2) (Jdt. 8:1).

ANANIEL: An ancestor of Tobit (Tob. 1:1).

ANATH: 1. A Canaanite goddess who figures in the Ras Shamra texts and whose name appears in the place-names Anathoth, Beth-anath and Beth-anoth.
  2. The father of Shamgar (Jg. 3:31, 5:6).

ANATHOTH: 1. A Benjaminite, son of Becher (1) (1 Chr. 7:8).
  2. One who sealed the covenant (Neh. 10:19).

ANDREW: Brother of Peter (Jn 1:40) and a disciple of John (6) the Baptist (Jn 1:35) and then of Jesus (1) (Mt. 10:2; Lk. 6:14). He was from Bethsaida (Jn 1:44), and lived with his brother in Capernaum (Mk 1:29), where they were fishermen (Mt. 4:18; Mk 1:16). He brought to Jesus the lad with the loaves and fishes (Jn 6:8), and introduced the Greeks to Jesus (Jn 12:22), and he was one of those who asked Jesus about the signs of the end (Mk 13:3).

ANDRONICUS: 1. An officer of Antiochus (4), who treacherously murdered Onias (3) and was put to death by Antiochus (2 Mac. 4:31ff.).

2. Another officer of Antiochus (4), left at Gerizim (2 Mac. 5:23).

3. A Roman Christian greeted by Paul (Rom. 16:7). Paul calls him a kinsman and a fellow-prisoner, who was a Christian before he himself was.

ANER: An Amorite and an ally of Abraham (Gen. 14:13).

ANIAM: A Manassite (1 Chr. 7:19).

ANNA: 1. Wife of Tobit (Tob. 1:9).

2. A pious prophetess who did not depart from the Temple and who spoke of the coming redemption when Jesus (1) was presented in the Temple (Lk. 2:36ff.).

ANNAN: One whose sons married foreign wives (1 Esd. 9:32).

ANNAS: High Priest of Jerusalem from A.D. 6 to 15, and father-in-law of Caiaphas (Jn 18:13). His influence continued and in Lk. 3:2 the high priesthood of Annas and Caiaphas is mentioned (cf. Ac. 4:6). Jesus (1) was tried before Annas (Jn 18:13ff.).

ANNIAS: Ancestor of a family which returned with Zerubbabel (1 Esd. 5:16).

ANNIUTH: A Levite who taught the Law (1 Esd. 9:48); called Bani (9) in Neh. 8:7.

ANNUNUS: A Levite (1 Esd. 8:48).

ANTHOTHIJAH: A Benjaminite (1 Chr. 8:24).

ANTIOCHIS: Concubine of Antiochus (4) (2 Mac. 4:30).

ANTIOCHUS: 1. Antiochus I, Soter, king of Syria, son of Seleucus (1), unmentioned in the Bible, save that he was one of the ten horns of Dan. 7:7.

2. Antiochus II, Theos, son of 1. He engaged in war with Ptolemy (2) and was compelled to replace his wife, Laodice, by Ptolemy's daughter, Berenice. Laodice poisoned him and had his son by Berenice killed. These events are referred to in Dan. 11:6.

3. Antiochus III, the Great, grandson of 2. He fought many wars, and in 198 B.C. he annexed Palestine from Egypt. These events are referred to in Dan. 11:11ff. His daughter married the Egyptian king (Dan. 11:17). He is mentioned in 1 Mac. 1:10, 8:6.

4. Antiochus IV, Epiphanes, son of 3. He had been a hostage in Rome (1 Mac. 1:10), but seized the Syrian throne when Heliodorus murdered Seleucus (4). He displaced Onias (3) from the high priesthood (2 Mac. 4:7) and appointed Jason (3), who was, however, soon replaced by Menelaus (2 Mac. 4:24). He is the 'contemptible person' of Dan. 11:21, who took action against the holy covenant when he returned in disappointment from Egypt

(Dan. 11:30; 2 Mac. 5:11). His persecution of the Jews is described in 1 Mac. 1:44ff. (cf. 2 Mac. 5:13ff.), as well as the rising of the Jews against him (1 Mac. 2ff.; 2 Mac. 5:27ff.). He sought to plunder the temple of Elymais (1 Mac. 6:1ff.) but failed and went to Babylon (1 Mac. 6:4), where he died (1 Mac. 6:16). A different account of his end is given in 2 Mac. 9.

5. Antiochus V, Eupator, son of 4. He became king when a boy and his father appointed Philip (2) as regent (1 Mac. 6:14f.), but Lysias (1) assumed the power (1 Mac. 6:17). Antiochus and Lysias marched against the Jews (2 Mac. 13:1) and defeated Judas (1) (1 Mac. 6:47; 2 Mac. 13:16f. represents Judas as victorious). Antiochus made peace with Judas (1 Mac. 6:59; 2 Mac. 13:23), but broke his oath (1 Mac. 6:62). He was killed by the orders of Demetrius (1), together with Lysias (1 Mac. 7:1ff.; 2 Mac. 14:1f.).

6. Antiochus VI, Epiphanes, son of Alexander (2). He was elevated to the throne by Trypho (1 Mac. 12:39) but Trypho later eliminated him and elevated himself to the throne instead (1 Mac. 13:31f.).

7. Antiochus VII, Sidetes, son of Demetrius (1). He invaded Syria and drove Trypho out (1 Mac. 15:10ff., 37). He confirmed the privileges of the Jews (1 Mac. 15:2ff.) and added the right to coin money (1 Mac. 15:6), and Simon (3) sent troops to his aid (1 Mac. 15:26). He declined the aid and made new demands on Simon (1 Mac. 15:27ff.), who resisted and was in consequence attacked by troops under Cendebaeus (1 Mac. 15:38ff., 16:1ff.).

8. Father of Numenius (1 Mac. 12:16, 14:22).

ANTIPAS: 1. *See* Herod (3).

2. A martyr of the church at Pergamum (Rev. 2:13).

ANTIPATER: Son of Jason (1), sent as a Jewish envoy to Rome (1 Mac. 12:16) and to Sparta (1 Mac. 14:22).

ANUB: A Judahite (1 Chr. 4:8).

APAME: Concubine of Darius (1) (1 Esd. 4:29).

APELLES: A Roman Christian greeted by Paul (Rom. 16:10).

APHERRA: Ancestor of some who returned with Zerubbabel (1 Esd. 5:34).

APHIAH: Ancestor of Saul (1) (1 Sam. 9:1).

APOLLONIUS: 1. Governor of Coele-Syria and Phoenicia (2 Mac. 3:5), at whose suggestion Seleucus (4) sent Heliodorus to rob the Temple (2 Mac. 3:4ff.). He was sent by Antiochus (4) to subdue Jerusalem and massacred large numbers on the sabbath (2 Mac. 5:24ff.). Judas (1) defeated and slew him (1 Mac. 3:10ff.).

2. An envoy of Antiochus (4) to Egypt (2 Mac. 4:21).

3. A district governor who molested the Jews (2 Mac. 12:2).

4. Governor of Coele-Syria appointed by Demetrius (2) (1 Mac. 10:69). He challenged Jonathan (3) (1 Mac. 10:70ff.), who resisted him and defeated him (1 Mac. 10:74ff.).

APOLLOPHANES: A Syrian slain at Gazara (2 Mac. 10:37).

APOLLOS: An Alexandrian Jewish Christian who taught in Ephesus (Ac. 18:24ff.) and Corinth (Ac. 19:1). In the Corinthian church there was an Apollos party opposed to a **Peter** party and a **Paul** party (1 C. 1:12), and Paul insists that Apollos only built on the foundation Paul laid (1 C. 3:3ff.). In Ephesus Apollos was instructed by **Aquila** and **Priscilla** (Ac. 18:24ff.).

APOLLYON: The angel of the bottomless pit (Rev. 9:11).

APPAIM: A Jerahmeelite (1 Chr. 2:30f.).

APPHIA: A Christian lady of Colossae (Phm. 2).

APPHUS: Epithet or surname applied to **Jonathan** (15) (1 Mac. 2:5).

AQUILA: A Jew of Pontus, who with his wife **Priscilla** went from Rome to Corinth while **Paul** was there (Ac. 18:2f.). They later went to Ephesus (Ac. 18:19) and there instructed **Apollos** (Ac. 18:24ff.). They were in Corinth when Paul wrote to the church there (1 C. 16:19) and in Rome when he wrote to the church there (Rom. 16:3ff.). In writing to **Timothy (2)** Paul greets, them (2 Tim. 4:19), but we do not know where they were then.

ARA: An Asherite (1 Chr. 7:38).

ARAD: A Benjaminite (1 Chr. 8:15).

ARAH: 1. An Asherite (1 Chr. 7:39).
2. Ancestor of a family which returned with **Zerubbabel** (Ezr. 2:5; Neh. 6:18, 7:10; 1 Esd. 5:10).

ARAM: 1. Son of **Shem** (Gen. 10:22f.; 1 Chr. 1:17). He was the eponymous ancestor of the Aramaeans.
2. Grandson of **Nahor (2)** (Gen. 22:21).
3. An Asherite (1 Chr. 7:34).

ARAN: A Horite (Gen. 36:28; 1 Chr. 1:42).

ARAUNAH: A Jebusite whose threshing floor **David** bought (2 Sam. 24:18ff.); called **Ornan** in 1 Chr. 21:15ff. On the site of this threshing floor **Solomon** built the Temple (2 Chr. 3:2).

ARBA: One who gave his name to the city of Kiriath-arba, which was later known as Hebron (Jos. 14:15, 15:13, 21:11).

ARCHELAUS: *See* **Herod (2)**.

ARCHIPPUS: One of the addressees of the Letter to Philemon (Phm. 2), there called **Paul**'s fellow soldier. He is also sent a message in Col. 4:17.

ARD: Son (Gen. 46:21) or grandson (Num. 26:40) of **Benjamin (1)**; called **Addar** in 1 Chr. 8:3.

ARDON: Son of **Caleb** (1 Chr. 2:18).

ARELI: Son of **Gad** (2) (Gen. 46:16; Num. 26:17).

ARETAS: The name of four rulers of the Nabataeans, of whom two are mentioned in the Bible:
1. Aretas I, before whom **Jason** (3) was accused (2 Mac. 5:8). He was friendly towards the Maccabees (1 Mac. 5:24ff., 9:35).
2. Aretas IV, who sought to capture **Paul** (2 C. 9:32f.; cf. Ac. 9:24f.).

ARIARATHES: King of Cappadocia, to whom the consul wrote announcing the friendship of the Romans for the Jews (1 Mac. 15:22).

ARIDAI: Son of **Haman**, slain by the Jews (Est. 9:9).

ARIDATHA: Son of **Haman**, slain by the Jews (Est. 9:8).

ARIEL: A supporter of **Ezra** (1) (Ezr. 8:16); called **Iduel** in 1 Esd. 8:43.

ARIOCH: 1. King of Ellasar (Gen. 14:1), one of the kings defeated by **Abraham** (Gen. 14:15, 17).
2. Captain of **Nebuchadnezzar**'s guard (Dan. 2:14f., 24f.).
3. King of the Elymaeans, i.e. Elam (Jdt. 1:6).

ARISAI: Son of **Haman**, slain by the Jews (Est. 9:8).

ARISTARCHUS: A Jew (Col. 4:10f.) from Thessalonica (Ac. 20:4, 27:2; cf. 19:29), who was **Paul**'s companion on his last journey to Jerusalem (Ac. 20:4) and on his journey to Rome (Ac. 27:2). Paul calls him his fellow prisoner (Col. 4:10) and his fellow worker (Phm. 24). At Ephesus he was dragged by the mob into the theatre (Ac. 19:29).

ARISTOBULUS: 1. The teacher of **Ptolemy** (6) (2 Mac. 1:10).
2. A Roman Christian whose family **Paul** greets (Rom. 16:10).

ARIUS: A king of the Spartans to whom **Onias** (1) had written (1 Mac. 12:7). **Jonathan** (3) wrote to Sparta quoting his letter and the reply it received (1 Mac. 12:7ff., 19ff.).

ARMONI: Son of **Saul** (1) and **Rizpah**, hanged in Gibeon (2 Sam. 21:8).

ARNA: An ancestor of **Ezra** (1) (2 Esd. 1:2); called **Zerahiah** (1) in Ezr. 7:4.

ARNAN: A descendant of **David** (1 Chr. 3:21).

ARNI: An ancestor of **Jesus** (1) (Lk. 3:33); called **Ram** in Mt. 1:3f. (cf. Ru. 4:19; 1 Chr. 2:9f.).

AROD: Son of **Gad** (2) (Num. 26:17); called **Arodi** in Gen. 46:16.

ARODI: *See* Arod.

AROM: Ancestor of some who returned with **Zerubbabel** (1 Esd. 5:16).

ARPACHSAD: Son of **Shem** (Gen. 10:22; 1 Chr. 1:17) and an ancestor of **Abraham** (Gen. 11:10ff.).

ARPHAXAD: King of the Medes (Jdt. 1:1ff.).

ARSACES: King of Parthia, who took **Demetrius (2)** prisoner (1 Mac. 14:1ff.).

ARTAXERXES: The name of three Persian kings, of whom two may be mentioned in the Bible:

1. Artaxerxes I, who figures in the correspondence of Ezr. 4:7ff., 1 Esd. 2:16ff., and in Ezr. 6:14. He was also the Artaxerxes who authorized the mission of **Nehemiah (2)** (Neh. 2:1, 5:14, 13:6).

2. Artaxerxes II, who is probably the king who authorized the mission of **Ezra (1)** (Ezr. 7:1ff., 8:1), though this is not certain, and many scholars think this was also 1.

ARTEMAS: A companion of **Paul's** (Tit. 3:12). Paul planned to send him or **Tychicus** to Crete.

ARTEMIS: An Anatolian goddess, worshipped in Ephesus, and identified with the Greek goddess Artemis (Ac. 19:24, 27f., 34f.).

ARZA: An officer of the royal household in whose house **Elah (2)** was murdered (1 Kg. 16:9).

ASA: 1. Son and successor of **Abijah (1)** (1 Kg. 15:8), who reigned forty-one years in Jerusalem (1 Kg. 15:10). He was the grandson of **Absalom (1)** (1 Kg. 15:10). He is praised for his piety (1 Kg. 15:11ff.). He was attacked by Israel and he sent the Temple treasures to Damascus in return for an attack on Israel from the north (1 Kg. 15:16ff.). The Chronicler records his victory over an Ethiopian army of a million men, of whom not a man survived (2 Chr. 14:9ff.), but this is unmentioned in Kings.

2. A Levite (1 Chr. 9:16).

ASAHEL: 1. Brother of **Joab (1)** and one of **David's** heroes (2 Sam. 23:24). He was killed by **Abner** in self-defence (2 Sam. 2:18ff.), and this gave rise to a blood feud. He was famous for his fleetness (2 Sam. 2:18). He commanded a division of David's army (1 Chr. 27:7).

2. A Levite whom **Jehoshaphat (4)** sent to teach the people the Law (2 Chr. 17:8).

3. One of the overseers appointed by **Hezekiah (1)** (2 Chr. 31:13).

4. Father of **Jonathan (10)** (Ezr. 10:15; 1 Esd. 9:14).

ASAIAH: 1. One of those sent to consult **Huldah** (2 Kg. 22:12, 14; 2 Chr. 34:20).

2. A Simeonite who joined in an attack on the people of Gedor (1 Chr. 4:36).

3. One who shared in bringing the Ark to Jerusalem (1 Chr. 6:30, 15:6, 11).

4. The firstborn of the Shilonites (1 Chr. 9:5).

ASAIAS: One who married a foreign wife (1 Esd. 9:32); perhaps the same as **Isshijah** in Ezr. 10:31.

ASAPH: 1. Father of Joah (1) (2 Kg. 18:18, 37; Isa. 36:3, 22).
   2. A seer of the time of David (2 Chr. 29:30), who gave his name to a guild of Temple singers (1 Chr. 15:16f., 25:1f.; cf. 6:39; 2 Chr. 35:15; Neh. 12:46). Their name figures in the heading of Pss. 50, 73–83.
   3. A Korahite (1 Chr. 26:1); perhaps the same as Abiasaph.
   4. Keeper of the king's forest (Neh. 2:8).

ASAREL: A Judahite (1 Chr. 4:16).

ASENATH: Daughter of Potiphera and wife of Joseph (1) (Gen. 41:45); she was the mother of Ephraim and Manasseh (1) (Gen. 41:50ff., 46:20).

ASHARELAH: An Asaphite (1 Chr. 25:2); called Jesharelah in 1 Chr. 25:14.

ASHBEL: Second (1 Chr. 8:1; Num. 26:38) or third (Gen. 46:21) son of Benjamin (1).

ASHER: Son of Jacob (1) by Zilpah (Gen. 30:13, 35:26). He gave his name to one of the twelve tribes of Israel.

ASHERAH: Canaanite goddess often worshipped in Israel (1 Kg. 18:19; 2 Kg. 23:4). Asa (1) demoted his mother for having an image made for her worship (1 Kg. 15:13; 2 Chr. 15:16). The name stands in the plural in Jg. 3:7 for localized cults of the goddess.

ASHHUR: Son of Caleb and founder of Tekoa (1 Chr. 2:24, 4:5).

ASHIMA: A god worshipped by colonists from Hamath brought to Samaria (2 Kg. 17:30). But already in the time of Amos this deity (here Ashimah) was worshipped in Samaria (Am. 8:14).

ASHIMAH: *See* Ashima.

ASHKENAZ: Son of Gomer (1) (Gen. 10:3; 1 Chr. 1:6), representing a people akin to the Cimmerians, probably the Scythians; mentioned also in Jer. 51:27.

ASHPENAZ: Chief eunuch of Nebuchadnezzar (Dan. 1:3).

ASHTORETH: Canaanite goddess (1 Kg. 11:5) sometimes worshipped in Israel (1 Kg. 11:33; 2 Kg. 23:13). The name stands in the plural in Jg. 10:6 for localized cults of the goddess.

ASHVATH: An Asherite (1 Chr. 7:33).

ASIBIAS: One who married a foreign wife (1 Esd. 9:26); called Hashabiah (9) in Ezr. 10:25.

ASIEL: 1. A Simeonite (1 Chr. 4:35).
   2. A scribe employed by Ezra (1) (2 Esd. 14:24).
   3. An ancestor of Tobit (Tob. 1:1).

ASMODEUS: An evil demon who had slain each of seven husbands of Sarah (2) (Tob. 3:8), and who was bound by Raphael (Tob. 3:17, 8:3).

ASNAH: Ancestor of some Temple servants who returned with Zerubbabel (Ezr. 2:50; 1 Esd. 5:31).

ASPATHA: Son of Haman, slain by the Jews (Est. 9:7).

ASRIEL: A Manassite (Num. 26:31; Jos. 17:2; 1 Chr. 7:14).

ASSHUR: Son of Shem (Gen. 10:22; 1 Chr. 1:17) and eponymous ancestor of the Assyrians.

ASSIR: 1. Son of Korah (2) (Exod. 6:24; 1 Chr. 6:22).
2. Great-grandson of 1 (1 Chr. 6:23).

ASTYAGES: The last king of Media (Bel 1:1), conquered by Cyrus.

ASUR: Ancestor of some Temple servants who returned with Zerubbabel (1 Esd. 5:31); perhaps the same as Harhur in Ezr. 2:51; Neh. 7:53.

ASYNCRITUS: A Roman Christian greeted by Paul (Rom. 16:14).

ATARAH: Wife of Jerahmeel (1) (1 Chr. 2:26).

ATARGATIS: A Syrian goddess, to whom there was a temple at Carnaim (2 Mac. 12:26), destroyed by Judas (1) (1 Mac. 5:43f.).

ATER: 1. Ancestor of some who returned with Zerubbabel (Ezr. 2:16; Neh. 7:21; 1 Esd. 5:15).
2. Head of a family of gatekeepers who returned with Zerubbabel (Ezr. 2:42; Neh. 7:45; 1 Esd. 5:28).
3. One who sealed the covenant (Neh. 10:17).

ATHAIAH: A Judahite who lived in Jerusalem (Neh. 11:4).

ATHALIAH: 1. Daughter of Ahab (1), who married Jehoram (2) (2 Kg. 8:18). She was the mother of Ahaziah (2) (2 Kg. 8:26, 11:1). She reigned over Judah for six years following the death of Ahaziah (2 Kg. 11:3), until she was slain by the orders of Jehoiada (3) (2 Kg. 11:15f.).
2. A Benjaminite (1 Chr. 8:26).
3. Father of Jeshaiah (4) (Ezr. 8:7); called Gotholiah in 1 Esd. 8:33.

ATHENOBIUS: A friend of Antiochus (7) sent to Simon (3) (1 Mac. 15:28ff.).

ATHLAI: One who married a foreign wife (Ezr. 10:28); called Emathis in 1 Esd. 9:29).

ATROTH-BETH-JOAB: A Calebite family (1 Chr. 2:54).

ATTAI: 1. A Jerahmeelite (1 Chr. 2:35f.).
2. A Gadite who joined David in the wilderness (1 Chr. 12:11).
3. Son of Rehoboam (2 Chr. 11:20).

ATTALUS: King of Pergamum, to whom the consul wrote announcing the friendship of the Romans for the Jews (1 Mac. 15:22).

ATTHARATES: Apparently a person's name (1 Esd. 9:49), but in reality a corruption of a Persian title; cf. Neh. 8:9, 'the governor'.

ATTHARIAS: Ostensibly a proper name (1 Esd. 5:40), but a corruption of a Persian title; cf. Ezr. 2:63, 'the governor'.

AUGUSTUS: The first Roman emperor, who issued the decree ordering the enrolment of the people of the empire (Lk. 2:1). He reigned from 27 B.C. to A.D. 14.

AURANUS: An old man who led an attack on the Jews who rose against the sacrilege of **Lysimachus (2)** (2 Mac. 4:40).

AVARAN: Surname of **Eleazar (8)** (1 Mac. 2:5, 6:43).

AZAEL: One who married a foreign wife (1 Esd. 9:34).

AZALIAH: Father of **Shaphan (1)** (2 Kg. 22:3; 2 Chr. 34:8).

AZANIAH: One who sealed the covenant (Neh. 10:7).

AZAREL: 1. A Korahite who joined **David** at Ziklag (1 Chr. 12:6).
2. A musician, son of **Heman (4)** (1 Chr. 25:18); called **Uzziel (4)** in 1 Chr. 25:4.
3. David's chief officer for Dan (1 Chr. 27:22).
4. One who married a foreign wife (Ezr. 10:41; 1 Esd. 9:34).
5. A priest (Neh. 11:13).
6. A Levite who shared in the dedication of the wall (Neh. 12:36).

AZARIAH: 1. *See* **Uzziah (1)**.
2. Son of **Zadok (1)** and priest under **Solomon** (1 Kg. 4:2).
3. Son of **Nathan (2)** and an officer of Solomon's (1 Kg. 4:5).
4. A Judahite, son of **Ethan (1)** (1 Chr. 2:8).
5. A descendant of **Jerahmeel (1)** (1 Chr. 2:38; cf. 2:34).
6. A priest, father of **Johanan (4)** (1 Chr. 6:9).
7. Another priest, son of **Johanan (4)** (1 Chr. 6:10).
8. Another priest, son of **Hilkiah (2)** (1 Chr. 6:13).
9. A Kohathite Levite (1 Chr. 6:36); called **Uzziah (2)** in 1 Chr. 6:24.
10. A priest, son of **Hilkiah (2)**, who lived in Jerusalem after the exile (1 Chr. 9:11). This may be the same as 8, but he is called **Seraiah (8)** in Neh. 11:11, and this may be his real name.
11. A prophet, who persuaded **Asa (1)** to undertake a reform (2 Chr. 15:1ff.).
12. Son of **Jehoshaphat (4)** (2 Chr. 21:2).
13. A brother of 12 (2 Chr. 21:2).
14. Son of **Jeroham (7)** and a military officer (2 Chr. 23:1).
15. Son of **Obed (5)** and a military officer (2 Chr. 23:1).

16. Priest in the reign of Uzziah (1) who opposed the king (2 Chr. 26:16ff.).

17. An Ephraimite who supported Oded (2) (2 Chr. 28:12f.).

18. A Kohathite Levite in the time of Hezekiah (1) (2 Chr. 29:12).

19. A Merarite Levite in the time of Hezekiah (1) (2 Chr. 29:12).

20. Chief priest in the reign of Hezekiah (1) (2 Chr. 31:10, 13).

21. One who shared in repairing the wall (Neh. 3:23, 12:33).

22. One who returned with Zerubbabel (Neh. 7:7); called Seraiah (6) in Ezr. 2:2; 1 Esd. 5:8.

23. One who expounded the Law (Neh. 8:7; 1 Esd. 9:48) and who sealed the covenant (Neh. 10:3).

24. Son of Hoshaiah (2) and one of those who carried Jeremiah (1) into Egypt (Jer. 42:1, 43:2).

25. The Hebrew name of Abednego (Dan. 1:6f.).

26. A priest who married a foreign wife (1 Esd. 9:21); called Uzziah (4) in Ezr. 10:21.

27. One who stood on the right of Ezra (1) at the reading of the Law (1 Esd. 9:43).

28. A captain of Judas (1) (1 Mac. 5:18).

AZARIAS: Name assumed by the angel Raphael (Tob. 5:12).

AZARU: Ancestor of some who returned with Zerubbabel (1 Esd. 5:15).

AZAZ: A Reubenite (1 Chr. 5:8).

AZAZEL: Probably the name of a desert demon to whom the goat bearing the sins of the people was sent in the ritual of the Day of Atonement (Lev. 16:8, 10, 26).

AZAZIAH: 1. A Levite musician (1 Chr. 15:21).

2. Father of Hoshea (3) (1 Chr. 27:20).

3. An overseer under Hezekiah (1) (2 Chr. 31:13).

AZBUK: Father of Nehemiah (3) (Neh. 3:16).

AZEL: A descendant of Jonathan (2) (1 Chr. 8:37f., 9:43f.).

AZETAS: Ancestor of some who returned with Zerubbabel (1 Esd. 5:15).

AZGAD: 1. Ancestor of some who returned with Zerubbabel (Ezr. 2:12; Neh. 7:17; 1 Esd. 5:13) and with Ezra (1) (Ezr. 8:12; 1 Esd. 8:38).

2. One who sealed the covenant (Neh. 10:15).

AZIEL: A Levite musician who accompanied the Ark (1 Chr. 15:20); called Jaaziel in 1 Chr. 15:18.

AZIZA: One who married a foreign wife (Ezr. 10:27); called Zerdaiah in 1 Esd. 9:28.

AZMAVETH: 1. One of David's heroes (2 Sam. 23:31; 1 Chr. 11:33); perhaps mentioned also in 1 Chr. 12:3 as the father of two who joined David at Ziklag.
2. A descendant of Jonathan (2) (1 Chr. 8:36).
3. One who was over the treasuries (1 Chr. 27:15); perhaps the same as 1.

AZOR: An ancestor of Jesus (1) (Mt. 1:13f.).

AZRIEL: 1. A Manassite (1 Chr. 5:24).
2. A Naphtalite (1 Chr. 27:19).
3. Father of Seraiah (9) (Jer. 36:26).

AZRIKAM: 1. A descendant of Solomon (1 Chr. 3:23).
2. A descendant of Jonathan (2) (1 Chr. 8:38, 9:44).
3. A Levite (1 Chr. 9:14; Neh. 11:15).
4. An officer under Ahaz (1) (2 Chr. 28:7).

AZUBAH: 1. Mother of Jehoshaphat (4) (1 Kg. 22:42; 2 Chr. 20:31).
2. Wife of Caleb (1 Chr. 2:18f.).

AZZAN: Father of Paltiel (1) (Num. 34:26).

AZZUR: 1. One who sealed the covenant (Neh. 10:17).
2. Father of Hananiah (12) (Jer. 28:1).
3. Father of Jaazaniah (4) (Ezek. 11:1).

B

BAAL: 1. A Canaanite fertility god, frequently worshipped in Israel (2 Kg. 3:2, 21:3; Jer. 7:9, 11:13), often under localized forms, called Baals (Jg. 2:11, 8:33; Jer. 9:14). Josiah (1) abolished Baal worship (2 Kg. 23:4f.).
2. A Reubenite (1 Chr. 5:5).
3. Uncle of Saul (1) (1 Chr. 8:30, 9:36).

BAAL-BERITH: God of Shechem (Jg. 8:33, 9:4); called El-berith (Jg. 9:46).

BAAL-HANAN: 1. King of Edom (Gen. 36:38f.; 1 Chr. 1:49f.).
2. An officer of David's (1 Chr. 27:28).

BAALIS: King of Ammon who instigated the murder of Gedaliah (1) (Jer. 40:14).

BAALSAMUS: One who stood on the right of Ezra (1) at the reading of the Law (1 Esd. 9:43); called Maaseiah (11) in Neh. 8:4.

BAALZEBUB: Philistine god worshipped at Ekron (2 Kg. 1:2). *See* **Beelzebul.**

BAANA: 1. Son of **Ahilud** (2) and officer of **Solomon** (1 Kg. 4:12).
2. Son of **Hushai** and officer of **Solomon** (1 Kg. 4:16).
3. Father of **Zadok** (5) (Neh. 3:4).

BAANAH: 1. One of the murderers of **Ishbosheth** (1) (2 Sam. 4:2, 5f., 9).
2. Father of **Heleb** (2 Sam. 23:29) or **Heled** (1 Chr. 11:30).
3. One who returned with **Zerubbabel** (Ezr. 2:2; Neh. 7:7; 1 Esd. 5:8).
4. One who sealed the covenant (Neh. 10:27).

BAARA: Wife of a Benjaminite (1 Chr. 8:8).

BAASEIAH: A Kohathite Levite (1 Chr. 6:40).

BAASHA: Murderer of **Nadab** (2) and of the family of **Jeroboam** (1) (1 Kg. 15:27, 29). He made himself king of Israel (1 Kg. 15:28), and reigned twenty-four years (1 Kg. 15:33). He attacked **Asa** (1), who invoked the aid of **Benhadad** (1) (1 Kg. 15:16ff.).

BACCHIDES: Friend of **Demetrius** (1) (1 Mac. 7:8). He was sent to support **Alcimus** (1 Mac. 7:9ff.) and fought against **Judas** (1) at the battle of Elasa, where Judas was slain (1 Mac. 9:1ff.). He defeated **Jonathan** (3) in a battle on the sabbath day (1 Mac. 9:43ff.) and later besieged Jonathan in Beth-basi, but was forced to agree to terms of peace (1 Mac. 9:62ff., 10:12).

BACENOR: An officer of **Judas** (1) (2 Mac. 12:35).

BAGOAS: A eunuch who served **Holofernes** (Jdt. 12:11, 13, 15, 13:3, 14:14).

BAITERUS: Ancestor of some who returned with **Zerubbabel** (1 Esd. 5:17).

BAKBAKKAR: A Levite (1 Chr. 9:15).

BAKBUK: Ancestor of a family of Temple servants who returned with **Zerubbabel** (Ezr. 2:51; Neh. 11:17; 1 Esd. 5:31).

BAKBUKIAH: 1. A Levite (Neh. 11:17).
2. A gatekeeper (Neh. 12:25).

BALAAM: A seer from Pethor (Num. 22:5), called by **Balak** to curse the Israelites (Num. 22:6). He declined at first (Num. 22:13), but later agreed to go (Num. 22:21). On the way his ass reproached him for beating it when an angel barred its way (Num. 22:22ff.). Arrived at the Moabite camp, Balaam several times pronounced oracles, but always failed to curse Israel (Num. 23f.). His death is recorded in Num. 31:8. In the NT he is accused of greed (2 Pet. 2:15) and is classed with **Cain** (Jude 11), and he is said to have taught Balak to tempt Israel to idolatry and immorality (Rev. 2:14).

BALADAN: Father of Merodach-baladan (2 Kg. 20:12; Isa. 39:1).

BALAK: King of Moab who sent for Balaam to curse Israel (Num. 22ff.).

BANI: 1. A Gadite, one of David's heroes (2 Sam. 23:36).
2. An ancestor of Asaph (2) (1 Chr. 6:46).
3. A Judahite (1 Chr. 9:4).
4. Ancestor of some who returned with Zerubbabel (Ezr. 2:10; 1 Esd. 5:12); called Binnui (3) in Neh. 7:15.
5. Ancestor of Shelomith (5) (Ezr. 8:10; 1 Esd. 8:36).
6. Ancestor of some who married foreign wives (Ezr. 10:29; 1 Esd. 9:30).
7. Ancestor of others who had married foreign wives (Ezr. 10:34; 1 Esd. 9:34); perhaps the same as Binnui (5) in Ezr. 10:38.
8. A Levite, father of one who helped repair the wall (Neh. 3:17).
9. A Levite who expounded the Law (Neh. 8:7, 9:4f.); called Anniuth in 1 Esd. 9:48.
10. One who sealed the covenant (Neh. 10:13); perhaps the same as 9.
11. Another who sealed the covenant (Neh. 10:14).
12. Father of an overseer of the Levites (Neh. 11:22).

BANNAS: A Levite who returned with Zerubbabel (1 Esd. 5:26).

BARABBAS: A revolutionary or robber who was released by Pilate when the crowd chose him in preference to Jesus (1) (Mt. 27:16f., 20f., 26; Mk 15:7, 11, 15; Lk. 23:18f.; Jn 18:40).

BARACHEL: Father of Elihu (5) (Job 32:2, 6).

BARACHIAH: Father of Zechariah (35) (Mt. 23:35); perhaps for Berechiah (7). See Zechariah (35).

BARAK: Son of Abinoam; he led the army of Zebulun and Naphtali against Jabin and Sisera (1) at the instigation of Deborah (2) (Jg. 4:6ff., 12ff., 5:1, 12, 15).

BARIAH: A descendant of Zerubbabel (1 Chr. 3:22).

BAR-JESUS: A Jewish magician, also called Elymas (Ac. 13:8), who opposed Paul at Paphos (Ac. 13:6ff.), and who was struck blind for a time (Ac. 13:11f.).

BAR-JONA: Name used of Peter (Mt. 16:17). The name means 'son of John' (8); cf. Jn 1:42, 21:15ff.

BARKOS: Ancestor of some Temple servants who returned with Zerubbabel (Ezr. 2:52; Neh. 7:55; 1 Esd. 5:32).

BARNABAS: Surname of a Levite named Joseph (16) from Cyprus (Ac. 4:36), who introduced Paul to the Apostles (Ac. 9:27) and who was sent to Antioch (Ac. 11:22ff.), and later fetched Paul from Tarsus to Antioch (Ac.

11:25f.). He and Paul carried relief to the church at Jerusalem (Ac. 11:30, 12:25), and then set out together on Paul's first missionary journey (Ac. 13f.). Together they went to the Jerusalem Council (Ac. 15), but after their return to Antioch (Ac. 15:30) they separated (Ac. 15:36ff.) and Barnabas returned to Cyprus (Ac. 15:39). He withdrew from Paul later, under the influence of Peter (Gal. 2:12f.), but they appear to have been reconciled (1 C. 9:6).

BARODIS: Ancestor of some who returned with Zerubbabel (1 Esd. 5:34).

BARSABBAS: 1. See Joseph (15).
  2. See Judas (10).

BARTACUS: Father of Apame (1 Esd. 4:29).

BARTHOLOMEW: One of the twelve Apostles (Mt. 10:3; Mk 3:18; Lk. 6:14; Ac. 1:13).

BARTIMAEUS: A blind beggar whom Jesus (1) healed at Jericho (Mk 10:46ff.; cf. Mt. 20:29ff.; Lk. 18:35ff.).

BARUCH: 1. Companion of Jeremiah (1) (Jer. 32:12f., 16), who wrote the scroll of Jeremiah's prophecies and read it in the Temple (Jer. 36:4ff.) and then wrote another scroll (Jer. 36:27ff.). He was carried into Egypt with Jeremiah (Jer. 43:6).
  2. One who helped repair the wall (Neh. 3:20).
  3. One who sealed the covenant (Neh. 10:6).
  4. Father of Maaseiah (14) (Neh. 11:5).

BARZILLAI: 1. A Gileadite who furnished David with supplies when he fled before Absalom (1) (2 Sam. 17:27ff.), but who declined to go to court when David returned to Jerusalem (2 Sam. 19:31ff.). David commended him to Solomon (1 Kg. 2:7). A family of priests traced their descent from his daughter Agia and took his name (Ezr. 2:61; Neh. 7:63). They are called 'sons of Jaddus' in 1 Esd. 5:38.
  2. Father of Adriel (2 Sam. 21:8).

BASEMATH: 1. Daughter of Elon (1) and wife of Esau (Gen. 26:34); called Adah (2) in Gen. 36:2.
  2. Daughter of Ishmael (1) and wife of Esau (Gen. 36:3); called Mahalath (1) in Gen. 28:9.
  3. Daughter of Solomon and wife of Ahimaaz (3) (1 Kg. 4:15).

BATHSHEBA: Wife of Uriah (1), seduced by David (2 Sam. 11:2ff.), and subsequently married by him (2 Sam. 11:27). She was the mother of Solomon (2 Sam. 12:24), and she collaborated with Nathan (2) to secure him the throne (1 Kg. 1:11ff.). Adonijah (1) sought her good offices to get Abishag as his wife, but it cost him his life (1 Kg. 2:13ff.). She is called Bathshua (2) in 1 Chr. 3:5.

BATHSHUA: 1. The Canaanite wife of **Judah** (1) (1 Chr. 2:3); called the daughter of **Shua** (1) in Gen. 38:12.
2. *See* **Bathsheba.**

BAVVAI: One who helped repair the wall (Neh. 3:18); called **Binnui** (2) in Neh. 3:24.

BAZLITH: *See* **Bazluth.**

BAZLUTH: Ancestor of some Temple servants who returned with **Zerubbabel** (Ezr. 2:52; 1 Esd. 5:31); called **Bazlith** in Neh. 7:54.

BEALIAH: A Benjaminite who joined **David** when he was an outlaw (1 Chr. 12:5).

BEBAI: 1. Ancestor of some who returned with **Zerubbabel** (Ezr. 2:11; Neh. 7:16; 1 Esd. 5:13) and with **Ezra** (1) (Ezr. 10:28; 1 Esd. 9:29).
2. One who sealed the covenant (Neh. 10:15).

BECHER: 1. Son of **Benjamin** (1) (Gen. 46:21; 1 Chr. 7:6, 8).
2. Head of a family of Ephraimites (Num. 26:35); called **Bered** in 1 Chr. 7:20.

BECORATH: Ancestor of **Saul** (1) (1 Sam. 9:1).

BEDAD: Edomite king who defeated Moab (Gen. 36:35; 1 Chr. 1:46).

BEDAN: A Manassite (1 Chr. 7:17).

BEDEIAH: One who married a foreign wife (Ezr. 10:35; 1 Esd. 9:34).

BEELIADA: Son of **David** (1 Chr. 14:7); called **Eliada** (1) in 2 Sam. 5:16.

BEELZEBUL: Prince of demons (Mt. 12:24), called the master of the house (Mt. 10:25); mentioned also in Mk 3:22; Lk. 11:15ff. *See* **Baalzebub.**

BEERA: An Asherite (1 Chr. 7:37).

BEERAH: A Reubenite carried captive by Assyria (1 Chr. 5:6).

BEERI: 1. A Hittite, father of **Judith** (1) (Gen. 26:34).
2. Father of **Hosea** (Hos. 1:1).

BEL: Babylonian god, named **Marduk** or **Merodach,** mentioned in Isa. 46:1; Jer. 50:2, 51:44; Ep. Jer. 6:41. In Bel and the Dragon he is ridiculed (Bel 3ff.).

BELA: 1. King of Edom (Gen. 36:32f.; 1 Chr. 1:43f.).
2. Son of **Benjamin** (1) (Gen. 46:21; Num. 26:38, 40; 1 Chr. 7:6f., 8:1, 3).
3. A Reubenite who dwelt in Moab (1 Chr. 5:8).

BELIAL: The arch-enemy of Christ in 2 C. 6:15.

BELNUUS: One who married a foreign wife (1 Esd. 9:31); called **Binnui** (4) in Ezr. 10:30.

BELSHAZZAR: Called son of Nebuchadnezzar (Dan. 5:1), at whose feast Daniel (2) interpreted the writing on the wall (Dan. 5:13ff.). Actually Belshazzar was the son of Nabonidus, the fourth successor of Nebuchadnezzar on the throne of Babylon, but unrelated to him. Belshazzar was regent for much of his father's reign.

BELTESHAZZAR: Name given to Daniel (5) (Dan. 1:7, 2:26, 4:8f., 18f., 5:12, 10:1).

BELTETHEMUS: Apparently the name of a Persian officer (1 Esd. 2:16, 25), but in fact the corruption of a Persian title of Rehum (2); cf. Ezr. 4:9.

BEN-ABINADAB: One of Solomon's officers (1 Kg. 4:11).

BENAIAH: 1. One of David's heroes (2 Sam. 23:20ff.) and captain of his bodyguard (2 Sam. 8:18, 20:23). He supported Solomon (1 Kg. 1:8, 38, 44) and slew Joab (1) at the king's command (1 Kg. 2:28ff.).
2. Another of David's heroes (2 Sam. 23:30; 1 Chr. 11:31), who was one of Solomon's officers (1 Chr. 27:14).
3. A Simeonite (1 Chr. 4:36).
4. A Levite musician (1 Chr. 15:18, 20, 16:5).
5. A priest (1 Chr. 15:24, 16:6).
6. An ancestor of Jahaziel (4) (2 Chr. 20:14).
7. An overseer under Hezekiah (1) (2 Chr. 31:13).
8. One who married a foreign wife (Ezr. 10:25; 1 Esd. 9:26).
9. Another who married a foreign wife (Ezr. 10:30); perhaps called Naidus in 1 Esd. 9:31.
10. Another who married a foreign wife (Ezr. 10:35), perhaps called Mamdai in 1 Esd. 9:34.
11. Another who married a foreign wife (Ezr. 10:43; 1 Esd. 9:35).
12. Father of Pelatiah (4) (Ezek. 11:1, 13).

BEN-AMMI: Son of Lot and his younger daughter (Gen. 19:38). He was the ancestor of the Ammonites.

BEN-DEKER: One of Solomon's officers (1 Kg. 4:9).

BEN-GEBER: One of Solomon's officers (1 Kg. 4:13).

BEN-HADAD: 1. Son of Tabrimmon and king of Damascus (1 Kg. 15:18), who helped Asa (1) against Israel (1 Kg. 15:20; 2 Chr. 16:4ff.).
2. Son of the preceding (1 Kg. 20:34), who fought against Ahab (1) (1 Kg. 20:1ff., 22:29ff.).
3. Son of Hazael and king of Damascus, who was thrice defeated by Jehoash (2) (2 Kg. 13:24f.). In Jer. 49:27 and Am. 1:4 Benhadad seems to be used as a general name for the kings of Damascus.

BEN-HAIL: One of the princes sent by Jehoshaphat (4) to teach (2 Chr. 17:7).

BEN-HANAN: A Judahite (1 Chr. 4:20).

BEN-HESED: One of Solomon's officers (1 Kg. 4:10).

BEN-HINNOM: One who gave his name to the valley near Jerusalem (Jer. 19:2, 6). It is elsewhere called the valley of Hinnom.

BEN-HUR: One of Solomon's officers (1 Kg. 4:8).

BENINU: One who sealed the covenant (Neh. 10:13).

BENJAMIN: 1. The youngest son of Jacob (1) by Rachel (Gen. 35:16ff.). He gave his name to one of the tribes of Israel. He was taken to Egypt on the insistence of Joseph (1) (Gen. 43:15), and Joseph's divining cup was put in his sack (Gen. 44:2), leading to the return of all the brothers to Egypt (Gen. 44:13) and Joseph's disclosure of his identity and embracing of Benjamin (Gen. 45:14).
    2. A descendant of 1 (1 Chr. 7:10).
    3. One who married a foreign wife (Ezr. 10:32).
    4. One who helped repair the wall (Neh. 3:23, 12:34).

BENO: A Merarite Levite (1 Chr. 24:26f.).

BENONI: Name first given to Benjamin (1) (Gen. 35:18).

BEN-ZOHETH: A Judahite (1 Chr. 4:20).

BEOR: 1. Father of Bela (1) (Gen. 36:32; 1 Chr. 1:43).
    2. Father of Balaam (Num. 22:5, 24:3, 15).

BERA: King of Sodom in the time of Abraham (Gen. 14:2).

BERACAH: A Benjaminite who joined David at Ziklag (1 Chr. 12:3).

BERAIAH: A Benjaminite (1 Chr. 8:21).

BERECHIAH: 1. Son of Zerubbabel (1 Chr. 3:20).
    2. Father of Asaph (2) (1 Chr. 6:39, 15:17).
    3. A Levite who dwelt in a village of the Netophathites (1 Chr. 9:16).
    4. A Levite gatekeeper (1 Chr. 15:23).
    5. An Ephraimite who supported Oded (2) (2 Chr. 28:12f.).
    6. Father of one who helped repair the wall (Neh. 3:4, 30, 6:18).
    7. Father of Zechariah (31) (Zech. 1:1).

BERED: Head of a family of Ephraimites (1 Chr. 7:20); called Becher (2) in Num. 26:35.

BERI: An Asherite (1 Chr. 7:36).

BERIAH: 1. Son of Asher (Gen. 46:17; Num. 26:44f.; 1 Chr. 7:30f.).
    2. Son of Ephraim (1 Chr. 7:23).
    3. A Benjaminite of Aijalon (1 Chr. 8:13, 16).
    4. A Levite (1 Chr. 23:10).

BERNICE: Sister of Herod (7) Agrippa, with whom she came to Caesarea (Ac. 25:13) and with whom she heard Paul's defence (Ac. 25:23, 26:30).

BESAI: Father of some Temple servants who returned with Zerubbabel (Ezr. 2:49; Neh. 7:52; 1 Esd. 5:31).

BESCASPASMYS: One who married a foreign wife (1 Esd. 9:31); called Mattaniah (8) in Ezr. 10:30.

BESODEIAH: Father of one who repaired the Old Gate (Neh. 3:6).

BETHEL: A god, whose name probably stands in Jer. 48:13.

BETHUEL: Son of Nahor (2) and Milcah (1) (Gen. 22:22, 24:24, 47) and nephew of Abraham (Gen. 24:15). He was the father of Laban (1) and Rebekah (Gen. 22:23, 25:20, 28:2, 5).

BEZAI: 1. Ancestor of some who returned with Zerubbabel (Ezr. 2:17; Neh. 7:23; 1 Esd. 5:16).
2. One who sealed the covenant (Neh. 10:18).

BEZALEL: 1. Craftsman who was chiefly responsible for the creation of the Tabernacle (Exod. 31:2, 35:30) and the Ark (Exod. 37:1).
2. One who married a foreign wife (Ezr. 10:30); called Sesthel in 1 Esd. 9:31.

BEZER: An Asherite (1 Chr. 7:37).

BICHRI: A Benjaminite, father of Sheba (1) (2 Sam. 20:1ff.).

BIDKAR: An officer of Jehu (2), who threw the body of Jehoram (1) into the plot of ground that belonged to Naboth (2 Kg. 9:25).

BIGTHA: One of the seven eunuchs of Ahasuerus (1) (Est. 1:10).

BIGTHAN: A eunuch of Ahasuerus (1) who plotted against the king (Est. 2:21); called Bigthana in Est. 6:2, and Gabatha in Ad. Est. 12:1.

BIGTHANA: See Bigthan.

BIGVAI: 1. One who returned with Zerubbabel (Ezr. 2:2; Neh. 7:7; 1 Esd. 5:8), and some of whose descendants returned with Ezra (1) (Ezr. 8:14; 1 Esd. 8:40).
2. One who sealed the covenant (Neh. 10:16).

BILDAD: One of the three friends of Job (Job 2:11), whose speeches stand in Job 8, 18, 25. He is condemned in Job 42:7 and Job intercedes for him (Job 42:9). He is described as a Shuhite.

BILGAH: 1. A priest in David's time (1 Chr. 24:14).
2. A priest who returned with Zerubbabel (Neh. 12:5).

BILGAI: One who sealed the covenant (Neh. 10:8).

BILHAH: Rachel's slave girl (Gen. 29:29; 46:25), who became the concubine of Jacob (1) (Gen. 30:3ff.) and the mother of Dan and Naphtali (Gen. 30:5ff., 35:25, 37:2). Reuben also had relations with her (Gen. 35:22).

BILHAN: 1. A Horite (Gen. 36:27; 1 Chr. 1:42).
2. A Benjaminite (1 Chr. 7:10).

BILSHAN: One who returned with Zerubbabel (Ezr. 2:2; Neh. 7:7; 1 Esd. 5:8).

BIMHAL: An Asherite (1 Chr. 7:33).

BINEA: A descendant of Saul (1) (1 Chr. 8:37, 9:43).

BINNUI: 1. A Levite, father of Noadiah (1) (Ezr. 8:33; 1 Esd. 8:63).
2. Son of Henadad and one who helped repair the wall (Neh. 3:24); called Bavvai in Neh. 3:18. He is perhaps the same as one who sealed the covenant (Neh. 10:9).
3. Ancestor of some who returned with Zerubbabel (Neh. 7:15); called Bani (4) in Ezr. 2:10; 1 Esd. 5:12.
4. One who married a foreign wife (Ezr. 10:30); called Belnuus in 1 Esd. 9:31.
5. Ancestor of some who married foreign wives (Ezr. 10:38); perhaps the same as Bani (7) in Ezr. 10:34; 1 Esd. 9:34.
6. A Levite who returned with Zerubbabel (Neh. 12:8).

BIRSHA: King of Gomorrah in Abraham's time (Gen. 14:2).

BIRZAITH: An Asherite (1 Chr. 7:31).

BISHLAM: An official under Artaxerxes (1) (Ezr. 4:7; 1 Esd. 2:16). It was understood by LXX in Ezr. 4:7 as a common noun, and it should perhaps be rendered 'with the approval of'.

BITHIAH: Daughter of Pharaoh who married Mered (1 Chr. 4:17).

BIZTHA: One of the seven eunuchs of Ahasuerus (1) (Est. 1:10).

BLASTUS: Chamberlain of Herod (6) (Ac. 12:20).

BOANERGES: A name given to James (1) and John (7) (Mk 3:17), and rendered 'sons of thunder'.

BOAZ: A Bethlehemite (Ru. 2:4), who married Ruth (Ru. 4:13) and became an ancestor of David (Ru. 4:17, 21f.; 1 Chr. 2:12ff.) and so of Jesus (1) (Mt. 1:5f.; Lk. 3:32).

BOCHERU: A descendant of Saul (1) (1 Chr. 8:38, 9:44).

BOHAN: Son of Reuben (Jos. 15:6, 18:17), after whom the Stone of Bohan was named.

BORITH: An ancestor of Ezra (1) (2 Esd. 1:2); called Bukki (2) in 1 Chr. 6:5, 51; Ezr. 7:4; 1 Esd. 8:2.

BUKKI: 1. A Danite who helped divide the land (Num. 34:22).
2. An ancestor of **Ezra** (1); *see* **Borith**.

BUKKIAH: A Levite of the sons of **Heman** (4) (1 Chr. 25:4, 13).

BUNAH: A Jerahmeelite (1 Chr. 2:25).

BUNNI: 1. A Levite who was present when **Ezra** (1) read the Law (Neh. 9:4).
2. One who sealed the covenant (Neh. 10:15).
3. A Levite (Neh. 11:15). 1 Chr. 9:14 has 'of the sons of **Merari**' (1) for 'son of Bunni'.

BUZ: 1. Son of **Nahor** (2) and nephew of **Abraham** (Gen. 22:21).
2. A Gadite (1 Chr. 5:14).

BUZI: Father of Ezekiel (Ezek. 1:3).

C

CAESAR: The surname of Julius Caesar, borne by the Roman emperors and used as a title. In the NT there are references to:
1. **Augustus** Caesar, who ordered the enrolment (Lk. 2:1).
2. **Tiberius** Caesar (Lk. 3:1 and all the remaining references in the Gospels).
3. **Claudius** Caesar (Ac. 11:28, 17:7, 18:2).
4. Perhaps Nero Caesar (Ac. 25:8, 11f., 21, 26:32, 27:24, 28:19). In Phil. 4:22 the reference may be to 3 or 4.

CAIAPHAS: Son-in-law of **Annas** (Jn 18:13) and High Priest A.D. 18-36. He advised that **Jesus** (1) should be put to death (Jn 11:49ff.), joined in planning the arrest of Jesus (Mt. 26:3), questioned Him at His trial (Mt. 26:57ff., cf. Mk 14:53ff.; Lk. 22:66ff.), and took part in the trial of **Peter** and John (7) (Ac. 4:6). He is referred to, though not by name, in Ac. 5:17, 27ff.

CAIN: Eldest son of **Adam** and **Eve** (Gen. 4:1). He offered unacceptable sacrifice to God (Gen. 4:3f.; cf. Heb. 11:4) and in consequence murdered his brother **Abel** (Gen. 4:8; 1 Jn 3:12). He became a wanderer (Gen. 4:11ff.), with the mark of Cain upon him (Gen. 4:15). He was the eponymous ancestor of the Kenites, who in the Hebrew are called Cain in Num. 24:23; Jg. 4:11, just as the Amalekites are called Amalek and the Moabites Moab.

CAINAN: 1. An ancestor of **Jesus** (1) (Lk. 3:37); called **Kenan** in Gen. 5:9ff.; 1 Chr. 1:2.

2. Another ancestor of Jesus (1) (Lk. 3:36), mentioned in LXX in Gen. 10:24, 11:12, but not in the Hebrew.

CALCOL: A Judahite (1 Chr. 2:6), whose wisdom was famed, but surpassed by Solomon's (1 Kg. 4:31).

CALEB: A Judahite (Num. 13:6) or Kenizzite (Num. 32:12; Jos. 14:6, 14), son of Jephunneh (1), who was one of the spies sent into Canaan (Num. 13:2ff.). He gave a favourable report (Num. 13:30ff.) and was promised entrance into the Promised Land (Num. 14:24). Joshua (1) assigned him Hebron as his portion (Jos. 14:13f.), and he in turn gave Debir to Othniel, together with the hand of his daughter Achsah (Jos. 15:15ff.; Jg. 1:11ff.). He is called the son of Hezron (2) in 1 Chr. 2:18, 24, 42, but the same person is intended (cf. 1 Chr. 2:49 and Jos. 15:16).

CALLISTHENES: A Syrian captured and burnt to death by the Jews, because he had set fire to the gates of the Temple (2 Mac. 8:33; cf. 1 Mac. 4:38).

CANAAN: Son of Ham and grandson of Noah (1) (Gen. 9:18, 10:6; 1 Chr. 1:8), and eponymous ancestor of the Canaanites (Gen. 10:15ff.). He is cursed by Noah (Gen. 9:25) because of his father's lack of modesty (Gen. 9:22ff.).

CANDACE The queen of Ethiopia, whose treasurer was baptized by Philip (6) (Ac. 8:27ff.). Candace is not a personal name, but a title like Pharaoh.

CARABASION: One who married a foreign wife (1 Esd. 9:34). The name appears to correspond to Meremoth (2) in Ezr. 10:36.

CARKAS: One of the seven eunuchs of Ahasuerus (1) (Est. 1:10).

CARMI: 1. A Reubenite (Gen. 46:9; Exod. 6:14; 1 Chr. 5:3).
2. A Judahite, father of Achan (Jos. 7:1, 18; 1 Chr. 2:7).
3. A Judahite (1 Chr. 4:1); perhaps the same as Chelubai (1 Chr. 2:9).

CARPUS: A man of Troas with whom Paul left his cloak (2 Tim. 4:13).

CARSHENA: One of the seven princes of Ahasuerus (1) (Est. 1:14).

CATHUA: Ancestor of some Temple servants who returned with Zerubbabel (1 Esd. 5:30); called Giddel (1) in Ezr. 2:47; Neh. 7:49.

CENDEBAEUS: Commander under Antiochus (7), sent against Simon (3) (1 Mac. 15:38ff.), who defeated him (1 Mac. 16:4ff.).

CEPHAS: *See* Peter.

CHABRIS: A magistrate of Bethulia (Jdt. 6:15, 8:10, 10:6).

CHAEREAS: Commander at Gazara, slain by Judas (1) (2 Mac. 10:32ff.).

CHALPHI: Father of Judas (2) (1 Mac. 11:70).

CHAREA: Ancestor of some Temple servants who returned with Zerubbabel (1 Esd. 5:32); perhaps called Harsha in Ezr. 2:52; Neh. 7:54.

CHARMIS: A magistrate of Bethulia (Jdt. 6:15, 8:10, 10:6).

CHEDORLAOMER: King of Elam in the time of Abraham (Gen. 14:1). He attacked Sodom and other cities and was pursued and routed by Abraham (Gen. 14:8ff.).

CHELAL: One who married a foreign wife (Ezr. 10:30).

CHELUB: 1. A Judahite (1 Chr. 4:11).
2. Father of Ezri (1 Chr. 27:26).

CHELUBAI: A Judahite (1 Chr. 2:9); called Caleb in 1 Chr. 2:18, 24, 42, and perhaps Carmi (3) in 1 Chr. 4:1.

CHELUHI: One who married a foreign wife (Ezr. 10:35).

CHEMOSH: God of the Moabites (Num. 21:29; Jg. 11:24; 1 Kg. 11:7, 33; Jer. 48:13).

CHENAANAH: 1. A Benjaminite (1 Chr. 7:10).
2. Father of Zedekiah (1) (1 Kg. 22:11, 24; 2 Chr. 18:10, 23).

CHENANI: A Levite in the time of Ezra (1) (Neh. 9:3).

CHENANIAH: 1. Leader of the music when David brought the Ark to Jerusalem (1 Chr. 15:22, 27).
2. An Izrahite appointed to administrative and judicial duties (1 Chr. 26:29); perhaps the same as 1.

CHERAN: A Horite (Gen. 36:26; 1 Chr. 1:41).

CHESED: Son of Nahor (2) and Milcah (1) (Gen. 22:22).

CHIDON: Owner of the threshing floor where Uzzah died (1 Chr. 13:9); called Nacon in 2 Sam. 6:6.

CHILEAB: Son of David by Abigail (1) (2 Sam. 3:3); called Daniel (1) in 1 Chr. 3:1.

CHILION: Son of Elimelech and Naomi (Ru. 1:2) and husband of Orpah (Ru. 1:4, 4:9). He died in Moab (Ru. 1:5).

CHIMHAM: Son of Barzillai (1) (cf. 1 Kg. 2:7). He accompanied David when he returned to Jerusalem after the rebellion of Absalom (1) (2 Sam. 19:37ff.). Geruth Chimham ('lodging place of Chimham'), mentioned in Jer. 41:17, may have been named after him.

CHISLON: Father of Elidad (Num. 34:21).

CHLOE: A woman whose slaves informed Paul of the strife in the church at Corinth (1 C. 1:11).

35

CHORBE: Ancestor of some who returned with Zerubbabel (1 Esd. 5:12); called Zaccai in Ezr. 2:9; Neh. 7:14.

CHOSAMAEUS: *See* Simon (1).

CHUZA: Steward of Herod (3) and husband of Joanna (Lk. 8:3).

CLAUDIA: A Roman Christian lady (2 Tim. 4:21).

CLAUDIUS: 1. Roman emperor (*see* Caesar, 3), in whose reign there was a great famine (Ac. 11:28), and who expelled the Jews from Rome (Ac. 18:2). He is referred to in Ac. 17:7.
2. *See* Lysias (2).

CLEMENT: A fellow worker with Paul (Phil. 4:3).

CLEOPAS: One of the disciples who went to Emmaus (Lk. 24:18); possibly, though not probably, the same as Clopas (Jn 19:25).

CLEOPATRA: The name of several queens of Egypt in the Ptolemaic period. The following appear to be referred to in the Bible:
1. Daughter of Antiochus (3) and wife of Ptolemy (5), whose marriage is alluded to in Dan. 11:17.
2. Daughter of Ptolemy (5) and wife of Ptolemy (6), referred to in Ad. Est. 11:1.
3. Daughter of Ptolemy (6) and wife of Alexander (2) (1 Mac. 10:57f.) and later of Demetrius (2) (1 Mac. 11:12).

CLOPAS: Husband of Mary (2) (Jn 19:25). The Aramaic underlying Clopas and Alphaeus is probably the same, and Clopas is sometimes identified with Alphaeus (1); also sometimes, improbably, with Cleopas.

COL-HOZEH: 1. Father of Shallum (14) (Neh. 3:15).
2. Father of Baruch (4) (Neh. 11:5); perhaps the same as 1.

CONANIAH: 1. A Levite in the time of Hezekiah (1) (2 Chr. 31:12f.). He had charge of the tithes.
2. A Levite chief in the time of Josiah (1) (2 Chr. 35:9); called Jeconiah (2) in 1 Esd. 1:9.

CONIAH: *See* Jehoiachin.

CORNELIUS: A Roman centurion whom Peter baptized and whose baptism was an important step in the admission of Gentiles to the Church (Ac. 10).

COSAM: An ancestor of Jesus (1) (Lk. 3:28).

COZBI: A Midianite woman killed by Phinehas (1) (Num. 25:7, 15).

CRESCENS: A companion of Paul's sent to Galatia (2 Tim. 4:10).

CRISPUS: A Corinthian Jew and leader of the synagogue who became a Christian (Ac. 18:8) and who was personally baptized by Paul (1 C. 1:14).

CUSH: 1. A son of Ham and ancestor of South Arabian tribes (Gen. 10:6ff.; 1 Chr. 1:8ff.), as well as of the Ethiopians, who are called Cush or Cushites in the Hebrew of the OT.

2. A Benjaminite, mentioned in the heading of Ps. 7.

CUSHAN-RISHATHAIM: King of Mesopotamia, from whose oppression Othniel delivered the Israelites (Jg. 3:8ff.).

CUSHI: 1. An ancestor of Jehudi (Jer. 36:14).

2. Father of Zephaniah (3) (Zeph. 1:1).

CUTHA: Ancestor of some Temple servants who returned with Zerubbabel (1 Esd. 5:32).

CYRUS: The founder of the Persian empire (2 Chr. 36:22f.; Dan. 1:21, 6:28, 10:1). He permitted the Jews to return to Palestine and to rebuild the Temple (Ezr. 1:1ff.; cf. 6:3, 14). He is called the shepherd (Isa. 44:28) and the anointed (Isa. 45:1) of God.

D

DABRIA: A scribe employed by Ezra (1) (2 Esd. 14:24).

DAGON: A Philistine god (Jg. 16:23; 1 Sam. 5:2ff.; 1 Mac. 10:83f., 11:4), who was perhaps also worshipped at Beth-shan when it was dominated by the Philistines (1 Chr. 10:10; but 1 Sam. 31:10 has 'the temple of Ashtaroth'). Dagon was not a fish-god, as was formerly supposed, but a Semitic corn-god.

DALPHON: Son of Haman, slain by the Jews (Est. 9:7).

DAMARIS: A convert of Paul's at Athens (Ac. 17:34).

DAN: Son of Jacob (1) by Bilhah (Gen. 30:5f., 35:25). He gave his name to one of the tribes of Israel.

DANIEL: 1. Son of David and Abigail (1) (1 Chr. 3:1); called Chileab in 2 Sam. 3:3.

2. A priest who returned with Ezra (1) (Ezr. 8:2); called Gamael in 1 Esd. 8:29.

3. One who sealed the covenant (Neh. 10:6).

4. An ancient worthy, renowned for righteousness and wisdom, mentioned with Noah (1) and Job (Ezek. 14:14, 20, 28:3). He is probably the person who figures in a Ras Shamra text.

5. The hero of the book of Daniel and its additions in the Apocrypha. He was a Jewish captive in Babylon (Dan. 1:3ff.) and was given the name

Belteshazzar (Dan. 1:7). He refused to eat forbidden food (Dan. 1:8ff.) and interpreted dreams for **Nebuchadnezzar** (Dan. 2, 4) and the writing on the wall for **Belshazzar** (Dan. 5). He was cast into the den of lions for persisting in praying in defiance of the order of **Darius** (3) and was delivered (Dan. 6), and had visions himself (Dan. 7ff.).

DARA: *See* **Darda.**

DARDA: A wise man whose wisdom was surpassed by **Solomon's** (1 Kg. 4:31); called **Dara** in 1 Chr. 2:6, where he is said to be a Judahite.

DARIUS: 1. Darius I, king of Persia, who suppressed the revolt that broke out on the death of Cambyses, the son and successor of **Cyrus**, and reorganized the Persian empire. He was contemporary with **Haggai** and **Zechariah** (31) (Hag. 1:1, 2:1, 10; Zech. 1:1, 7, 7:1) and he confirmed the authority to rebuild the Temple (Ezr. 5f.), and the return of **Zerubbabel** may have taken place in his reign (1 Esd. 3ff.).

2. Darius III, the last king of Persia, who was defeated by **Alexander** (1). He is probably referred to in Neh. 12:22, as well as in 1 Mac. 1:1.

3. Darius the Mede, who figures in the book of Daniel (Dan. 5:31, 6:1ff., 9:1, 11:1), who would appear to have reigned between **Belshazzar** and **Cyrus**. He is said to be the son of **Ahasuerus** (2) (Dan. 9:1). But no Darius reigned before Cyrus, and there is some confusion in the account.

DARKON: One whose descendants returned with **Zerubbabel** (Ezr. 2:56; Neh. 7:58); called **Lozon** in 1 Esd. 5:33.

DATHAN: A Reubenite, son of **Eliab** (2), who conspired against **Moses** with **Abiram** (1) (Num. 16:1, 26:9; Dt. 11:6), and who was swallowed up (Num. 16:31; Ps. 106:17).

DAVID: Youngest son of **Jesse** (1 Sam. 16:1ff.), who was anointed by **Samuel** (1 Sam. 16:13). He was brought to **Saul** (1) as a skilled musician (1 Sam. 16:18ff.). He slew **Goliath** (1 Sam. 17) and aroused the envy of Saul (1 Sam. 18:8ff.), who sought to bring about his death (1 Sam. 18:20ff.). He became the friend of **Jonathan** (1) (1 Sam. 18:1ff.) and married **Michal** (1 Sam. 18:27). When Saul sought to kill him he was saved by Jonathan (1 Sam. 19:1ff., 20:1ff.) and by Michal (1 Sam. 19:11ff.) and became an outlaw until Saul died (1 Sam. 21ff.). For a time he was dependent on **Achish** (1) (1 Sam. 21:10ff., 27:1ff.). On the death of Saul and Jonathan he composed an elegy on them (2 Sam. 1:19ff.) and became king of Judah (2 Sam. 2:1ff.) until the elimination of **Ish-bosheth** (2 Sam. 3:5ff.), when he became king of all Israel (2 Sam. 5:1ff.). He conquered Jerusalem and made it his capital (2 Sam. 5:6ff.) and brought the Ark into the city (2 Sam. 6). He defeated the Philistines (2 Sam. 5:17ff.) and other neighbouring states (2 Sam. 8, 10ff.) and added them to his kingdom. His adultery with **Bathsheba** and elimination of **Uriah** (1) (2 Sam. 11:2ff.) brought on him the condemnation of **Nathan** (2) (2 Sam. 12:1ff.). During his reign there were rebellions by **Absalom** (1) (2 Sam. 15ff.) and **Sheba** (1) (2 Sam. 20). At an unknown point in his reign there was a famine which led to the killing of seven of Saul's descendants (2 Sam. 21:1ff.), and at another point a pestilence following a census, which led to the purchase of the site of the future Temple (2 Sam. 24; 1 Chr. 21). At the end of his reign there was a struggle for the succession which he resolved by elevating **Solomon** to the throne (1 Kg. 1f.). In 1 Chr. 11ff. there is an account of his reign with some additions and modifications and with the omission of the story of his adultery and of the rebellions. The Chronicler gives an account of his organization of the Temple worship (2 Chr. 22ff.) which is absent from the earlier account. That David was a poet and a musician is certain, but tradition has ascribed to him the composition of many psalms which he did not compose.

DEBIR: King of Eglon, who joined the alliance against **Joshua** (1) (Jos. 10:3), and who was put to death when defeated and captured (Jos. 10:26f.).

DEBORAH: 1. The nurse of **Rebekah** (Gen. 24:59), who died at Bethel (Gen. 35:8).

2. A prophetess (Jg. 4:4) who supported **Barak** in arousing the Israelite tribes against **Jabin** and **Sisera** (1) (Jg. 4:6ff., 12ff.) and to whom is ascribed the magnificent poem celebrating the victory (Jg. 5).

3. **Tobit's** grandmother, who taught him charity (Tob. 1:8).

DEDAN: Grandson of **Cush** (1) (Gen. 10:7; 1 Chr. 1:9) or grandson of **Abraham** and **Keturah** (Gen. 25:3; 1 Chr. 1:32), and eponymous ancestor of an Arabian people.

DELAIAH: 1. A descendant of **Solomon** (1 Chr. 3:24).

2. A priest in **David's** time (1 Chr. 24:18).

3. Ancestor of some who returned with **Zerubbabel** but were unable to prove their Israelite descent (Ezr. 2:60; Neh. 7:62; 1 Esd. 5:37).

4. Father of **Shemaiah** (19) (Neh. 6:10).

5. One of the princes who heard **Baruch** (1) read the scroll of **Jeremiah** (1) (Jer. 36:12) and who were sent to arrest Baruch and Jeremiah (Jer. 36:25).

DELILAH: A Philistine woman whom **Samson** loved (Jg. 16:4) and who betrayed him to the Philistines (Jg. 16:5ff.).

DEMAS: A companion of **Paul** in imprisonment (Col. 4:14; Phm. 24), who deserted him and went to Thessalonica (2 Tim. 4:10).

DEMETRIUS: 1. Demetrius I, Soter, king of Syria, son of **Seleucus** (4). He was a hostage in Rome when his father was assassinated and his uncle **Antiochus** (4) seized the throne. After the death of Antiochus he escaped from Rome and landed at Tripolis to dispute the throne with **Antiochus** (5) (1 Mac. 7:1ff.; 2 Mac. 14:1f.). Seven years later **Alexander** (2) claimed the throne and he and Demetrius competed for the support of **Jonathan** (3) (1 Mac. 10:3ff., 15ff., 22ff., 46f.). Demetrius was defeated and killed by Alexander (1 Mac. 10:48ff.).

2. Demetrius II, Nicator, son of 1. He was sent abroad for safety by his father, but was recalled by **Ptolemy** (6) when the latter attacked **Alexander** (2), and became king of Syria (1 Mac. 11:9ff.). He married **Cleopatra** (3) (1 Mac. 11:12). Involved in war with **Trypho** (1 Mac. 11:39ff.), he competed with the latter for the support of **Jonathan** (3) (1 Mac. 11:41ff., 54ff.), but before the dispute with Trypho was resolved he was captured by **Arsaces** (1 Mac. 14:1ff.).

3. A silversmith of Ephesus, who led the riot against **Paul** (Ac. 19:24ff.).

4. A Christian commended in 3 Jn 12.

DEMOPHON: A Syrian governor in the time of **Judas** (1) (2 Mac. 12:2).

DEUEL: Father of **Eliasaph** (1) (Num. 1:14, 7:42, 47, 10:20); called **Reuel** (3) in Num. 2:14.

DIBLAIM: Father of **Gomer** (2) (Hos. 1:3).

DIBRI: A Danite, whose grandson blasphemed and was stoned (Lev. 24:10ff.).

DIDYMUS: *See* **Thomas**.

DIKLAH: Son of **Joktan** (Gen. 10:27; 1 Chr. 1:21).

DINAH: Daughter of **Jacob** (1) by **Leah** (Gen. 30:21). She was violated by **Shechem** (Gen. 34:2), and her brothers, **Simeon** (1) and **Levi** (1), avenged the deed (Gen. 34:25ff.).

DIONYSIUS THE AREOPAGITE: A member of the Athenian court of the Areopagus, who was converted by **Paul** (Ac. 17:34).

DIONYSUS: Commonly called Bacchus, a Thracian vegetation god who became connected with the vine and whose festivals were orgiastic. In the time of **Antiochus** (4) Jews were compelled to share in the celebration of his festival (2 Mac. 6:7) and **Nicanor** (1) threatened to erect a temple in his honour on the site of the Temple (2 Mac. 14:33).

DIOTREPHES: A Christian who liked to put himself first and who resisted authority (3 Jn 9f.).

DIPHATH: Son of **Gomer** (1) (1 Chr. 1:6); called **Riphath** in Gen. 10:3.

DISHAN: A Horite (Gen. 36:21, 28, 30; 1 Chr. 1:38, 42).

DISHON: 1. A Horite, son of **Seir** (1) (Gen. 36:21; 1 Chr. 1:38).

2. A Horite, son of **Anah** (2) (Gen. 36:25f., 30; 1 Chr. 1:41).

DODAI: *See* **Dodo**.

DODAVAHU: Father of **Eliezer** (7) (2 Chr. 20:37).

DODO: 1. Grandfather of **Tola** (Jg. 10:1).

2. Father of **Eleazar** (3) (2 Sam. 23:9; 1 Chr. 11:12). He is called **Dodai** in 1 Chr. 27:4, where 'Eleazar the son of' has perhaps been omitted.

3. Father of Elhanan (2) (2 Sam. 23:24; 1 Chr. 11:26).

DOEG: An Edomite who reported to **Saul** (1) on **David's** visit to Nob (1 Sam. 21:7, 22:9), and then slew all the priests of Nob at Saul's command (1 Sam. 22:18). He is mentioned in the heading of Ps. 52.

DORCAS: A Christian woman of Joppa, who was full of good deeds, and who was raised from the dead by **Peter** (Ac. 9:36ff.). She was also called **Tabitha.**

DORYMENES: Father of **Ptolemy** (8) (1 Mac. 3:38; 2 Mac. 4:45).

DOSITHEUS: 1. A priest who brought to **Ptolemy** (6) the Letter of Purim (Ad. Est. 11:1).
2. One of the men of **Bacenor.** who tried to capture **Gorgias** (2 Mac. 12:35).
3. A captain under **Judas** (1) (2 Mac. 12:19, 24).

DRUSILLA: Wife of **Felix** (Ac. 24:24). She was the daughter of **Herod** (6).

DUMAH: Son of Ishmael (1) (Gen. 25:14; 1 Chr. 1:30), who gave his name to a region.

E

EBAL: 1. A Horite (Gen. 36:23; 1 Chr. 1:40).
2. Son of **Joktan** (1 Chr. 1:22); called **Obal** in Gen. 10:28.

EBED: 1. Father of **Gaal** (Jg. 9:26ff.).
2. One who returned with **Ezra** (1) (Ezr. 8:6); called **Obed** (6) in 1 Esd. 8:32.

EBED-MELECH: An Ethiopian eunuch who rescued **Jeremiah** (1) from the cistern (Jer. 38:7ff.) and who was promised divine protection (Jer. 39:15ff.).

EBER: 1. The eponymous ancestor of the Hebrews (Gen. 10:21, 24f., 11:14ff.; 1 Chr. 1:18ff.); named in the genealogy of **Jesus** (1) (Lk. 3:35).
2. In Num. 24:24 Eber is of uncertain meaning, and is perhaps not a personal name.
3. A Gadite (1 Chr. 5:13).
4. A Benjaminite (1 Chr. 8:12).
5. Another Benjaminite (1 Chr. 8:22).
6. A priestly head (Neh. 12:20).

EBIASAPH: A descendant of **Korah** (2) (1 Chr. 6:23, 37, 9:19); called Abiasaph in Exod. 6:24.

EDDINUS: A Temple singer (1 Esd. 1:15). The name replaces **Jeduthun** of the parallel 2 Chr. 35:15.

EDEN: 1. A Levite, son of **Joah** (2) (2 Chr. 29:12).
  2. A Levite who assisted in distributing portions to the priests (2 Chr. 31:15); possibly the same as 1.

EDER: 1. A Benjaminite (1 Chr. 8:15).
  2. A Merarite Levite (1 Chr. 23:23, 24:30).

EDNA: Wife of **Raguel** (Tob. 7:2, 8) and mother of **Sarah** (2) (Tob. 7:16f.).

EDOM: Alternative name for **Esau** (Gen. 25:30). He was the eponymous ancestor of the Edomites.

EGLAH: One of David's wives (2 Sam. 3:5; 1 Chr. 3:3).

EGLON: King of Moab, who oppressed Israel and was assassinated by **Ehud** (1) (Jg. 3:12ff.).

EHI: Son of **Benjamin** (1) (Gen. 46:21); perhaps the same as **Ahiram** (Num. 26:38).

EHUD: 1. A left-handed Benjaminite who stabbed **Eglon** and delivered the Israelites from the Moabites (Jg. 3:12ff.).
  2. A Benjaminite (1 Chr. 7:10, 8:6).

EKER: A Jerahmeelite (1 Chr. 2:27).

ELA: Father of **Shimei** (4) (1 Kg. 4:18).

ELAH: 1. An Edomite chief (Gen. 36:41; 1 Chr. 1:52).
  2. Son and successor of **Baasha**, king of Israel (1 Kg. 16:8ff.). He was assassinated by **Zimri** (4) after a reign of two years.
  3. Father of **Hoshea** (2) (2 Kg. 15:30, 17:1).
  4. Son of **Caleb** (1 Chr. 4:15).
  5. A Benjaminite (1 Chr. 9:8).

ELAM: 1. Son of **Shem** (Gen. 10:22; 1 Chr. 1:17) and eponymous ancestor of the Elamites.
  2. A Benjaminite (1 Chr. 8:24).
  3. A Korahite (1 Chr. 26:3).
  4. Ancestor of some who returned with **Zerubbabel** (Ezr. 2:7; Neh. 7:12; 1 Esd. 5:12) and with **Ezra** (1) (Ezr. 8:7; 1 Esd. 8:33). Six members of the family married foreign wives (Ezr. 10:26; 1 Esd. 9:27), and one urged Ezra to deal with the problem of mixed marriages (Ezr. 10:2ff.).
  5. Ancestor of another group, curiously of the same number (but cf. 1 Esd. 5:22), which returned with **Zerubbabel** (Ezr. 2:31; Neh. 7:34).
  6. One who sealed the covenant (Neh. 10:14).

7. A priest who was present at the dedication of the wall (Neh. 12:42).

ELASAH: 1. One who married a foreign wife (Ezr. 10:22; 1 Esd. 9:22).
2. One of the bearers of the message of Zedekiah (2) to Babylon (Jer. 29:3).

EL-BERITH: *See* Baal-berith.

ELDAAH: Son of Midian (Gen. 25:4; 1 Chr. 1:33).

ELDAD: One who prophesied in the camp in the wilderness (Num. 11:26ff.).

ELEAD: An Ephraimite (1 Chr. 7:21).

ELEADAH: An Ephraimite (1 Chr. 7:20).

ELEASAH: 1. A Judahite (1 Chr. 2:39f.).
2. A descendant of Saul (1) (1 Chr. 8:37, 9:43).

ELEAZAR: 1. Son of Aaron (Exod. 6:23; Num. 3:2), who was consecrated to the priesthood with him (Exod. 28:1). He married a daughter of Putiel and was the father of Phinehas (1) (Exod. 6:25; Jos. 24:33). He had oversight of the Levites (Num. 3:32) and succeeded Aaron as chief priest (Num. 20:25ff.; Dt. 10:6). He took part in the census in Moab (Num. 26:1, 3, 63) and assisted Joshua (1) in the allotment of the land (Num. 34:17; Jos. 14:1, 17:4, 19:51, 21:1). He died and was buried at Gibeah (Jos. 24:33). The Zadokites traced their descent through him (1 Chr. 6:3ff.).
2. One who had charge of the Ark at Kiriath-jearim (1 Sam. 7:1).
3. One of David's heroes (2 Sam. 23:9; 1 Chr. 11:12). He fought heroically at the battle of Pas-dammim (1 Chr. 11:13f.), but this feat is attributed to Shammah (3) in 2 Sam. 23:11f.
4. A Levite of the sons of Merari (1) (1 Chr. 23:21f.). He had no sons (1 Chr. 24:28).
5. A priest in the time of Ezra (1) (Ezr. 8:33; 1 Esd. 8:63).
6. One who married a foreign wife (Ezr. 10:25; 1 Esd. 9:26).
7. A priest who was present at the dedication of the wall (Neh. 12:42).
8. Brother of Judas (1) (1 Mac. 2:5, 6:43ff.; 2 Mac. 8:23), surnamed Avaran.
9. An aged martyr (2 Mac. 6:18ff.).
10. Father of Jason (1) (1 Mac. 8:17).
11. Father of Sirach (Sir. 50:27).
12. An ancestor of Jesus (1) (Mt. 1:15).

EL-HANAN: 1. Son of Jaare-oregim the Bethlehemite (2 Sam. 21:19) or of Jair (3) (1 Chr. 20:5). In the former passage he is credited with slaying Goliath, in the latter with slaying Lahmi the brother of Goliath. 'Lahmi' is probably a corruption of 'Bethlehemite' and 'oregim' means 'weavers' and is probably a duplicate of the word which occurs later in the verse in both versions. It is possible that 'the brother of' is an insertion to harmonize with the tradition that David slew Goliath, though some scholars hold that El-hanan is David, the latter being his throne name.

2. Son of **Dodo** (3) and one of David's heroes (2 Sam. 23:24; 1 Chr. 11:26).

ELI: Priest of Shiloh (1 Sam. 1:9) who judged Israel forty years (1 Sam. 4:18). He spoke to **Hannah** (1 Sam. 1:12ff.) and to him **Samuel** was brought (1 Sam. 1:28, 2:11). His sons were worthless (1 Sam. 2:12ff.) and a prophet predicted the supersession of his line (1 Sam. 2:27ff.). This was repeated in substance through Samuel (1 Sam. 3). When the Ark was taken from Shiloh to the battlefield (1 Sam. 4:4) and was captured by the Philistines (1 Sam. 4:11), Eli, now aged ninety-eight (1 Sam. 4:15), died of shock (1 Sam. 4:18).

ELIAB: 1. Representative of Zebulun at the census in the wilderness (Num. 1:9) and on other occasions (Num. 2:7, 7:24, 29, 10:16).

2. Father of **Dathan** and **Abiram** (1) (Num. 16:1, 12, 26:9).

3. David's eldest brother (1 Sam. 16:6f.), who fought against the Philistines and rebuked David for going to the camp (1 Sam. 17:28ff.); possibly the same as **Elihu** (4).

4. A Levite (1 Chr. 6:27); called **Eliel** (2) in 1 Chr. 6:34, and **Elihu** (1) in 1 Sam. 1:1.

5. A Gadite who joined David in the wilderness (1 Chr. 12:9).

6. A Levite musician (1 Chr. 15:18).

7. An ancestor of **Judith** (2) (Jdt. 8:1).

ELIADA: 1. Son of David (2 Sam. 5:16); called **Beeliada** in 1 Chr. 14:7.

2. Father of **Rezon** (1 Kg. 11:23).

3. A Benjaminite officer under **Jehoshaphat** (4) (2 Chr. 17:17).

ELIAHBA: One of David's heroes (2 Sam. 23:32; 1 Chr. 11:33).

ELIAKIM: 1. Major-domo of Hezekiah (1) who was sent to parley with the emissaries of **Sennacherib** (Isa. 36:3; cf. 2 Kg. 18:18). He is commended by Isaiah (Isa. 22:20ff.).

2. Son of **Josiah** (1) (2 Kg. 23:34) who was placed on the throne by Neco with the throne name of **Jehoiakim** (1).

ELIALIS: One who married a foreign wife (1 Esd. 9:34).

ELIAM: 1. Father of **Bathsheba** (2 Sam. 11:3); called **Ammiel** (3) in 1 Chr. 3:5.

2. One of David's heroes (2 Sam. 23:34). He was the son of **Ahithophel.**

ELIASAPH: 1. Representative of Gad at the census in the wilderness (Num. 1:14) and on other occasions (Num. 2:14, 7:42, 47, 10:20).

2. Leader of the Gershonites (Num. 3:24).

ELIASHIB: 1. A descendant of **Solomon** (1 Chr. 3:24).

2. Head of a priestly course (1 Chr. 24:12).

3. Father of Jehohanan (4) (Ezr. 10:6; Neh. 12:23; 1 Esd. 9:1); probably the same as 7.
4. One who married a foreign wife (Ezr. 10:24; 1 Esd. 9:24).
5. Another who married a foreign wife (Ezr. 10:27; 1 Esd. 9:28).
6. Another who married a foreign wife (Ezr. 10:36; 1 Esd. 9:34).
7. High Priest contemporary with Nehemiah (2) and who assisted in repairing the wall (Neh. 3:1). He later allowed Tobiah (2) to use a room in the Temple (Neh. 13:4). He was the father of Joiada (2) (Neh. 12:10, 13:28), who was the father of Jehohanan (4) (Neh. 12:11, 22; *see* Jonathan, 11). Hence in Ezr. 10:6; Neh. 12:23; 1 Esd. 9:1 'father' may mean 'grandfather' and Eliashib be the same as 3.

ELIASIS: One who married a foreign wife (1 Esd. 9:34); perhaps the same as Jaasu in Ezr. 10:37.

ELIATHAH: A Temple musician (1 Chr. 25:4, 27).

ELIDAD: Representative of Benjamin for the allotment of the land (Num. 34:21).

ELIEHOENAI: 1. A Korahite gatekeeper (1 Chr. 26:3).
2. One who returned with Ezra (1) (Ezr. 8:4; 1 Esd. 8:31).

ELIEL: 1. A Manassite (1 Chr. 5:24).
2. A Kohathite (1 Chr. 6:34); called Eliab (4) in 1 Chr. 6:27 and Elihu (1) in 1 Sam. 1:1.
3. A Benjaminite (1 Chr. 8:20).
4. Another Benjaminite (1 Chr. 8:22).
5. One of David's heroes (1 Chr. 11:46).
6. Another of David's heroes (1 Chr. 11:47).
7. A Gadite who joined David in the wilderness (1 Chr. 12:11).
8. A Levite who helped to bring the Ark to Jerusalem (1 Chr. 15:9, 11).
9. A Levite in the time of Hezekiah (1) (2 Chr. 31:13).

ELIENAI: A Benjaminite (1 Chr. 8:20).

ELIEZAR: 1. One of those sent to Iddo (6) (1 Esd. 8:43); called Eliezer (8) in Ezr. 8:16.
2. A priest who married a foreign wife (1 Esd. 9:19); called Eliezer (9) in Ezr. 10:18.

ELIEZER: 1. Abraham's servant (Gen. 15:2). It was probably he who was sent to bring a wife for Isaac (Gen. 24).
2. Son of Moses by Zipporah (Exod. 18:4; 1 Chr. 23:15, 17).
3. A Benjaminite (1 Chr. 7:8).
4. A priest who shared in bringing the Ark to Jerusalem (1 Chr. 15:24).
5. A Levite (1 Chr. 26:25).
6. Chief officer for the Reubenites in David's reign (1 Chr. 27:16).

45

7. One who prophesied the destruction of the fleet of **Jehoshaphat** (4) (2 Chr. 20:37).

8. One of those sent to **Iddo** (6) (Ezr. 8:16); called **Eliezar** (1) in 1 Esd. 8:43.

9. A priest who married a foreign wife (Ezr. 10:18); called **Eliezar** (2) in 1 Esd. 9:19.

10. A Levite who married a foreign wife (Ezr. 10:23); called **Jonah** (2) in 1 Esd. 9:23.

11. A layman who married a foreign wife (Ezr. 10:31); called **Elionas** in 1 Esd. 9:32.

12. An ancestor of **Jesus** (1) (Lk. 3:29).

ELIHOREPH: A secretary of Solomon's (1 Kg. 4:3); brother of Ahijah (2).

ELIHU: 1. An ancestor of **Samuel** (1 Sam. 1:1); called **Eliab** (4) in 1 Chr. 6:27 and **Eliel** (2) in 1 Chr. 6:34.

2. A Manassite who joined **David** at Ziklag (1 Chr. 12:20).

3. A Korahite gatekeeper (1 Chr. 26:7).

4. A brother of **David's** (1 Chr. 27:18); possibly the same as **Eliab** (3).

5. A young man who addressed **Job** after the three friends had finished (Job 32ff.).

ELIJAH: 1. Prophet from Tishbe in Gilead (1 Kg. 17:1), who opposed the promotion of the cult of **Baal** (1) by **Jezebel** (1) in the reign of **Ahab** (1). He predicted a three years' drought (1 Kg. 17:1), and at the end of the period he challenged the prophets of Baal to a contest on Carmel (1 Kg. 18) in which the Lord vindicated Himself against Baal. The prophets of Baal were slain (1 Kg. 18:40) and the drought was ended (1 Kg. 18:41ff.). Threatened by Jezebel, he went to Horeb and received comfort and direction from God (1 Kg. 19). During the period of drought he was fed by ravens (1 Kg. 17:4ff.) and later by a widow of Zarephath (1 Kg. 17:8ff.), whose son he raised from the dead (1 Kg. 17:17ff.). He rebuked Ahab after the judicial murder of **Naboth** (1 Kg. 21) and **Ahaziah** (1) for inquiring of **Baalzebub** (2 Kg. 1). He was taken up to heaven by a whirlwind after anointing **Elisha** as his successor (2 Kg. 2). He was expected to return before the day of the Lord (Mal. 4:5) and to be the herald of the Messiah (Mt. 11:14, 17:10ff.).

2. A Benjaminite (1 Chr. 8:27).

3. A priest who married a foreign wife (Ezr. 10:21).

4. A layman who married a foreign wife (Ezr. 10:26; 1 Esd. 9:27).

5. An ancestor of **Judith** (2) (Jdt. 8:1).

ELIKA: One of David's heroes (2 Sam. 23:25).

ELIMELECH: Husband of Naomi (Ru. 1:2), who went to Moab and died there (Ru. 1:3). He was a kinsman of **Boaz** (Ru. 2:1, 3, 4:3).

ELIOENAI: 1. A descendant of **David** (1 Chr. 3:23f.).

2. A Simeonite (1 Chr. 4:36).

3. A Benjaminite (1 Chr. 7:8).
4. A priest who married a foreign wife (Ezr. 10:22; 1 Esd. 9:22).
5. A layman who married a foreign wife (Ezr. 10:27; 1 Esd. 9:28).
6. A priest in the time of Nehemiah (2) (Neh. 12:41).

ELIONAS: A layman who married a foreign wife (1 Esd. 9:32); called Eliezer (11) in Ezr. 10:31.

ELIPHAL: One of David's heroes (1 Chr. 11:35); perhaps called Eliphelet (3) in 2 Sam. 23:34.

ELIPHAZ: 1. Son of Esau by Adah (2) (Gen. 36:4, 10) and father of Amalek by Timna (1) (Gen. 36:12).
2. One of Job's three friends (Job 2:11), whose speeches stand in Job 4f., 15, 22. He is condemned in Job 42:7 and Job intercedes for him (Job 42:9). He is described as a Temanite.

ELIPHELEHU: A Levite musician (1 Chr. 15:18, 21).

ELIPHELET: 1. Son of David (2 Sam. 5:16; 1 Chr. 3:8, 14:7).
2. A second son of David with the same name (1 Chr. 3:6); called Elpelet in 1 Chr. 14:5.
3. One of David's heroes (2 Sam. 23:34); perhaps called Eliphal in 1 Chr. 11:35.
4. A descendant of Saul (1) (1 Chr. 8:39).
5. One who returned with Ezra (1) (Ezr. 8:13; 1 Esd. 8:39).
6. One who married a foreign wife (Ezr. 10:33; 1 Esd. 9:33).

ELISHA: A prophet from Abelmeholah (1 Kg. 19:16), son of Shaphat (2) (1 Kg. 19:16, 19; 2 Kg. 3:11, 6:31). He succeeded Elijah (1) (2 Kg. 2). He performed various miracles (2 Kg. 4, 6:1ff.), including the raising of the son of a Shunammite woman (2 Kg. 4:18ff.), and by obeying his word Naaman (4) was cleansed of leprosy (2 Kg. 5). He helped the king of Israel in his Syrian wars (2 Kg. 6:8ff., 7:1ff.), and incited Hazael to seize the throne of Damascus (2 Kg. 8:7ff.) and Jehu (2) to seize the throne of Samaria (2 Kg. 9:1ff.). On his death bed he promised Jehoash (2) victory over the Syrians (2 Kg. 13:14ff.).

ELISHAH: Son of Javan (Gen. 10:4; 1 Chr. 1:7), who gave his name to a district whence Tyre obtained purple dye (Ezek. 27:7).

ELISHAMA: 1. An Ephraimite, grandfather of Joshua (1) (Num. 1:10, 2:18, 7:48, 53, 10:22; 1 Chr. 7:26).
2. Son of David (2 Sam. 5:16; 1 Chr. 3:8, 14:7).
3. Another son of David (1 Chr. 3:6); called Elishua in 2 Sam. 5:15; 1 Chr. 14:5.
4. Grandfather of Ishmael (2) (2 Kg. 25:25; Jer. 41:1).
5. A Jerahmeelite (1 Chr. 2:41).
6. A priest whom Jehoshaphat (4) sent to teach the people (2 Chr. 17:8).
7. A secretary to Jehoiakim (1) (Jer. 36:12, 20f.).

ELISHAPHAT: One of the commanders who helped to make **Jehoash** (1) king (2 Chr. 23:1).

ELISHEBA: Daughter of **Amminadab** (1) and wife of **Aaron** (Exod. 6:23).

ELISHUA: Son of **David** (2 Sam. 5:15; 1 Chr. 14:5); called **Elishama** (3) in 1 Chr. 3:6.

ELIUD: An ancestor of **Jesus** (1) (Mt. 1:14f.).

ELIZABETH: Wife of **Zechariah** (34) and mother of **John** (6) the Baptist (Lk. 1:5ff.). She was a kinswoman of **Mary** (1) (Lk. 1:36).

ELIZAPHAN: 1. A Kohathite Levite (Num. 3:30; 1 Chr. 15:8; 2 Chr. 29:13); called **Elzaphan** in Exod. 6:22; Lev. 10:4. He helped to remove the bodies of **Nadab** (1) and **Abihu** (Lev. 10:4f.).
　　2. Representative of Zebulun for allotting the land (Num. 34:25).

ELIZUR: Representative of Reuben at the census in the wilderness (Num. 1:5) and on other occasions (Num. 2:10, 7:30, 35, 10:18).

ELKANAH: 1. Son of **Korah** (2) (Exod. 6:24).
　　2. Father of **Samuel** (1 Sam. 1). He was an Ephraimite according to 1 Sam. 1:1, but a Levite according to 1 Chr. 6:27, 34.
　　3. A Levite (1 Chr. 6:23).
　　4. Another Levite, descendant of 3 (1 Chr. 6:26, 35).
　　5. Another Levite, who dwelt in a village of the Netophathites (1 Chr. 9:16).
　　6. A Benjaminite who joined **David** in Ziklag (1 Chr. 12:6).
　　7. A Levite gatekeeper (1 Chr. 15:23).
　　8. An officer of **Ahaz** (1) (2 Chr. 28:7).

ELKIAH: An ancestor of **Judith** (2) (Jdt. 8:1).

ELMADAM: An ancestor of **Jesus** (1) (Lk. 3:28).

ELNAAM: Father of two of **David's** heroes (1 Chr. 11:46).

ELNATHAN: 1. Father of **Nehushta** (2 Kg. 24:8).
　　2. One who was sent by **Jehoiakim** (1) to Egypt to fetch **Uriah** (5) (Jer. 26:22f.). He urged the king not to burn the scroll of **Jeremiah** (1) (Jer. 36:25). He may be the same as 1.
　　3. Three persons sent for by **Ezra** (1) from Ahava (Ezr. 8:16). In 1 Esd. 8:44 only two persons of this name are mentioned.

ELON: 1. A Hittite, father-in-law of **Esau** (Gen. 26:34, 36:2).
　　2. Son of **Zebulun** (Gen. 46:14; Num. 26:26).
　　3. One of the Judges (Jg. 12:11f.). He was a Zebulunite and judged Israel for ten years.

ELPAAL: A Benjaminite (1 Chr. 8:11f., 18).

ELPELET: Son of **David** (1 Chr. 14:5); called **Eliphelet** (2) in 1 Chr. 3:6.

ELUZAI: A Benjaminite who joined David at Ziklag (1 Chr. 12:3).

ELYMAS: *See* Bar-Jesus.

ELZABAD: 1. A Gadite who joined David at Ziklag (1 Chr. 12:12).
2. A Korahite gatekeeper (1 Chr. 26:7).

ELZAPHAN: A Korahite Levite (Exod. 6:22; Lev. 10:4); called **Elizaphan** (1) in Num. 3:30; 1 Chr. 15:8; 2 Chr. 29:13. He helped to remove the bodies of **Nadab** (1) and **Abihu** (Lev. 10:4).

EMADABUN: Surname of a Levite named **Jeshua** (12), whose sons shared in the work on the Temple (1 Esd. 5:58).

EMATHIS: One who married a foreign wife (1 Esd. 9:29); called **Athlai** in Ezr. 10:28.

EMMANUEL: *See* Immanuel.

ENAN: Representative of Naphtali at the census in the wilderness (Num. 1:15), and on other occasions (Num. 2:29, 7:78, 83, 10:27).

ENOCH: 1. Son of **Cain** and father of **Irad** (Gen. 4:17f.).
2. Son of **Jared** (Gen. 5:19) and father of **Methuselah** (Gen. 5:21; 1 Chr. 1:3) and 'in the seventh generation from **Adam**' (Jude 14) through **Seth** (Gen. 5:6). He lived 365 years (Gen. 5:22) and then 'he was not, for God took him' (Gen. 5:24; Heb. 11:5). He figures in the ancestry of **Jesus** (1) (Lk. 3:37).

ENOS: *See* Enosh.

ENOSH: Son of **Seth** (Gen. 4:26, 5:6) and grandson of **Adam**. He lived 905 years (Gen. 5:11). He is called **Enos** in Lk. 3:38.

EPAENETUS: The first convert in the Roman province of Asia, and greeted by **Paul** in Rom. 16:5.

EPAPHRAS: Fellow prisoner of **Paul** (Phm. 23), called 'beloved fellow servant' and 'faithful minister of Christ' (Col. 1:7). He was a native of Colossae and sent greetings to the church there (Col. 4:12).

EPAPHRODITUS: Called 'brother and fellow worker and fellow soldier' by **Paul** (Phil. 2:25). He brought a gift from the Philippian church to Paul (Phil. 4:18) and was sent by Paul to Philippi (Phil. 2:25) after he had recovered from an illness of which he almost died (Phil. 2:26ff.).

EPHAH: 1. Son of **Midian** (Gen. 25:4; 1 Chr. 1:33); eponymous ancestor of a tribe (Isa. 60:6).
2. A concubine of **Caleb** (1 Chr. 2:46).
3. A Calebite (1 Chr. 2:47).

EPHAI: A Netophathite who joined **Gedaliah** (1) at Mizpah (Jer. 40:8).

49

EPHER: 1. Son of **Midian** (Gen. 25:4; 1 Chr. 1:33).
2. Son of **Ezrah** (1 Chr. 4:17).
3. A Manassite (1 Chr. 5:24).

EPHLAL: A Jerahmeelite (1 Chr. 2:37).

EPHOD: Father of **Hanniel** (1) (Num. 34:23).

EPHRAIM: Son of **Joseph** (1) by **Asenath** (Gen. 41:50, 52, 46:20). He gave his name to one of the tribes of Israel.

EPHRATH: Wife of **Caleb** (1 Chr. 2:19).

EPHRATHAH: Another wife of **Caleb** (1 Chr. 2:24). In 1 Chr. 2:50 Ephrathah would appear to be a man, and in 1 Chr. 4:4 he is described as the founder of Bethlehem.

EPHRON: A Hittite from whom **Abraham** bought the cave of Machpelah (Gen. 23:8ff., 25:9, 49:29f., 50:13).

ER: 1. Son of **Judah** (1) (Gen. 38:3, 6f.; Num. 26:19; 1 Chr. 2:3).
2. Grandson of **Judah** (1) (1 Chr. 4:21).
3. An ancestor of **Jesus** (1) (Lk. 3:28).

ERAN: An Ephraimite (Num. 26:36).

ERASTUS: 1. City treasurer of Corinth, who sent greetings to the church at Rome (Rom. 16:23).
2. One sent by **Paul** from Ephesus to Macedonia (Ac. 19:22) and later found in Corinth (2 Tim. 4:20); possiby the same as 1.

ERI: Son of **Gad** (2) (Gen. 46:16; Num. 26:16).

ESARHADDON: Son and successor of **Sennacherib** (2 Kg. 19:37; Isa. 37:38). His transfer of people to Samaria is mentioned in Ezr. 4:2.

ESAU: Son of **Isaac** (Gen. 25:25), also called **Edom** (Gen. 25:30) and ancestor of the Edomites. He was the elder twin of **Jacob** (1) (Gen. 25:25), to whom he later sold his birthright (Gen. 25:29ff.). The blessing his father thought to pronounce on him was fraudulently obtained by Jacob (Gen. 27:1ff.), and for this he planned to kill Jacob (Gen. 27:41). When Jacob returned from his sojourn with **Laban** (1), however, the brothers were reconciled (Gen. 33:4ff.). In the NT he is called 'immoral and irreligious' (Heb. 12:16).

ESDRIS: A Syrian commander against **Judas** (1) (2 Mac. 12:36).

ESHBAAL: *See* **Ishbosheth.**

ESHBAN: A Horite (Gen. 36:22; 1 Chr. 1:41).

ESHCOL: One who aided **Abraham** in pursuing **Chedorlaomer** and his allies (Gen. 14:13, 24). He may have given his name to the valley of Eshcol.

ESHEK: A descendant of Saul (1) (1 Chr. 8:39).

ESHTEMOA: 1. A Calebite (1 Chr. 4:17).
2. A Maacathite (1 Chr. 4:19).

ESHTON: A Judahite (1 Chr. 4:11f.).

ESLI: An ancestor of Jesus (1) (Lk. 3:25).

ESTHER: Jewish queen of Ahasuerus (1) (Est. 2:17), also called Hadassah (Est. 2:7), who had been brought up by her cousin Mordecai (2) (Est. 2:7). She is the heroine of the book of Esther, who by her courage and skill averted the peril to the Jews from the malice of Haman.

ETAM: A Judahite (1 Chr. 4:3).

ETHAN: 1. A wise man, whose wisdom was surpassed by Solomon's (1 Kg. 4:31). He is called the 'Ezrahite' (1 Kg. 4:31; Ps. 89 Heading). He was a Judahite, son of Zerah (3) (1 Chr. 2:6).
2. An ancestor of Asaph (2) (1 Chr. 6:42).
3. A Levite musician (1 Chr. 6:44).

ETHANUS: A scribe employed by Ezra (1) (2 Esd. 14:24).

ETHBAAL: King of the Sidonians and father of Jezebel (1) (1 Kg. 16:31).

ETHNAN: A Judahite (1 Chr. 4:7).

ETHNI: An ancestor of Asaph (2) (1 Chr. 6:41).

EUBULUS: A Christian who sent greetings to Timothy (2) (2 Tim. 4:21).

EUMENES: A king to whom the Romans gave territory taken from Antiochus (3) (1 Mac. 8:8). He was Eumenes II, king of Pergamum.

EUNICE: A Jewess, mother of Timothy (2) (2 Tim. 1:5; Ac. 16:1).

EUODIA: A Christian woman of Philippi (Phil. 4:2f.), whom Paul urges to be reconciled to Syntyche.

EUPATOR: See Antiochus (5).

EUPOLEMUS: An ambassador sent by Judas (1) to Rome (1 Mac. 8:17ff.; 2 Mac. 4:11).

EUTYCHUS: A young man who fell from a third storey while Paul was speaking at Troas and was killed (Ac. 20:9ff.), and whom Paul restored to life.

EVE: The first woman and wife of Adam (Gen. 3:20, 4:1). She was deceived by the serpent (Gen. 3:1ff.; 2 C. 11:3) and tempted Adam to eat the forbidden fruit (Gen. 3:6, 14), and in consequence punishment was pronounced upon her (Gen. 3:16).

EVI: A Midianite king who was slain by the Israelites (Num. 31:8; Jos. 13:21).

EVIL-MERODACH: Son and successor of Nebuchadrezzar (2 Kg. 25:27; Jer. 52:31). He freed Jehoiachin from prison (2 Kg. 25:27ff.; Jer. 52:31ff.). He was killed by Neriglissar after reigning two years.

EZBAI: Father of Naarai (1 Chr. 11:37).

EZBON: 1. A Gadite (Gen. 46:16); called Ozni in Num. 26:16.
2. A Benjaminite (1 Chr. 7:7).

EZEKIEL: The prophet, son of the priest Buzi (Ezek. 1:3). He was among the exiles taken to Babylonia with Jehoiachin (Ezek. 1:2) and he received his call by the river Chebar in the fifth year of the captivity (Ezek. 1:2f.). He performed many symbolical actions and prophesied the fall of Jerusalem. When his wife died, he refrained from mourning as a sign to his people (Ezek. 24:15ff.). In the last nine chapters of the book of Ezekiel he outlines a plan for the building of a new Temple and the organization of its priesthood and cultus (Ezek. 40–48).

EZER: 1. A Horite (Gen. 36:21, 27, 30; 1 Chr. 1:38, 42).
2. A Judahite (1 Chr. 4:4).
3. An Ephraimite cattle raider who was slain by the men of Gath (1 Chr. 7:21).
4. A Gadite who joined David in the wilderness (1 Chr. 12:9).
5. A Levite who helped to repair the wall (Neh. 3:19).
6. A priest who shared in the dedication of the wall (Neh. 12:42).

EZORA: Ancestor of some who married foreign wives (1 Esd. 9:34).

EZRA: 1. A priest (Ezr. 7:1ff., 10:16; Neh. 8:2) and scribe (Ezr. 7:6; cf. Neh. 8:2, 9, 12:26), who was authorized by Artaxerxes (2) (Ezr. 7:1ff., 8:1) to lead a party of Jews from Babylonia to Jerusalem and to put into practice the Law which he carried (Ezr. 7:11ff.). He read the Law (Neh. 7:73–8:12) and the Feast of Tabernacles was observed (Neh. 8:13ff.) and this was followed by fasting and penitence (Neh. 9:1ff.). Ezra also dealt with the problem of mixed marriages (Ezr. 9f.).
2. A priest who returned with Zerubbabel (Neh. 12:1).
3. Ancestor of a priest in the days of Joiakim (Neh. 12:13).
4. A priest who shared in the dedication of the wall (Neh. 12:33).

EZRAH: A Judahite (1 Chr. 4:17).

EZRI: Minister of agriculture under David (1 Chr. 27:26).

F

FELIX, ANTONINUS: The Roman governor to whom **Paul** was sent by Claudius **Lysias** from Jerusalem to Caesarea (Ac. 23:23ff.). Paul was tried before him (Ac. 24:1ff.) and again before him and his Jewish wife **Drusilla** (Ac. 24f.). He kept Paul in prison for two years, hoping for a bribe (Ac. 24:26), and left him in prison when he was succeeded by **Festus** (Ac. 24:27).

FESTUS, PORCIUS: Successor of **Felix** (Ac. 24:27). **Paul** was tried before him (Ac. 25:6ff.) and he proposed to transfer the trial to Jerusalem (Ac. 25:9), whereupon Paul appealed to **Caesar** (Ac. 25:10f.). When **Herod** (7) and **Bernice** came to Caesarea (Ac. 25:13ff.), Paul was brought before them and before Festus and heard again (Ac. 26).

FORTUNATUS: A Corinthian Christian with **Paul** (1 C. 16:16) in Ephesus (1 C. 16:8).

G

GAAL: One who led the revolt of Shechem against **Abimelech** (2) (Jg. 9:26ff.), which Abimelech crushed (Jg. 9:34ff.).

GABAEL: 1. An ancestor of **Tobit** (Tob. 1:1).
2. A friend of **Tobit**, who left ten talents of silver with him in Rages (Tob. 1:14). **Tobias** (1) was sent to collect the silver (Tob. 4:20f.) and took as guide the angel **Raphael** in disguise (Tob. 5:4ff.). Raphael went from Ecbatana, where Tobias married **Sarah** (2), to Rages and collected the silver (Tob. 9:2ff.).

GABATHA: A eunuch of **Ahasuerus** (1) who plotted against the king (Ad. Est. 12:1); called **Bigthan** in Est. 2:21 and **Bigthana** in Est. 6:2.

GABBAI: A Benjaminite (Neh. 11:8).

GABRIAS: Brother of **Gabael** (2) (Tob. 1:14); called the father of Gabael in Tob. 4:20.

GABRIEL: An angel who interprets the vision of **Daniel** (5) (Dan. 8:15ff.) and tells him of the seventy weeks (Dan. 9:22ff.). He also announced the birth of **John** (6) the Baptist (Lk. 1:11ff.) and of **Jesus** (1) (Lk. 1:26ff.).

GAD: 1. A god, rendered 'Good Fortune' in Gen. 30:11, and 'Fortune' in Isa. 65:11.

2. Son of Jacob (1) by Zilpah (Gen. 30:10f., 35:26). He gave his name to one of the tribes of Israel.

3. A seer in the time of David (2 Sam. 24:11; 1 Chr. 21:9, 29:29; 2 Chr. 29:25). He gave advice to David when he was an outlaw (1 Sam. 22:5) and rebuked him for taking a census (2 Sam. 24:11ff.; 1 Chr. 21:9ff.). He wrote a record of David's reign (1 Chr. 29:29) and advised on the musical arrangements of the worship (2 Chr. 29:25).

GADDI: 1. The Manassite spy (Num. 13:11).

2. Surname of Jonathan (3) (1 Mac. 2:2).

GADDIEL: The Zebulunite spy (Num. 13:10).

GADI: Father of Menahem (2 Kg. 15:14, 17).

GAHAM: Son of Nahor (2) by Reumah (Gen. 22:24).

GAHAR: Ancestor of some Temple servants who returned with Zerubbabel (Ezr. 2:47; Neh. 7:49; 1 Esd. 5:30).

GAIUS: 1. Paul's host in Corinth (Rom. 16:23), whom Paul baptized (1 C. 1:14).

2. Companion of Paul, who was seized by the mob at Ephesus (Ac. 19:29).

3. A Christian of Derbe, who accompanied Paul (Ac. 20:4).

4. The Christian to whom 3 John was addressed (3 Jn 1).

GALAL: 1. A Levite in post-exilic times (1 Chr. 9:15).

2. Ancestor of another Levite (1 Chr. 9:16; Neh. 11:17).

GALLIO: Proconsul of Achaia before whom Paul was brought (Ac. 18:12ff.) and who dismissed the case (Ac. 18:15). He was the brother of Seneca, the Roman philosopher.

GAMAEL: A priest who returned with Ezra (1) (1 Esd. 8:29); called Daniel (2) in Ezr. 8:2.

GAMALIEL: 1. Representative of Manasseh at the census in the wilderness (Num. 1:10) and on other occasions (Num. 2:20, 7:54, 59, 10:23).

2. A leading Pharisee who was a member of the Council and under whom Paul studied (Ac. 22:3). He advised caution in dealing with the Christians (Ac. 5:34ff.).

GAMUL: A Levite head (1 Chr. 24:17).

GAREB: One of David's heroes (2 Sam. 23:38; 1 Chr. 11:40).

GAS: Father of some of Solomon's servants who returned with Zerubbabel (1 Esd. 5:34).

GATAM: An Edomite (Gen. 36:11, 16; 1 Chr. 1:36).

GAZEZ: 1. Son of **Caleb** by **Ephah** (2) (1 Chr. 2:46).
2. Grandson of **Caleb** (1 Chr. 2:46).

GAZZAM: Father of some Temple servants who returned with **Zerubbabel** (Ezr. 2:48; Neh. 7:51; 1 Esd. 5:31).

GEBER: An administrator under **Solomon** (1 Kg. 4:19).

GEDALIAH: 1. Son of **Ahikam** (2 Kg. 25:22; Jer. 40:7ff.). He was made governor by **Nebuchadrezzar** (2 Kg. 25:22ff.; Jer. 40:7ff.), but was murdered by **Ishmael** (2) (2 Kg. 25:25; Jer. 41:1ff.).
2. Head of a family of Temple musicians (1 Chr. 25:3, 9).
3. A priest who married a foreign wife (Ezr. 10:18); called **Jodan** in 1 Esd. 9:19.
4. One who urged **Zedekiah** (2) to put **Jeremiah** (1) to death (Jer. 38:1ff.).
5. A priest who married a foreign wife (1 Esd. 9:22); called **Jozabad** (7) in Ezr. 10:22.
6. Grandfather of **Zephaniah** (3) (Zeph. 1:1).

GEDOR: A Benjaminite (1 Chr. 8:31, 9:37).

GEHAZI: Servant of **Elisha** (2 Kg. 4:12, 25). He figures in the story of the birth, death, and raising of the Shunammite's son (2 Kg. 4:8ff.), in the story of the cleansing of **Naaman** (4) (2 Kg. 5), and in the story of the restoration of the Shunammite's land (2 Kg. 8:1ff.).

GEMALLI: Father of **Ammiel** (1) (Num. 13:12).

GEMARIAH: 1. Son of **Shaphan** (1) (Jer. 36:10). He was one who urged **Jehoiakim** (1) not to burn the scroll of **Jeremiah** (1) (Jer. 36:25).
2. One of the bearers of the message of **Zedekiah** (2) to Babylon (Jer. 29:3).

GENNAEUS: Father of **Apollonius** (3) (2 Mac. 12:2).

GENUBATH: Son of **Hadad** (5) by the sister of **Tahpenes** (1 Kg. 11:20).

GERA: 1. Son of **Benjamin** (1) (Gen. 46:21).
2. Son of **Bela** (2) and grandson of **Benjamin** (1) (1 Chr. 8:3). The name is repeated in 1 Chr. 8:5, where the same person may be intended.
3. Father of **Ehud** (1) (Jg. 3:15).
4. Father of **Shimei** (2) (2 Sam. 16:5, 19:16, 18; 1 Kg. 2:8).
5. Son of **Ehud** (2) (1 Chr. 8:7).

GERSHOM: 1. Son of **Moses** by **Zipporah** (Exod. 2:22, 18:2f.).
2. Son of **Levi** (1) (1 Chr. 6:1, 16f., 20, 43, 23:6f.); elsewhere called **Gershon**.
3. One who returned with **Ezra** (1) (Ezr. 8:2; 1 Esd. 9:29).

GERSHON: Son of **Levi** (1) (Gen. 46:11; Exod. 6:16f.; Num. 3:17f.); also called **Gershom** (2). A section of the Levites were called after his name.

GESHAN: A Calebite (1 Chr. 2:47).

GESHEM: An Arabian who opposed Nehemiah (2) (Neh. 2:19, 6:1f., 6).

GETHER: Son of Aram (1) (Gen. 10:23). In 1 Chr. 1:17 he is said to be a son of Shem.

GEUEL: The Gadite spy (Num. 13:15).

GIBBAR: Ancestor of some who returned with Zerubbabel (Ezr. 2:20); called Gibeon in Neh. 7:25.

GIBEA: A Calebite (1 Chr. 2:49).

GIBEON: Ancestor of some who returned with Zerubbabel (Neh. 7:25); called Gibbar in Ezr. 2:20.

GIDDALTI: A Levite musician (1 Chr. 25:4, 29).

GIDDEL: 1. Ancestor of some Temple servants who returned with Zerubbabel (Ezr. 2:47; Neh. 7:49); called Cathua in 1 Esd. 5:30.
2. Ancestor of some of Solomon's servants who returned with Zerubbabel (Ezr. 2:56; Neh. 7:58; 1 Esd. 5:33).

GIDEON: One of the Judges (Jg. 6ff.). He was a man of Ophrah who was called to deliver Israel from the Midianites (Jg. 6:11ff.). He broke down the local Baal altar (Jg. 6:25ff.) and called out the Israelites to face the foe (Jg. 6:33ff.). He asked for a sign of divine support (Jg. 6:36ff.) and routed the Midianites (Jg. 7f.). He rejected an appeal to become king (Jg. 8:22f.), but made an ephod with the offerings of the people (Jg. 8:23ff.), and this became a snare. He had many wives and seventy sons (Jg. 8:30). Abimelech (2) was one of his sons.

GIDEONI: Father of Abidan (Num. 1:11, 2:22, 7:60, 65, 10:24).

GILALAI: A Levite musician in the time of Nehemiah (2) (Neh. 12:36).

GILEAD: 1. Son of Machir (Num. 26:29; 1 Chr. 2:21, 7:17); he gave his name to an Israelite clan.
2. Father of Jephthah (Jg. 11:1).
3. A Gadite (1 Chr. 5:14).

GINATH: Father of Tibni (1 Kg. 16:21f.).

GINNETHOI: A priest who returned with Zerubbabel (Neh. 12:4).

GINNETHON: 1. One who sealed the covenant (Neh. 10:6).
2. A priest in the days of Joiakim (Neh. 12:16).

GISHPA: One who was over the Temple servants (Neh. 11:21).

GOG: 1. A Reubenite (1 Chr. 5:4).
2. Prince of Meshech and Tubal (Ezek. 38:2f.) and leader of the hosts of evil against God and His people (Ezek. 38f.). He is from the land of Magog

(Ezek. 38:2). In Rev. 20:8 Gog and Magog are equated with the nations which Satan will lead.

GOLIATH: A giant from Gath who challenged any Israelite to meet him in single combat (1 Sam. 17:4ff.). He was killed by David (1 Sam. 17:49). In 2 Sam. 21:9 he is said to have been slain by Elhanan (1).

GOMER: 1. Son of Japheth (Gen. 10:2f.; 1 Chr. 1:5f.). He gave his name to a people (Ezek. 38:6), i.e. the Cimmerians.

2. Wife of Hosea (Hos. 1:3). She was unfaithful to her husband and left him, but was reclaimed by him (Hos. 3:1ff.).

GORGIAS: Army commander of Antiochus (4) (1 Mac. 3:38; 2 Mac. 8:9). He fought against Judas (1) (1 Mac. 3:40ff., 4:1ff., 5:55ff.; 2 Mac. 10:14ff., 12:32ff.).

GOTHOLIAH: Father of Jeshaiah (4) (1 Esd. 8:33); called Athaliah (3) in Ezr. 8:7.

GOTHONIEL: Father of Chabris (Jdt. 6:15).

GUNI: 1. Son of Naphtali (Gen. 46:24; Num. 26:48; 1 Chr. 7:13).

2. A Gadite (1 Chr. 5:15).

H

HAAHASHTARI: A Judahite (1 Chr. 4:6).

HABAIAH: Ancestor of some who returned with Zerubbabel but who were unable to establish their priestly descent (Ezr. 2:61; 1 Esd. 5:38); called Hobaiah in Neh. 7:63.

HABAKKUK: One of the Minor Prophets, of whom nothing is known. Even his father's name is unrecorded (Hab. 1:1). In Bel and the Dragon there is a legend that he was carried by his hair to Babylon to feed Daniel (5) (Bel 33ff.).

HABAZZINIAH: Grandfather of Jaazaniah (2) (Jer. 35:3).

HACALIAH: Father of Nehemiah (2) (Neh. 1:1, 10:1).

HACHMONI: Father of Jehiel (3) (1 Chr. 27:32). But instead of 'son of Hachmoni' the rendering should be 'the Hachmonite', as in 1 Chr. 11:11, where the Hebrew is the same.

HADAD: 1. A Syrian storm god, whose name is found in Zech. 12:11 combined with the name Rimmon (1). Hadad is the proper name of Baal (1) in the Ras Shamra texts.

2. Son of Ishmael (1) (Gen. 25:15; 1 Chr. 1:30).

3. Fourth king of Edom (Gen. 36:35; 1 Chr. 1:46).

4. Eighth king of Edom (1 Chr. 1:50); called **Hadar** in Gen. 36:39.

5. An Edomite prince who fled to Egypt in **David**'s time and returned in **Solomon**'s (1 Kg. 11:14ff.).

HADADEZER: King of Zobah, who was defeated by **David** (2 Sam. 8:3ff., 10:15ff.; 1 Chr. 18:3ff., 19:16ff.). **Rezon** fled from him and made himself king of Damascus (1 Kg. 11:23ff.).

HADAD-RIMMON: A combination of the names of two deities (*see* Hadad, 1, and Rimmon, 1), who were equated.

HADAR: *See* Hadad (4).

HADASSAH: The Jewish name of **Esther** (Est. 2:7).

HADLAI: Father of **Amasa** (2) (2 Chr. 28:12).

HADORAM: 1. Son of **Joktan** (Gen. 10:27; 1 Chr. 1:21).

2. Son of **Tou**, king of Hamath (1 Chr. 18:10); called **Joram** (3) in 2 Sam. 8:10.

3. An official in charge of forced labour under **Solomon** and **Rehoboam** (2 Chr. 10:18); called **Adoram** in 2 Sam. 20:24; 1 Kg. 12:18, and **Adoniram** in 1 Kg. 4:6, 5:14.

HAGAB: Ancestor of some Temple servants who returned with **Zerubbabel** (Ezr. 2:46; 1 Esd. 5:30).

HAGABA: Ancestor of some Temple servants who returned with **Zerubbabel** (Neh. 7:48); called **Hagabah** in Ezr. 2:45; 1 Esd. 5:29.

HAGABAH: *See* Hagaba.

HAGAR: The Egyptian slave of **Sarah** (1) (Gen. 16:1, 3, 21:9, 25:12). She was given to **Abraham** by Sarah to be his concubine (Gen. 16:3), but Sarah treated her so hardly that she fled before her child was born (Gen. 16:6ff.). She returned and bore **Ishmael** (1) (Gen. 16:15), but after the birth of Sarah's child, **Isaac**, Sarah persuaded Abraham to send Hagar and her son away (Gen. 21:8ff.). In Gal. 4:24f. **Paul** uses her allegorically.

HAGGAI: One of the Minor Prophets, whose parentage is unrecorded, but who prophesied in the reign of **Darius** (1) (Hag. 1:1, 2:1, 10; Ezr. 5:1, 6:14). Nothing is known of him save what is learned from his book, which shows that he encouraged the rebuilding of the Temple.

HAGGEDOLIM: Father of **Zabdiel** (2) (Neh. 11:14).

HAGGI: Son of **Gad** (2) (Gen. 46:16; Num. 26:15).

HAGGIAH: A Levite (1 Chr. 6:30).

HAGGITH: Wife of David and mother of Adonijah (1) (2 Sam. 3:4; 1 Kg. 1:5, 11, 2:13; 1 Chr. 3:2).

HAGRI: Father of Mibhar (1 Chr. 11:38). 2 Sam. 23:26 has Bani (1) 'the Gadite'.

HAKKATAN: Father of Johanan (8) (Ezr. 8:12; 1 Esd. 8:38).

HAKKOZ: 1. The head of a priestly course (1 Chr. 24:10).
2. Ancestor of some who returned with Zerubbabel but who were unable to establish their priestly descent (Ezr. 2:61; Neh. 7:63; 1 Esd. 5:38); perhaps the same as the grandfather of Meremoth (1) (Neh. 3:4, 21).

HAKUPHA: Ancestor of some Temple servants who returned with Zerubbabel (Ezr. 2:51; Neh. 7:53; 1 Esd. 5:31).

HALLOHESH: Father of Shallum (13) (Neh. 3:12); perhaps the same as one who sealed the covenant (Neh. 10:24).

HAM: Son of Noah (1) (Gen. 5:32, 6:10; 1 Chr. 1:4) and father of Canaan (Gen. 9:18, 22), and ancestor of peoples associated with Egypt (Gen. 10:6ff.).

HAMAN: The great enemy of the Jews in the book of Esther (Est. 3:6), whose plan to destroy the Jews was thwarted by Esther and who was hanged on the gallows he had prepared for Mordecai (2) (Est. 7:10). In Ad. Est. 16:10 he is said to have been a Macedonian.

HAMMATH: An ancestor of Rechab (2) (1 Chr. 2:55).

HAMMEDATHA: Father of Haman (Est. 3:1, 10, 8:5).

HAMMOLECHETH: Daughter of Machir (1) and sister of Gilead (1 Chr. 7:17f.).

HAMMUEL: A Simeonite (1 Chr. 4:26).

HAMOR: Father of Shechem (Gen. 33:19, 34:2, 4). He was killed (Gen. 34:26) when Simeon (1) and Levi (1) avenged the violation of Dinah (Gen. 34:2ff.).

HAMRAN: An Edomite (1 Chr. 1:41); called Hemdan in Gen. 36:26.

HAMUL: A Judahite (Gen. 46:12; Num. 26:21; 1 Chr. 2:5).

HAMUTAL: Wife of Josiah (1) and mother of Jehoahaz (2) and Zedekiah (2) (2 Kg. 23:31, 24:18; Jer. 52:1).

HANA: Ancestor of some Temple servants who returned with Zerubbabel (1 Esd. 5:30); called Hanan (4) in Ezr. 2:46; Neh. 7:49.

HANAMEL: Cousin of Jeremiah (1) (Jer. 32:7ff., 12).

HANAN: 1. A Benjaminite (1 Chr. 8:23).
2. A descendant of Saul (1) (1 Chr. 8:38, 9:44).
3. One of David's heroes (1 Chr. 11:43).

4. Ancestor of some Temple servants who returned with **Zerubbabel** (Ezr. 2:46; Neh. 7:49); called **Hana** in 1 Esd. 5:30.

5. A Levite who helped to expound the Law (Neh. 8:7; 1 Esd. 9:48).

6. One who sealed the covenant (Neh. 10:10); perhaps the same as 5.

7. Another who sealed the covenant (Neh. 10:22).

8. Another who sealed the covenant (Neh. 10:26).

9. An assistant treasurer appointed by **Nehemiah** (2) (Neh. 13:13).

10. One whose sons had a room in the Temple (Jer. 35:4).

HANANI: 1. Father of **Jehu** (1) (1 Kg. 16:1, 7; 2 Chr. 19:2, 20:34). He rebuked **Asa** (1) and was imprisoned (2 Chr. 16:7).

2. A Levite musician (1 Chr. 25:4, 25).

3. A priest who married a foreign wife (Ezr. 10:20; 1 Esd. 9:21).

4. A relative of **Nehemiah** (2) who brought news from Jerusalem (Neh. 1:2). He was given an administrative office in Jerusalem (Neh. 7:2).

5. A musician who shared in the dedication of the wall (Neh. 12:36).

HANANIAH: 1. Son of **Zerubbabel** (1 Chr. 3:19).

2. A Benjaminite (1 Chr. 8:24).

3. A Levite musician (1 Chr. 25:4).

4. A commander under **Uzziah** (1) (2 Chr. 26:11).

5. A layman who returned with **Zerubbabel** (Ezr. 10:28; 1 Esd. 9:29).

6. A perfumer who helped to repair the wall (Neh. 3:8).

7. Another who helped to repair the wall (Neh. 3:30).

8. One who was given an administrative office in Jerusalem (Neh. 7:2).

9. One who sealed the covenant (Neh. 10:23).

10. A priest in the days of **Joiakim** (Neh. 12:12).

11. A priest who shared in the dedication of the wall (Neh. 12:41); possibly the same as 10.

12. A priest whom **Jeremiah** (1) denounced for prophesying falsely (Jer. 28:1ff.). Jeremiah predicted his death (Jer. 28:16), which took place two months later (Jer. 28:17).

13. Father of **Zedekiah** (5) (Jer. 36:12).

14. Grandfather of **Irijah** (Jer. 37:13).

15. The Hebrew name of **Shadrach** (Dan. 1:6f., 11, 19).

16. A Levite whose sons were brought to **Ezra** (1) (1 Esd. 8:48); called **Merari** (2) in Ezr. 8:19.

HANNAH: Wife of **Elkanah** (2) (1 Sam. 1:1f.) and mother of **Samuel** (1 Sam. 1:20). She dedicated her son to the Lord at Shiloh (1 Sam. 1:28) and visited him every year, taking a new robe (1 Sam. 2:19). The Song of Hannah (1 Sam. 2:1ff.) is attributed to her. Subsequently she had five other children (1 Sam. 2:21).

HANNIEL: 1. Representative of Manasseh for the allotment of the land (Num. 34:23).

2. An Asherite (1 Chr. 7:39).

HANOCH: 1. Grandson of Abraham and Keturah (Gen. 25:4; 1 Chr. 1:33).
   2. Son of Reuben (Gen. 46:9; Exod. 6:14; Num. 26:5; 1 Chr. 5:3).

HANUN: 1. King of the Ammonites, who insulted David's messengers when they brought him condolence on the death of his father (2 Sam. 10:1ff., 11:1, 12:26ff.; 1 Chr. 19:1ff., 20:1ff.), and so provoked a war with Israel (2 Sam. 10:6ff.; 1 Chr. 19:6ff.).
   2. One who helped to repair the wall (Neh. 3:13).
   3. Another who helped to repair the wall (Neh. 3:30).

HAPPIZZEZ: Head of a priestly course (1 Chr. 24:15).

HARAN: 1. Brother of Abraham and father of Lot (Gen. 11:26ff.).
   2. Son of Caleb by Ephah (2) (1 Chr. 2:46).
   3. A Levite (1 Chr. 23:9).

HARBONA: One of the seven eunuchs of Ahasuerus (1) (Est. 1:10). It was at his suggestion that Haman was hanged on the gallows he had prepared for Mordecai (2) (Est. 7:9).

HAREPH: A descendant of Hur (2) (1 Chr. 2:51).

HARHAIAH: Father of Uzziel (6) (Neh. 3:8).

HARHAS: Ancestor of Shallum (3) (2 Kg. 22:14); called Hasrah (1) in 2 Chr. 34:22.

HARHUR: Ancestor of some Temple servants who returned with Zerubbabel (Ezr. 2:51; Neh. 7:53); called Asur in 1 Esd. 5:31.

HARIM: 1. Head of a priestly course (1 Chr. 24:8).
   2. Ancestor of some laymen who returned with Zerubbabel (Ezr. 2:32; Neh. 7:35). Some of his descendants married foreign wives (Ezr. 10:31).
   3. Ancestor of some priests who returned with Zerubbabel (Ezr. 2:39; Neh. 7:42; 1 Esd. 5:25). Some of his descendants married foreign wives (Ezr. 10:21). One of his descendants was a priestly head in the days of Joiakim (Neh. 12:15).
   4. One who sealed the covenant (Neh. 10:5).
   5. A layman who sealed the covenant (Neh. 10:27).

HARIPH: 1. Ancestor of some who returned with Zerubbabel (Neh. 7:24); called Jorah in Ezr. 2:18; 1 Esd. 5:16.
   2. One who sealed the covenant (Neh. 10:19).

HARNEPHER: An Asherite (1 Chr. 7:36).

HAROEH: A Judahite (1 Chr. 2:52); called Reaiah (1) in 1 Chr. 4:2.

HARSHA: Ancestor of some Temple servants who returned with Zerubbabel (Ezr. 2:52; Neh. 7:54); perhaps called Charea in 1 Esd. 5:32.

HARUM: A Judahite (1 Chr. 4:8).

HARUMAPH: Father of Jedaiah (5) (Neh. 3:10).

HARUZ: Maternal grandfather of Amon (1) (2 Kg. 21:19).

HASADIAH: 1. Son of Zerubbabel (1 Chr. 3:20).
  2. Ancestor of Baruch (1) (Bar. 1:1).

HASHABIAH: 1. A Levite (1 Chr. 6:45).
  2. Another Levite (1 Chr. 9:14; Neh. 11:15).
  3. A Levite musician (1 Chr. 25:3, 19).
  4. An official under David (1 Chr. 26:30).
  5. An officer over the Levites under David (1 Chr. 27:17).
  6. A Levite chief under Josiah (1) (2 Chr. 35:9; 1 Esd. 1:9).
  7. A Levite who returned with Ezra (1) (Ezr. 8:19; 1 Esd. 8:48); possibly the same as Hashabneiah (2).
  8. One of the priests in charge of the sacred vessels (Ezr. 8:24; 1 Esd. 8:54).
  9. A layman who returned with Ezra (1) (Ezr. 10:25); called Asibias in 1 Esd. 9:26.
  10. One who helped to repair the wall (Neh. 3:17).
  11. One who sealed the covenant (Neh. 10:11).
  12. Ancestor of an overseer of the Levites (Neh. 11:22).
  13. A priest in the days of Joiakim (Neh. 12:21).
  14. A Levite who shared in the dedication of the wall (Neh. 12:24).

HASHABNAH: One who sealed the covenant (Neh. 10:25).

HASHABNEIAH: 1. Father of Hattush (2) (Neh. 3:10).
  2. A Levite (Neh. 9:5); possibly the same as Hashabiah (7).

HASHBADDANAH: One who stood on the left hand of Ezra (1) when the Law was read (Neh. 8:4); called Nabariah in 1 Esd. 9:44.

HASHEM: One of David's heroes (1 Chr. 11:34); called Jashen in 2 Sam. 23:32.

HASHUBAH: Son of Zerubbabel (1 Chr. 3:20).

HASHUM: 1. Ancestor of some who returned with Zerubbabel (Ezr. 2:19; Neh. 7:22) and of some who married foreign wives (Ezr. 10:33; 1 Esd. 9:33).
  2. One who stood on the left of Ezra (1) when the Law was read (Neh. 8:4); called Lothasubus in 1 Esd. 9:44.
  3. One who sealed the covenant (Neh. 10:18).

HASRAH: 1. Ancestor of Shallum (3) (2 Chr. 34:22); called Harhas in 2 Kg. 22:14.
  2. Ancestor of some Temple servants who returned with Zerubbabel (1 Esd. 5:31).

HASSENAAH: One whose sons built the Fish Gate (Neh. 3:3); perhaps the same as Senaah (Ezr. 2:35; Neh. 7:38; 1 Esd. 5:23).

HASSENUAH: 1. A Benjaminite (1 Chr. 9:7).
2. Father of Judah (4) (Neh. 11:9).

HASSHUB: 1. A Levite (1 Chr. 9:14; Neh. 11:15).
2. One who helped to repair the wall (Neh. 3:11).
3. Another who helped to repair the wall (Neh. 3:23).
4. One who sealed the covenant (Neh. 10:23).

HASSOPHERETH: Ancestor of some of Solomon's servants who returned with Zerubbabel (Ezr. 2:55; 1 Esd. 5:33); called **Sophereth** in Neh. 7:57.

HASUPHA: Ancestor of some Temple servants who returned with **Zerubbabel** (Ezr. 2:43; Neh. 7:46; 1 Esd. 5:29).

HATHACH: A eunuch who attended on **Esther** (Est. 4:5) and who was sent to **Mordecai (2)** (Est. 4:5).

HATHATH: Son of **Othniel** (1 Chr. 4:13).

HATIPHA: Ancestor of some Temple servants who returned with **Zerubbabel** (Ezr. 2:54; Neh. 7:56; 1 Esd. 5:32).

HATITA: Ancestor of some gatekeepers who returned with **Zerubbabel** (Ezr. 2:42; Neh. 7:45; 1 Esd. 5:28).

HATTIL: Ancestor of some of Solomon's servants who returned with **Zerubbabel** (Ezr. 2:57; Neh. 7:59; 1 Esd. 5:34).

HATTUSH: 1. A descendant of **David** who returned with **Ezra (1)** (Ezr. 8:2; 1 Esd. 8:29; cf. 1 Chr. 3:22).
2. One who helped to repair the wall (Neh. 3:10).
3. One who sealed the covenant (Neh. 10:4).
4. A priest who returned with **Zerubbabel** (Neh. 12:2).

HAVILAH: 1. Son of **Cush (1)** (Gen. 10:7; 1 Chr. 1:9).
2. Son of Joktan (Gen. 10:29; 1 Chr. 1:23).

HAZAEL: A Syrian who was sent to **Elisha** by **Ben-hadad (2)** (2 Kg. 8:10ff.), and who was incited by Elisha to seize the throne (2 Kg. 8:13ff.). Hazael then suffocated Ben-hadad and became king (2 Kg. 8:15). He soon attacked Israel (2 Kg. 8:28f., 10:32f., 13:3ff., 22) and also attacked Judah and Gath (2 Kg. 12:17f.).

HAZAIAH: A Judahite (Neh. 11:5).

HAZARMAVETH: A Son of Joktan (Gen. 10:26; 1 Chr. 1:20).

HAZIEL: A Levite (1 Chr. 23:9).

HAZO: Son of **Nahor (2)** and **Milcah (1)** (Gen. 22:22).

HAZZELELPONI: A Judahite woman (1 Chr. 4:3).

HEBER: 1. An Asherite (Gen. 46:17; Num. 26:45; 1 Chr. 7:31f.).

2. A Kenite, husband of Jael (Jg. 4:17, 5:24). He had separated himself from his clan (Jg. 4:11).

3. A Judahite, who founded Soco (1 Chr. 4:18).

4. A Benjaminite (1 Chr. 8:17).

HEBRON: 1. A Levite, son of **Kohath** (Exod. 6:18; Num. 3:19; 1 Chr. 6:2, 18, 15:9, 23:12, 19, 24:23).

2. A Calebite (1 Chr. 2:42f.).

HEGAI: Eunuch of **Ahasuerus** (1) (Est. 2:3, 8, 15).

HEGEMONIDES: An officer of **Lysias** (1) (2 Mac. 13:24).

HEGLAM: Son of **Ehud** (2), equated with **Gera** (5) (1 Chr. 8:7).

HELAH: One of the wives of **Ashhur** (1 Chr. 4:5, 7).

HELDAI: 1. One of the monthly commanders in the time of **David** (1 Chr. 27:15). He is perhaps the same as **Heleb** (2 Sam. 23:29) or **Heled** (1 Chr. 11:30), one of David's heroes.

2. One of those who brought gifts from Babylon for a crown for **Joshua** (4) (Zech. 6:10, 14).

HELEB: *See* **Heldai** (1).

HELED: *See* **Heldai** (1).

HELEK: A Manassite (Num. 26:30; Jos. 17:2).

HELEM: An Asherite (1 Chr. 7:35); called **Hotham** (1) in 1 Chr. 7:32.

HELEZ: 1. One of **David's** heroes (2 Sam. 23:26; 1 Chr. 11:27).

2. One of the monthly commanders in the time of **David** (1 Chr. 27:10); probably the same as 1.

3. A Judahite (1 Chr. 2:39).

HELI: An ancestor of **Jesus** (1) (Lk. 3:23).

HELIODORUS: An officer of **Seleucus** (4), sent to plunder the Temple (2 Mac. 3:7), but prevented from doing so by an apparition (2 Mac. 3:14ff.). He murdered Seleucus, and this may be referred to in Dan. 11:20.

HELKAI: A priest in the days of **Joiakim** (Neh. 12:15).

HELON: Father of **Eliab** (1) (Num. 1:9, 2:7, 7:24, 29, 10:16).

HEMAN: 1. A Horite (Gen. 36:22); called **Homam** in 1 Chr. 1:39.

2. A wise man whose wisdom was excelled by **Solomon's** (1 Kg. 4:31).

3. A Judahite, son of **Zerah** (3) (1 Chr. 2:6); perhaps referred to in Ps. 88 Heading as Heman the Ezrahite (**Ezrah** being equated with Zerah).

4. A Levite musician (1 Chr. 6:33, 15:17, 16:41, 25:1; 2 Chr. 5:12, 35:15). In 1 Esd. 1:15 **Zechariah** (32) stands instead of Heman (cf. 2 Chr. 35:15).

HEMDAN: An Edomite (Gen. 36:26); called **Hamran** in 1 Chr. 1:41.

HENADAD: Ancestor of some Levites who returned with **Zerubbabel** (Ezr. 3:9), of two who helped to repair the wall (Neh. 3:18, 24), and of one who sealed the covenant (Neh. 10:9).

HEPHER: 1. A Manassite (Num. 26:32f., 27:1; Jos. 17:2f.).
2. A Judahite (1 Chr. 4:6).
3. One of David's heroes (1 Chr. 11:36).

HEPHZIBAH: Mother of **Manasseh** (2) (2 Kg. 21:1).

HERCULES: Greek god, to whose temple in Tyre **Jason** (3) sent an offering (2 Mac. 4:19f.). The carriers of the offering devoted it to the construction of triremes.

HERESH: A Levite (1 Chr. 9:15).

HERMAS: A Roman Christian to whom **Paul** sent greetings (Rom. 16:14)

HERMES: 1. Greek god of eloquence, with whom **Paul** was identified at Lystra, because he was the chief speaker (Ac. 14:12).
2. A Roman Christian to whom **Paul** sent greetings (Rom. 16:14).

HERMOGENES: One who deserted **Paul** (2 Tim. 1:15).

HEROD: 1. Herod the Great, son of Antipater, who became king of Palestine (37–4 B.C.), and in whose reign **Jesus** (1) was born (Mt.2:1; Lk. 1:5). He sent the wise men to Bethlehem (Mt. 2:7ff.), and afterwards killed all male children at Bethlehem who were two years old or under (Mt. 2:16).
2. Herod Archelaus, son of 1, who became tetrarch of Judaea, Samaria and Idumaea on the death of his father (4 B.C.–A.D. 6). He is mentioned in Mt. 2:22, and perhaps alluded to in Lk. 19:14, where the reference may be to a Jewish mission sent to Rome to oppose his succession to Herod the Great.
3. Herod Antipas, younger brother of 2. He became tetrarch of Galilee and Peraea (Lk. 3:1), and retained his position until A.D. 39, when he was banished. He was rebuked by **John** (6) the Baptist for taking his brother's wife, **Herodias** (Mt. 14:3f.; Mk 6:16ff.; Lk. 3:19f.), and later had John beheaded (Mt. 14:6ff.; Mk 6:16ff.). He heard the fame of Jesus (1) (Mt. 14:1) and sought to see Him (Lk. 9:1), but later he sought to kill Him (Lk. 13:21). Jesus was tried before him (Lk. 23:7ff.). **Manaen**, a Christian at Antioch, had been a member of his court or brought up with him (Ac. 13:1).
4. Herod Philip, tetrarch of Ituraea and Trachonitis (Lk. 3:1) from 4 B.C. to A.D. 34, when he died. He founded the city of Caesarea Philippi. He married **Salome** (1).
5. Another Philip, son of 1 by another wife, and first husband of **Herodias** (Mt. 14:3; Mk 6:17; Lk. 3:19).
6. Herod Agrippa I, who was given the tetrarchy of 4 and that of **Lysanias** in A.D. 37, with the title of king. In A.D. 40 the tetrarchy of 3 was added, and the next year the tetrarchy of 2. He put **James** (1) to death (Ac. 12:2) and in A.D. 44 he died in great agony (Ac. 12:20ff.).

7. Herod Agrippa II, son of 6. He was a minor when his father died. In A.D. 50 he became king of Chalcis and three years later he exchanged this for the former tetrarchy of 4, and to this was added later the former tetrarchy of 3. He died in A.D. 100. When Paul was imprisoned in Caesarea in the procuratorship of Festus, Agrippa and his sister Bernice came there (Ac. 25:13) and Paul was heard before them (Ac. 25:23ff., 26:1ff.).

HERODIAS: Granddaughter of Herod (1), who married Herod (5) and then left him for Herod (3). She resented John (6) the Baptist's condemnation of this and moved her daughter, Salome (1), to demand the death of John when opportunity offered (Mt. 14:3ff.; Mk 6:16ff.; Lk. 3:19).

HERODION: A Roman Christian greeted by Paul (Rom. 16:11).

HETH: Son of Canaan (Gen. 10:15; 1 Chr. 1:13) and eponymous ancestor of the Hittites.

HEZEKIAH: 1. Son and successor of Ahaz (1), king of Judah (2 Kg. 16:20; 2 Chr. 28:27). He reigned twenty-nine years (2 Kg. 18:2; 2 Chr. 29:1), and during his reign he reformed the worship (2 Kg. 18:4ff.) and rebelled against Sennacherib (2 Kg. 18:7, 13ff.). The embassy from Merodach-baladan (2 Kg. 20:12ff.; Isa. 39:1ff.), which was sent on Hezekiah's recovery from illness (2 Kg. 20:1ff.), was probably connected with this rebellion. In preparation for the conflict Hezekiah cut the tunnel to the pool of Siloam (2 Kg. 20:20; 2 Chr. 32:3ff.). Sennacherib overran the country (2 Kg. 18:13; Isa. 36:1), and Hezekiah submitted and paid an indemnity (2 Kg. 18:14ff.). Later Sennacherib dispatched an army to occupy Jerusalem and, encouraged by Isaiah (2 Kg. 19:1ff.; Isa. 37:1ff.), Hezekiah resisted and Jerusalem was miraculously delivered (2 Kg. 19:35; Isa. 37:36). The reform of Hezekiah is much expanded in the Chronicler's account (2 Chr. 29ff.). A psalm attributed to Hezekiah stands in Isa. 38:9ff.

2. An ancestor of Zephaniah (3) (Zeph. 1:1).

3. Ancestor of some who returned with Zerubbabel (Ezr. 2:16; Neh. 7:21).

4. One who sealed the covenant (Neh. 10:17).

5. One who accompanied Ezra (1) at the reading of the Law (1 Esd. 9:43); called Hilkiah (6) in Neh. 8:4.

HEZION: Grandfather of Ben-hadad (1) (1 Kg. 15:18).

HEZIR: 1. Head of a priestly course (1 Chr. 24:15).

2. One who sealed the covenant (Neh. 10:20).

HEZRO: One of David's heroes (2 Sam. 23:35; 1 Chr. 11:37).

HEZRON: 1. A Reubenite (Gen. 46:9; Exod. 6:14; Num. 26:6; 1 Chr. 5:3).

2. A Judahite (Gen. 46:12; Num. 26:21; Ru. 4:18f.; 1 Chr. 2:5, 9, 18, 4:1). He stands in the genealogy of Jesus (1) (Mt. 1:3; Lk. 3:33).

HIDDAI: One of David's heroes (2 Sam. 23:30); called **Hurai** in 1 Chr. 11:32.

HIEL: A Bethelite who rebuilt Jericho in the time of Ahab (1) (1 Kg. 16:34).

HIERONYMUS: A Syrian officer under **Antiochus** (5) who harried the Jews (2 Mac. 12:2).

HILKIAH: 1. Father of Eliakim (1) (2 Kg. 18:18, 26, 37; Isa. 22:20, 36:3, 22).

2. High Priest under Josiah (1). He found the book of the Law (2 Kg. 22:3ff.; 2 Chr. 34:8ff.). He was sent to Huldah (2 Kg. 22:14ff.; 2 Chr. 34:22ff.) and supervised the renovation of the Temple (2 Kg. 23:4ff.). He made a voluntary contribution for the Passover celebration (2 Chr. 35:8; 1 Esd. 1:8). He was an ancestor of Ezra (1) (Ezr. 7:1; 1 Esd. 8:1) and the father of Jehoiakim (2) (Bar. 1:7).

3. Ancestor of a Levite who stood on the left (1 Chr. 6:45).

4. Another Levite (1 Chr. 26:11).

5. A priest who returned with **Zerubbabel** (Neh. 12:7, 21).

6. One who accompanied **Ezra** (1) at the reading of the Law (Neh. 8:4); called Hezekiah (5) in 1 Esd. 9:43.

7. Father of Jeremiah (1) (Jer. 1:1).

8. Father of Gemariah (2) (Jer. 29:3).

9. Ancestor of **Baruch** (1) (Bar. 1:1).

10. Father of **Susanna** (1) (Sus. 2:29).

HILLEL: Father of Abdon (1) (Jg. 12:13, 15).

HINNOM: One who gave his name to the Valley of the (son of) Hinnom (Jos. 15:8, 18:6; 2 Kg. 23:10; 2 Chr. 28:3, 33:6; Neh. 11:30; Jer. 7:31f., 32:35). Here child sacrifices were offered and the valley gave its name to Gehenna.

HIRAH: An Adullamite with whom **Judah** (1) was friendly (Gen. 38:1, 12).

HIRAM: 1. King of Tyre, with whom **David** and **Solomon** were friendly (2 Sam. 5:11, 18; 1 Kg. 5:1ff., 9:26ff., 10:1; 1 Chr. 14:1; 2 Chr. 2:3, 11f., 8:18, 9:10, 21). Solomon had to cede some territory to him (1 Kg. 9:10, 14), but the Chronicler reverses this (2 Chr. 8:2). He is called **Huram** (2) in 2 Chr. 2:3, 11f., 8:2, 18, 9:10, 21.

2. A Tyrian artificer who was employed in the building of the Temple (1 Kg. 7:13ff.; 2 Chr. 2:13ff., 4:11). According to 1 Kg. 7:14 his mother belonged to the tribe of Naphtali, but according to 2 Chr. 2:14 to the tribe of Dan. He is called **Huram** (3) in 2 Chr. 4:11 and **Huram-abi** in 2 Chr. 2:13, 4:16.

HIZKI: A Benjaminite (1 Chr. 8:17).

HIZKIAH: A descendant of **David** (1 Chr. 3:23).

HOBAB: Father-in-law of Moses (Num. 10:29; Jg. 4:11). According to Exod. 2:18 Reuel (2), the father of Hobab (Num. 10:29), was the father-in-law of Moses. In Exod. 3:1, 4:18, 18:1ff. the father-in-law of Moses is named Jethro.

HOBAIAH: Ancestor of some who returned with Zerubbabel and who were unable to establish their priestly descent (Neh. 7:63); called Habaiah in Ezr. 2:61; 1 Esd. 5:38.

HOD: An Asherite (1 Chr. 7:37).

HODAVIAH: 1. A descendant of David (1 Chr. 3:24).
2. A Manassite head (1 Chr. 5:24).
3. A Benjaminite (1 Chr. 9:7).
4. Ancestor of some Levites who returned with Zerubbabel (Ezr. 2:40); called Hodevah in Neh. 7:43, Judah (2) in Ezr. 3:9, Sudias in 1 Esd. 5:26, and Joda (1) in 1 Esd. 5:58.

HODESH: Wife of Shaharaim (1 Chr. 8:9).

HODEVAH: *See* Hodaviah (4).

HODIAH: 1. A Judahite (1 Chr. 4:19).
2. A Levite who helped to explain the Law (Neh. 8:7, 9:5; 1 Esd. 9:48).
3. A Levite who sealed the covenant (Neh. 10:10).
4. Another Levite who sealed the covenant (Neh. 10:13).
5. A layman who sealed the covenant (Neh. 10:18).

HOGLAH: Daughter of Zelophehad (Num. 26:33, 27:1, 36:11; Jos. 17:3).

HOHAM: King of Hebron, who joined the alliance against Joshua (1) (Jos. 10:3), and who was put to death when defeated and captured (Jos. 10:26f.).

HOLOFERNES: The general of Nebuchadnezzar (Jdt. 2:4) who was outwitted and beheaded by Judith (2) (Jdt. 13:8).

HOMAM: A Horite (1 Chr. 1:39); called Heman (1) in Gen. 36:22.

HOPHNI AND PHINEHAS: Sons of Eli, whose evil deeds were condemned by an unnamed prophet (1 Sam. 2:27ff.) and through Samuel (1 Sam. 3:11ff.), and who were killed when the Ark was taken by the Philistines (1 Sam. 4:11).

HOPHRA: Pharaoh of Egypt who is referred to by name in Jer. 44:30, where Jeremiah (1) prophesies disaster for him. He incited Zedekiah (2) to rebel against Babylon (Jer. 37:3ff.), but gave him no effective support. The prophecy in Ezek. 29:3ff. is directed against him.

HORAM: King of Gezer, who came against Joshua (1) and who was defeated (Jos. 10:33).

HORI: 1. A Horite (Gen. 36:22; 1 Chr. 1:39).

2. Father of Shaphat (1) (Num. 13:5).

HOSAH: A Levite gatekeeper (1 Chr. 16:38, 26:10f., 16).

HOSEA: One of the Minor Prophets, son of Beeri (2) (Hos. 1:1). He married Gomer (2) (Hos. 1:3), whom he loved despite her infidelity (Hos. 3:1), and through his own experience he learned some of the profounder elements of his message. His name in Hebrew is the same as the shorter form of the name of Joshua (1) and the name Hoshea.

HOSHAIAH: 1. Leader of half the procession at the dedication of the wall (Neh. 12:32).

2. Father of Azariah (24) (Jer. 42:1, 43:2).

HOSHAMA: Descendant of David and Jehoiachin (1 Chr. 3:18).

HOSHEA: 1. Name by which Joshua (1) is called in Num. 13:8, 16.

2. The last king of Israel, who assassinated Pekah (2 Kg. 15:30) and reigned for nine years (2 Kg. 17:1). For a few years he paid tribute to Assyria (2 Kg. 17:3), but then intrigued with Egypt and revolted (2 Kg. 17:4). Assyrian forces came against him and after a siege of three years (2 Kg. 18:10) Samaria was taken and its inhabitants deported (2 Kg. 17:6), and the northern kingdom came to an end.

3. Leader of the Ephraimites in the time of David (1 Chr. 27:20).

4. One who sealed the covenant (Neh. 10:23).

HOTHAM: 1. An Asherite (1 Chr. 7:32); called Helem in 1 Chr. 7:35.

2. Father of two of David's heroes (1 Chr. 11:44).

HOTHIR: A Levite of the sons of Heman (4) (1 Chr. 25:4, 28).

HUL: A son of Aram (1) (Gen. 10:23) or of Shem (1 Chr. 1:17).

HULDAH: A prophetess consulted by Josiah (1) about the book of the Law found in the Temple (2 Kg. 22:14ff.; 2 Chr. 34:22ff.).

HUPHAM: A Benjaminite (Num. 26:39); called Huppim in Gen. 46:21; 1 Chr. 7:12, 15.

HUPPAH: Head of a priestly course (1 Chr. 24:13).

HUPPIM: *See* Hupham.

HUR: 1. One who, with Aaron, upheld the hands of Moses during the battle with the Amalekites (Exod. 17:10ff.) and who took charge with Aaron while Moses was up the mountain (Exod. 24:14).

2. A Judahite (Exod. 31:2, 35:30, 38:22), grandfather of Bezalel (1) (Exod. 31:2; 1 Chr. 2:20). In 1 Chr. 2:19 he is said to be a son of Caleb by Ephrath, but in 1 Chr. 4:1 he is said to be a son of Judah (1), and in 1 Chr. 2:50, 4:4 he is called the son of Ephrathah, the founder of Bethlehem.

3. King of Midian, killed after the sin of Peor (Num. 31:8; cf. Jos. 13:21).

4. Father of Rephaiah (5) (Neh. 3:9).

HURAI: One of David's heroes (1 Chr. 11:32); called **Hiddai** in 2 Sam. 23:30.

HURAM: 1. A Benjaminite (1 Chr. 8:5).
   2. *See* Hiram (1).
   3. *See* Hiram (2).

HURAM-ABI: *See* Hiram (2).

HURI: A Gadite (1 Chr. 5:14).

HUSHAH: A Judahite (1 Chr. 4:4).

HUSHAI: David's friend (2 Sam. 15:37), who would have accompanied David when he fled from **Absalom** (1) (2 Sam. 15:33) but who was persuaded to return to Jerusalem and counter the advice of **Ahithophel** (2 Sam. 15:33), which he successfully did (2 Sam. 17:5ff.).

HUSHAM: King of Edom (Gen. 36:34f.; 1 Chr. 1:45f.).

HUSHIM: 1. Son of **Dan** (Gen. 46:23); called **Shuham** in Num. 26:42.
   2. A Benjaminite (1 Chr. 7:12).
   3. Wife of **Shaharaim** (1 Chr. 8:8, 11).

HYMENAEUS: A false teacher condemned by **Paul** (1 Tim. 1:19f.; 2 Tim. 2:17f.).

HYRCANUS: One who had money deposited in the Temple (2 Mac. 3:11).

I

IBHAR: Son of **David** (2 Sam. 5:15; 1 Chr. 3:6, 14:5).

IBNEIAH: A Benjaminite (1 Chr. 9:8).

IBNIJAH: A Benjaminite (1 Chr. 9:8).

IBRI: A Levite (1 Chr. 24:27).

IBSAM: Grandson of Issachar (1 Chr. 7:2).

IBZAN: A minor Judge, who judged Israel seven years (Jg. 12:8ff.). He was from Bethlehem, probably the Bethlehem in Zebulun (Jos. 19:15).

ICHABOD: Grandson of **Eli** (1 Sam. 4:21). His mother died in childbirth (1 Sam. 4:19).

IDBASH: A Judahite, son of **Etam** (1 Chr. 4:3).

IDDO: 1. Father of Ahinadab (1 Kg. 4:14).

2. A Levite (1 Chr. 6:21); called Adaiah (2) in 1 Chr. 6:41.

3. Officer for half the tribe of Manasseh in David's time (1 Chr. 27:21); perhaps the same as 1.

4. A seer who wrote a history of the reigns of Solomon (2 Chr. 9:29), Rehoboam (2 Chr. 12:15), and Abijah (1) (2 Chr. 13:22).

5. Grandfather (Zech. 1:1, 7) or father (Ezr. 5:1, 6:14; 1 Esd. 6:1) of Zechariah (31).

6. Chief of the Temple servants at Casiphia (Ezr. 8:17; 1 Esd. 8:45f.).

7. One who returned with Zerubbabel (Neh. 12:4).

8. One who married a foreign wife (1 Esd. 9:35); called Jaddai in Ezr. 10:43.

9. Father of a priest in the days of Joiakim (Neh. 12:16).

IDUEL: A supporter of Ezra (1) (1 Esd. 8:43); called Ariel in Ezr. 8:16.

IEZER: A Manassite (Num. 26:30); called Abiezer (1) in Jos. 17:2; 1 Chr. 7:18.

IGAL: 1. The spy representing Issachar (Num. 13:7).

2. One of David's heroes (2 Sam. 23:26); called Joel (8) in 1 Chr. 11:38.

3. Descendant of David (1 Chr. 3:22).

IGDALIAH: Father of Hanan (10) (Jer. 35:4).

IKKESH: Father of Ira (2) (2 Sam. 23:26; 1 Chr. 11:28, 27:9).

ILAI: One of David's heroes (1 Chr. 11:29); called Zalmon in 2 Sam. 23:28.

ILIADUN: Father of Joda (1) (1 Esd. 5:58).

IMALKUE: An Arab to whom Alexander (2) sent his son (1 Mac. 11:39).

IMLAH: Father of Micaiah (1) (1 Kg. 22:8f.; 2 Chr. 18:7f.).

IMMANUEL: Symbolic name given by Isaiah to the child whose birth he predicted (Isa. 7:14; cf. 8:8). In Mt. 1:23 it is applied to Jesus (1) (there written Emmanuel).

IMMER: 1. Head of a priestly course (1 Chr. 24:14).

2. A priest, some of whose descendants returned with Zerubbabel (Ezr. 2:37; Neh. 7:40; 1 Esd. 5:24); perhaps the same as 1.

3. A priest, some of whose descendants married foreign wives (Ezr. 10:20; 1 Esd. 9:21); perhaps the same as 1.

4. Father or ancestor of a priest who helped to repair the wall (Neh. 3:29); perhaps the same as 1.

5. Ancestor of some priests who lived in Jerusalem (Neh. 11:13); perhaps the same as 1.

6. Father of Pashhur (3) (Jer. 20:1).

IMNA: An Asherite (1 Chr. 7:35).

IMNAH: 1. Son of Asher (Gen. 46:17; Num. 26:44; 1 Chr. 7:30).
2. A Levite in the time of Hezekiah (1) (2 Chr. 31:14).

IMRAH: An Asherite (1 Chr. 7:36).

IMRI: 1. A Judahite (1 Chr. 9:4).
2. Father of Zaccur (6) (Neh. 3:2).

IOB: Son of Issachar (Gen. 46:13); called **Jashub** (1) in Num. 26:24; 1 Chr. 7:1.

IPHDEIAH: A Benjaminite (1 Chr. 8:25).

IR: A Benjaminite (1 Chr. 7:12); called **Iri** in 1 Chr. 7:7.

IRA: 1. David's priest (2 Sam. 20:26).
2. One of David's heroes (2 Sam. 23:26; 1 Chr. 11:28). He was one of David's monthly commanders (1 Chr. 27:9).
3. Another of David's heroes (2 Sam. 23:38; 1 Chr. 11:40).

IRAD: Grandson of Cain (Gen. 4:18).

IRAM: A chief of Edom (Gen. 36:43).

IRI: A Benjaminite (1 Chr. 7:7); called **Ir** in 1 Chr. 7:12.

IRIJAH: A sentry who arrested **Jeremiah** (1) (Jer. 37:13f.).

IRU: Son of Caleb (1 Chr. 4:15).

ISAAC: Son of Abraham and Sarah (1) (Gen. 17:19, 21:3). His father planned to sacrifice him to God in the land of Moriah, but was prevented from doing so (Gen. 22). He married **Rebekah**, who was of his father's kin (Gen. 24) and who bore him Esau and Jacob (1) (Gen. 25:21ff.). He passed his wife off as his sister in Gerar (Gen. 26:1ff.) and his herdsmen quarrelled with the herdsmen of Gerar (Gen. 26:17ff.) until he moved to Beersheba (Gen. 26:23ff.). He planned to bless Esau, but Jacob deceived him and secured the blessing (Gen. 27:1ff.). He died at Hebron when he was 180 years old (Gen. 35:27ff.).

ISAIAH: The prophet, son of Amoz (Isa. 1:1). He was called in the year that Uzziah (1) died (Isa. 6:1), and in the reign of **Ahaz** (1) he encouraged the king with the prophecy of the birth of **Immanuel** (Isa. 7:1ff.). His sons were **Shear-jashub** (Isa. 7:3) and **Maher-shalal-hash-baz** (Isa. 8:3). In the reign of Hezekiah (1) he strengthened the king with the promise of the deliverance of Jerusalem from **Sennacherib** (2 Kg. 19:14ff.; 2 Chr. 32:20f.; Isa. 37), and when Hezekiah was ill he promised him recovery (2 Kg. 20:1ff.; Isa. 38:1ff.), but rebuked him for his reception of the ambassadors of **Merodach-baladan** (2 Kg. 20:12ff.; Isa. 39). He is credited with a history of the reigns of Uzziah (2 Chr. 26:22) and Hezekiah (2 Chr. 32:32).

ISCAH: Daughter of **Haran** (1) and sister of **Milcah** (1) (Gen. 11:29).

ISCARIOT: *See* Judas (5).

ISHBAH: A Judahite (1 Chr. 4:17).

ISHBAK: Son of Abraham by Keturah (Gen. 25:2; 1 Chr. 1:32).

ISHBI-BENOB: A Philistine giant who was slain by Abishai (2 Sam. 21:16f.).

ISHBOSHETH: Son of Saul (1) (2 Sam. 2:8, 10, 12), who succeeded Saul, with his capital at Mahanaim (2 Sam. 2:8). There was a long war between him and David (2 Sam. 2:12ff., 3:1ff.), until Ishbosheth was murdered (2 Sam. 5:5ff.). He is called Eshbaal in 1 Chr. 8:33, 9:39 and is probably the same as Ishvi (2) in 1 Sam. 14:49. In 2 Sam. 2:10 he is said to have reigned for two years.

ISHHOD: A Manassite (1 Chr. 7:18).

ISHI: 1. A Jerahmeelite (1 Chr. 2:31).
   2. A Judahite (1 Chr. 4:20).
   3. Father of the leaders of the Simeonites who defeated the Amalekites (1 Chr. 4:42).
   4. A Manassite (1 Chr. 5:24).

ISHMA: Son of Etam (1 Chr. 4:3).

ISHMAEL: 1. Son of Abraham by Hagar (Gen. 16:15; 1 Chr. 1:28). He gave his name to the Ishmaelites. He was driven out with his mother (Gen. 21:14f.). He was circumcised on the same day as his father (Gen. 17:24ff.) and married an Egyptian wife (Gen. 21:21). He died at the age of 137 (Gen. 25:17).
   2. A member of the royal family who murdered Gedaliah (1) (2 Kg. 25:23ff.; Jer. 40:8–41:3).
   3. A descendant of Saul (1) through Jonathan (1) (1 Chr. 8:38, 9:44).
   4. Father of Zebadiah (7) (2 Chr. 19:11).
   5. A military officer who supported Jehoiada (3) (2 Chr. 23:1).
   6. A priest who married a foreign wife (Ezr. 10:22; 1 Esd. 9:22).

ISHMAIAH: 1. One of David's heroes (1 Chr. 12:4). He was a Benjaminite who joined David at Ziklag.
   2. David's commander for the tribe of Zebulun (1 Chr. 27:19).

ISHMERAI: A Benjaminite (1 Chr. 8:18).

ISHPAH: A Benjaminite (1 Chr. 8:16).

ISHPAN: A Benjaminite (1 Chr. 8:22).

ISHVAH: Son of Asher (Gen. 46:17; 1 Chr. 7:30).

ISHVI: 1. Son of Asher (Gen. 46:17; 1 Chr. 7:30).
   2. Son of Saul (1) by Ahinoam (1) (1 Sam. 14:49f.).

ISMACHIAH: A Levite contemporary of Hezekiah (1) (2 Chr. 31:13).

ISRAEL: Name given to Jacob (1) (Gen. 32:28, 35:10), after which the Israelites were called.

ISSACHAR: Son of Jacob (1) by Leah (Gen. 30:18, 35:23; 1 Chr. 2:1). He gave his name to one of the tribes of Israel.

ISSHIAH: 1. A man of Issachar (1 Chr. 7:3).
   2. A Korahite who joined David at Ziklag (1 Chr. 12:6).
   3. A Kohathite Levite (1 Chr. 23:20, 24:25).
   4. A Levite (1 Chr. 24:21).

ISSHIJAH: One who married a foreign wife (Ezr. 10:31); perhaps called **Asaias** in 1 Esd. 9:32.

ISTALCURUS: Ancestor of some who returned with **Ezra** (1) (1 Esd. 8:40); called **Zaccur** (5) in Ezr. 8:14.

ITHAI: One of David's heroes (1 Chr. 11:31); called **Ittai** (2) in 2 Sam. 23:29.

ITHAMAR: Son of Aaron and Elisheba (Exod. 6:23, 28:1; 1 Chr. 6:23, 24:1). He was consecrated to the priesthood (Num. 3:2f.), and priestly dues were assigned (Lev. 10:12ff.). He was rebuked for failing to observe the correct ritual (Lev. 10:16ff.). He was put in charge of the Gershonites and the Merarites (Lev. 4:28, 33). His descendants provided eight of the twenty-four courses of priests, the remaining sixteen coming from the house of **Eleazar** (1) (1 Chr. 24:4). One of his descendants returned with **Ezra** (1) (Ezr. 8:2).

ITHIEL: 1. A Benjaminite (Neh. 11:2).
   2. One of two persons to whom **Agur's** words were addressed (Prov. 30:1).

ITHMAH: One of David's heroes (1 Chr. 11:46).

ITHRA: Father of **Amasa** (1) (2 Sam. 17:25); called **Jether** (2) in 1 Kg. 2:5, 32; 1 Chr. 2:17.

ITHRAN: 1. A Horite (Gen. 36:26; 1 Chr. 1:41).
   2. An Asherite (1 Chr. 7:37); called **Jether** (5) in 1 Chr. 7:38.

ITHREAM: Son of David (2 Sam. 3:5; 1 Chr. 3:3).

ITTAI: 1. A man of Gath who led 600 Philistines to support **David** against **Absalom** (1) (2 Sam. 15:18ff.). He was made commander of one third of the army (2 Sam. 18:2).
   2. One of David's heroes (2 Sam. 23:29); called **Ithai** in 1 Chr. 11:31.

IZHAR: 1. Son of Kohath (Exod. 6:18, 21; Num. 3:19, 16:1; 1 Chr. 6:2, 18, 38, 23:12, 18).
   2. A Judahite (1 Chr. 4:7).

IZLIAH: A Benjaminite (1 Chr. 8:18).

IZRAHIAH: A man of Issachar (1 Chr. 7:3). The same name, borne by a different person, is rendered Jezrahiah in Neh. 12:42.

IZRI: A Levite musician (1 Chr. 25:11); perhaps the same as Zeri in 1 Chr. 25:3.

IZZIAH: One who married a foreign wife (Ezr. 10:10, 25; 1 Esd. 9:26).

J

JAAKAN: A Horite (1 Chr. 1:42); called Akan in Gen. 36:27.

JAAKOBAH: A Simeonite (1 Chr. 4:36).

JAALA: Ancestor of some of Solomon's servants who returned with Zerubbabel (Neh. 7:58); called Jaalah in Ezr. 2:56; 1 Esd. 5:33.

JAALAH: See Jaala.

JAARE-OREGIM: Father of El-hanan (1) (2 Sam. 21:19); called Jair (3) in 1 Chr. 20:5. See El-hanan (1).

JAARESHIAH: A Benjaminite (1 Chr. 8:27).

JAASIEL: 1. One of David's heroes (1 Chr. 11:47).
2. One who was over the Benjaminites (1 Chr. 27:21); perhaps the same as 1.

JAASU: One who married a foreign wife (Ezr. 10:37); perhaps the same as Eliasis in 1 Esd. 9:34.

JAAZANIAH: 1. One who came with Ishmael (2) to Gedaliah (1) (2 Kg. 25:23); called Jezaniah in Jer. 40:8.
2. A Rechabite (Jer. 35:3).
3. An idolatrous elder (Ezek. 8:11).
4. An evil counsellor (Ezek. 11:1ff.).

JAAZIAH: A Merarite (1 Chr. 24:26f.).

JAAZIEL: A Levite musician who accompanied the Ark (1 Chr. 15:18); called Aziel in 1 Chr. 15:20.

JABAL: Son of Lamech (1) by Adah (1) (Gen. 4:20).

JABESH: Father of Shallum (1) (2 Kg. 15:10, 13f.). It is possible that 'son of Jabesh' means 'inhabitant of Jabesh' (1 Sam. 11:1).

JABEZ: A Judahite (1 Chr. 4:9f.).

JABIN: King of Hazor (Jos. 11:1), whom **Joshua** (1) defeated and killed (Jos. 11:11). He destroyed the city and left no survivor (Jos. 11:13f.). A variant tradition says that Jabin oppressed Israel in the time of **Deborah** and **Barak** (Jg. 4:2), and that his army under **Sisera** (1) was defeated by Zebulun and Naphtali under their leadership (Jg. 4:12ff.) and Jabin destroyed (Jg. 4:23f.). But the Song of Deborah (Jg. 5) makes no mention of Jabin or of Hazor.

JACAN: A Gadite (1 Chr. 5:13).

JACHIN: Son of Simeon (1) (Gen. 46:10; Exod. 6:15; Num. 26:12); called **Jarib** (1) in 1 Chr. 4:24.

JACOB: 1. Son of **Isaac** and **Rebekah** (Gen. 25:26), and younger twin of **Esau**. He acquired the birthright from Esau (Gen. 25:29ff.) and by deceit obtained the blessing designed for Esau (Gen. 27:1ff.). Driven to flight (Gen. 27:41ff.), he went to his mother's kindred and there served **Laban** (1) (Gen. 29ff.). On his journey to Laban he had his dream at Bethel (Gen. 28:11ff.). He married **Leah** and **Rachel** (Gen. 29:15ff.) and acquired much cattle (Gen. 30:25ff.). Escaping from Laban to return to Palestine (Gen. 31:1ff.), he was pursued by Laban to Galeed (Gen. 31:22ff.), where they made a treaty. Jacob encountered an angel at Peniel, where his name was changed to **Israel** (Gen. 32:22ff.), and became reconciled to his brother (Gen. 33:4ff.). After a stay in Shechem (Gen. 33:18ff., 34:1ff., 35:1ff.) he moved to Bethel (Gen. 35:5ff.), and then farther south (Gen. 35:16ff.). He was deceived by his other sons into thinking his son **Joseph** (1) was dead (Gen. 37:31ff.), and continued to live in the south until famine caused him to send his sons to Egypt for food (Gen. 42ff.), until Joseph revealed himself to his brothers (Gen. 45:1ff.) and sent for Jacob to come to Egypt (Gen. 45:13ff.), where he died (Gen. 49:33). He was buried in the cave of Machpelah (Gen. 50:13).

2. Father of **Joseph** (11) (Mt. 1:15f.).

JADA: A Jerahmeelite (1 Chr. 2:28, 32).

JADDAI: One who married a foreign wife (Ezr. 10:43); called **Iddo** (8) in 1 Esd. 9:35.

JADDUA: 1. One who sealed the covenant (Neh. 10:21).

2. High Priest (Neh. 12:11, 22). He was still in office in the time of **Alexander** (1).

JADDUS: Ancestor of some who returned with **Zerubbabel**, who were unable to establish their priestly descent (1 Esd. 5:38); called **Barzillai** (1) in Ezr. 2:61; Neh. 7:63.

JADON: One who helped to repair the wall (Neh. 3:7).

JAEL: Wife of **Heber** (2) (Jg. 4:17, 21). She killed **Sisera** (1) (Jg. 4:17ff., 5:24ff.).

JAHATH: 1. A Judahite (1 Chr. 4:2).
  2. A Levite (1 Chr. 6:20, 43).
  3. Another Levite (1 Chr. 23:10); perhaps the same as 2.
  4. Another Levite (1 Chr. 24:22).
  5. A Levite who supervised the restoration of the Temple in the time of Josiah (1) (2 Chr. 34:12).

JAHAZIEL: 1. A Benjaminite who joined David at Ziklag (1 Chr. 12:4).
  2. A priest who accompanied the Ark (1 Chr. 16:6).
  3. A Levite in the time of David (1 Chr. 23:19, 24:23).
  4. A Levite who prophesied in the time of Jehoshaphat (4) (2 Chr. 20:14).
  5. Father of one who returned with Ezra (1) (Ezr. 8:5; 1 Esd. 8:32).

JAHDAI: A Calebite (1 Chr. 2:47).

JAHDIEL: A Manassite (1 Chr. 5:24).

JAHDO: A Gadite (1 Chr. 5:14).

JAHLEEL: Son of Zebulun (Gen. 46:14; Num. 26:26).

JAHMAI: A man of Issachar (1 Chr. 7:2).

JAHZEEL: Son of Naphtali (Gen. 46:24; Num. 26:48); called **Jahziel** in 1 Chr. 7:13.

JAHZEIAH: One who opposed **Ezra** (1) over mixed marriages (Ezr. 10:15; cf. 1 Esd. 9:14, where he and **Jonathan,** (10, are represented as supporting Ezra).

JAHZERAH: A priest (1 Chr. 9:12); called **Ahzai** in Neh. 11:13.

JAHZIEL: Son of Naphtali (1 Chr. 7:13); called **Jahzeel** in Gen. 46:24; Num. 26:48.

JAIR: 1. Son of Manasseh (Num. 32:41; 1 Kg. 4:13). He gave his name to a clan. In 1 Chr. 2:22 he is said to be son of **Segub** (2).
  2. A minor Judge (Jg. 10:3ff.).
  3. Father of **El-hanan** (1) (1 Chr. 20:5); called **Jaare-oregim** in 2 Sam. 21:19.
  4. Father of **Mordecai** (2) (Est. 2:5).

JAIRUS: Ruler of the synagogue whose daughter **Jesus** (1) raised from the dead (Mk 5:22; Lk. 8:41).

JAKEH: Father of **Agur** (Prov. 30:1).

JAKIM: 1. A Benjaminite (1 Chr. 8:19).
  2. Head of a priestly course (1 Chr. 24:12).

JALAM: Son of Esau (Gen. 36:5, 14, 18; 1 Chr. 1:35).

JALON: A Calebite (1 Chr. 4:17).

JAMBRES: *See* **Jannes and Jambres.**

JAMBRI: The 'sons of Jambri' who slew **John (2)** were an Arab tribe (1 Mac. 9:35f.). The deed was avenged by John's brothers (1 Mac. 9:37ff.).

JAMES: 1. Son of Zebedee and brother of **John (7)** (Mt. 4:21, 10:2; Mk 1:19, 3:17; Lk. 5:10). He was one of the twelve Apostles of **Jesus (1)** (Mt. 10:2; Mk 3:17; Lk. 6:14; Ac. 1:13), and he belonged to the inner group of three (Mt. 17:1, 26:37; Mk 5:37, 9:2, 14:33; Lk. 8:51, 9:28). He and his brother asked Jesus to promise them special positions in His Kingdom (Mk 10:35ff.; cf. Mt. 20:20ff.), and they were called **Boanerges** (Mk 3:17). They were fishermen before they became disciples (Mt. 4:21f.; Mk 1:19f.; Lk. 5:10f.), and after the Crucifixion they returned to that occupation (Jn 21:2f.). James was martyred by **Herod (6)** (Ac. 12:2).

2. Son of **Alphaeus (1)** (Mt. 10:3; Mk 3:18; Lk. 6:15; Ac. 1:13), another of the twelve Apostles. If Alphaeus is the same as **Clopas**, his mother was **Mary (2)**.

3. Brother of **Jesus (1)** (Mt. 13:55; Mk 6:3), who did not believe in the Lord before the Crucifixion (Jn. 7:5), but to whom Jesus appeared after the Resurrection (1 C. 15:7). He became the leader of the Jerusalem church, and when **Paul** went there after his conversion he saw him (Gal. 1:19). He presided at the Council of Jerusalem (Ac. 15:6ff.), and Paul reported to him and the elders after his third missionary journey (Ac. 21:17ff.). He was martyred shortly before the fall of Jerusalem, but his death is not recorded in the NT. The Epistle of James is attributed to him.

4. Father of **Judas (6)** (Lk. 6:16).

5. Son of **Mary (2)** (Mt. 27:56; Mk 15:40); possibly the same as **2**.

JAMIN: 1. Son of **Simeon (1)** (Gen. 46:10; Exod. 6:15; Num. 26:12; 1 Chr. 4:24).

2. A Jerahmeelite (1 Chr. 2:27).

3. One who helped to expound the Law (Neh. 8:7; 1 Esd. 9:48).

JAMLECH: A Simeonite (1 Chr. 4:34).

JANAI: A Gadite (1 Chr. 5:12).

JANNAI: An ancestor of **Jesus (1)** (Lk. 3:24).

JANNES AND JAMBRES: Two who opposed **Moses** (2 Tim. 3:8). Their names are not mentioned in the OT.

JAPHETH: Son of **Noah (1)** (Gen. 5:32, 6:10, 7:13, 9:18, 10:1; 1 Chr. 1:4). He is presented in Gen. 10:2ff. as the ancestor of the peoples in the northern part of the world then known. He showed modesty when his father was drunk (Gen. 9:23).

JAPHIA: 1. King of Lachish who joined a coalition against **Joshua (1)** (Jos. 10:3ff.), and who was defeated and slain (Jos. 10:26f.).

2. Son of **David** (2 Sam. 5:15; 1 Chr. 3:7, 14:6).

JAPHLET: An Asherite (1 Chr. 7:32f.).

JARAH: A descendant of Saul (1) (1 Chr. 9:42); called **Jehoaddah** in 1 Chr. 8:36.

JARED: Father of Enoch (2) (Gen. 5:15f., 18ff.; 1 Chr. 1:2). He figures in the ancestry of Jesus (1) (Lk. 3:37).

JARHA: An Egyptian slave who married the daughter of Sheshan (1 Chr. 2:34f.).

JARIB: 1. Son of Simeon (1) (1 Chr. 4:24); called **Jachin** in Gen. 46:10; Exod. 6:15; Num. 26:12.

2. One of those sent to Iddo (6) (Ezr. 8:16; 1 Esd. 8:44).

3. A priest who married a foreign wife (Ezr. 10:18; 1 Esd. 9:19).

JAROAH: A Gadite (1 Chr. 5:14).

JASHEN: Father of some of David's heroes (2 Sam. 23:32); called **Hashem** in 1 Chr. 11:34, where RSV omits 'sons of'.

JASHOBEAM: One of David's heroes (1 Chr. 11:11); called **Josheb-basshebeth** in 2 Sam. 23:8. He was a Korahite who joined David at Ziklag (1 Chr. 12:6), and he became one of David's monthly commanders (1 Chr. 27:2).

JASHUB: 1. Son of Issachar (Num. 26:24; 1 Chr. 7:1); called **Iob** in Gen. 46:13.

2. One who married a foreign wife (Ezr. 10:29; 1 Esd. 9:30).

JASON: 1. An ambassador sent by Judas (1) to Rome (1 Mac. 8:17ff.). He was the father of Antipater (1 Mac. 12:16, 14:22).

2. Jason of Cyrene, whose history in five volumes is condensed in 2 Maccabees (2 Mac. 2:23).

3. Brother of Onias (3), whom he displaced from the high priesthood (2 Mac. 4:7ff.). He was himself displaced by Menelaus and came to a miserable end (2 Mac. 5:5ff.).

4. Paul's host at Thessalonica (Ac. 17:6ff.). He was probably the Jason who sent greetings to the church in Rome in Rom. 16:21.

JATHAN: A kinsman of Tobit (Tob. 5:12f.).

JATHNIEL: A Levite gatekeeper (1 Chr. 26:2).

JAVAN: Son of Japheth (Gen. 10:2, 4; 1 Chr. 1:5, 7), who gave his name to the Ionians.

JAZIZ: One who was over the flocks of David (1 Chr. 27:30).

JEATHERAI: An ancestor of Asaph (2) (1 Chr. 6:21).

JEBERECHIAH: Father of Zechariah (19) (Isa. 8:2).

JECHONIAH: An ancestor of Jesus (1) (Mt. 1:11f.); *see* Jehoiachin.

JECOLIAH: Mother of Uzziah (1) (2 Kg. 15:2; 2 Chr. 26:3).

JECONIAH: 1. The name of Jehoiachin found in 1 Chr. 3:16f.; Est. 2:5; Jer. 24:1, 27:20, 28:4, 29:2; Ad. Est. 11:4; Bar. 1:3, 9.

2. A Levite in the time of Josiah (1) (1 Esd. 1:9); called **Conaniah** (2) in 2 Chr. 35:9.

3. The name for **Jehoahaz** (2) found in 1 Esd. 1:34.

JEDAIAH: 1. A Simeonite (1 Chr. 4:37).

2. Head of a priestly course (1 Chr. 24:7).

3. A Jerusalem priest (1 Chr. 9:10; Neh. 11:10).

4. Ancestor of some priests who returned with **Zerubbabel** (Ezr. 2:36; Neh. 7:39; 1 Esd. 5:24).

5. One who helped to repair the wall (Neh. 3:10).

6. A priest who returned with **Zerubbabel** (Neh. 12:6, 19).

7. Another priest who returned with **Zerubbabel** (Neh. 12:7, 21).

8. One who brought gifts for the Temple (Zech. 6:10, 14).

JEDIAEL: 1. A Benjaminite (1 Chr. 7:6, 10f.).

2. One of David's heroes (1 Chr. 11:45); probably the same as the Jediael who joined David at Ziklag (1 Chr. 12:20).

3. A Korahite gatekeeper (1 Chr. 26:2).

JEDIDAH: Mother of Josiah (1) (2 Kg. 22:1).

JEDIDIAH: Name given by **Nathan** (2) to **Solomon** (2 Sam. 12:25).

JEDUTHUN: A Levite musician of David's time (1 Chr. 16:41f., 25:1, 3, 6; 2 Chr. 5:12). He gave his name to a guild of singers. The name stands in the Headings of Pss. 39, 62, 77. A son of Jeduthun is described as a gatekeeper (1 Chr. 16:38). In 1 Esd. 1:15 **Eddinus** stands instead of Jeduthun (cf. 2 Chr. 35:15).

JEHALLELEL: 1. A Judahite (1 Chr. 4:16).

2. A Levite (2 Chr. 29:12).

JEHDEIAH: 1. A Levite (1 Chr. 24:20).

2. Officer of David in charge of she-asses (1 Chr. 27:30).

JEHEZKEL: Head of a priestly course (1 Chr. 24:16).

JEHIAH: A Levite gatekeeper for the Ark (1 Chr. 15:24).

JEHIEL: 1. A Levite musician (1 Chr. 15:18, 20, 16:5).

2. A Levite chief (1 Chr. 23:8), who had charge of the treasury (1 Chr. 29:8).

3. One who was charged with the care of **David's** sons (1 Chr. 27:32).

4. Son of **Jehoshaphat** (4) (2 Chr. 21:2).

5. A Levite officer under **Hezekiah** (1) (2 Chr. 31:13).

6. A Temple officer in the time of **Josiah** (1) (2 Chr. 35:8; 1 Esd. 1:8).

7. Father of **Obadiah** (10) (Ezr. 8:9; 1 Esd. 8:35).

8. Father of **Shecaniah** (6) (Ezr. 10:2; 1 Esd. 8:92).

9. One who married a foreign wife (Ezr. 10:26; 1 Esd. 9:27).

10. A priest who married a foreign wife (Ezr. 10:21; 1 Esd. 9:21).

JEHIELI: Not a proper name, but a patronymic from Jehiel (2) (1 Chr. 26:21f.).

JEHIZKIAH: An Ephraimite who supported Oded (2) (2 Chr. 28:12ff.).

JEHOADDAH: A descendant of Saul (1) (1 Chr. 8:36); called Jarah in 1 Chr. 9:42.

JEHOADDAN: Mother of Amaziah (1) (2 Chr. 25:1); called Jehoaddin in 2 Kg. 14:2.

JEHOADDIN: *See* Jehoaddan.

JEHOAHAZ: 1. Son and successor of Jehu (2), king of Israel (2 Kg. 13:1). He had to face Syrian inroads (2 Kg. 13:3ff.) and reigned seventeen years (2 Kg. 13:1). He is called Joahaz (2) in 2 Kg. 14:1.

2. Son of Josiah (1), made king of Judah at his father's death (2 Kg. 23:30), but deposed by Neco, who made Jehoiakim (1) king (2 Kg. 23:34). Jehoahaz was taken to Egypt and died there (2 Kg. 23:34). He is called Shallum (2) in Jer. 22:10ff., and Jeconiah (3) in 1 Esd. 1:34.

3. Youngest son and successor of Jehoram (2) (2 Chr. 21:17). He is called Ahaziah (2) in 2 Chr. 22:1, 25:23, as in 2 Kg. 8:25f., 29, 9:27, 10:12ff.

JEHOASH: 1. Son of Ahaziah (2), king of Judah (2 Kg. 11:1). He was an infant when his father died and he was hidden by his aunt for six years (2 Kg. 11:2f.; 2 Chr. 22:11f.) and then set on the throne by Jehoiada (3) (2 Kg. 11:4ff.; cf. 2 Chr. 23:1ff.). He later had a dispute with Jehoiada about the repairs of the Temple (2 Kg. 12:4ff.) and an arrangement which held in the time of Josiah (1) (2 Kg. 22:4ff.) was made (2 Kg. 12:9ff.). After reigning forty years (2 Kg. 12:1), Jehoash was assassinated (2 Kg. 12:20f.). The variant form of his name, Joash, is frequently used.

2. Son and successor of Jehoahaz (1), king of Israel (2 Kg. 13:10). He visited Elisha on his death-bed and was promised victory over Syria (2 Kg. 13:14ff.), and he stemmed the tide of Syrian aggression (2 Kg. 13:22ff.). He also defeated Judah (2 Kg. 13:12, 14:8ff.). The variant form of his name, Joash, is sometimes used.

JEHOHANAN: 1. A Levite gatekeeper (1 Chr. 26:3).

2. A commander in the time of Jehoshaphat (4) (2 Chr. 17:15).

3. Father of Ishmael (5) (2 Chr. 23:1).

4. High Priest (Ezr. 10:6; 1 Esd. 9:1), called Jonathan (11) in Neh. 12:11 and Johanan (9) in Neh. 12:22f. He is called son of Eliashib (2) (Ezr. 10:6; Neh. 12:23), but this stands, as frequently, for grandson, Joiada (2), the son of Eliashib (Neh. 12:10, 13:28) being his father (Neh. 12:11, 22).

5. One who married a foreign wife (Ezr. 10:28; 1 Esd. 9:29).

6. Son of Tobiah (2) (Neh. 6:18).

7. A priest in the days of Joiakim (Neh. 12:13).

8. A priest who shared in the dedication of the wall (Neh. 12:42).

JEHOIACHIN: Son and successor of Jekoiakim (1), king of Judah (2 Kg. 24:6; 2 Chr. 36:8). He became king when eighteen years old (2 Kg. 24:8; 2 Chr. 36:9 says eight years old) and reigned for three months and then surrendered to Nebuchadrezzar (2 Kg. 24:12). He was carried to Babylon (2 Kg. 24:15; 2 Chr. 36:10), where he remained in prison until the death of Nebuchadrezzar (2 Kg. 25:27ff.; Jer. 52:31ff.). He is called Jeconiah (1) in 1 Chr. 3:16f.; Est. 2:5; Jer. 24:1, 27:20, 28:4, 29:2; Ad. Est. 11:4; Bar. 1:3, 9, Jechoniah in Mt. 1:11f., and Coniah in Jer. 22:24, 28, 37:1.

JEHOIADA: 1. Father of Benaiah (1) (2 Sam. 8:18, 23:20; 1 Kg. 1:8); probably referred to in 1 Chr. 12:27.

2. Son of Benaiah (1) (1 Chr. 27:34). But perhaps the names have been reversed and this is the same as 1.

3. Priest in Jerusalem in the time of Athaliah (1) and Jehoash (1) (2 Kg. 11:4ff.). He married Jehosheba (2 Chr. 22:11), the aunt of Jehoash, and he placed the young prince on the throne (2 Kg. 11:4ff.; 2 Chr. 23:1ff.). Subsequently he had a dispute with Jehoash about the repair of the Temple (2 Kg. 12:4ff.).

4. Grandson of Eliashib (7) (Neh. 13:28). *See* Joiada (2).

JEHOIAKIM: 1. Son of Josiah (1), originally named Eliakim (2) (2 Kg. 23:34; 2 Chr. 36:4), placed on the throne with the name Jehoiakim by Neco, who set him in place of his brother Jehoahaz (2) (2 Kg. 23:33; 2 Chr. 36:4). He reigned eleven years (2 Kg. 23:36; 2 Chr. 36:5). After the battle of Carchemish he submitted to Nebuchadrezzar, but later rebelled and called a punitive expedition on himself (2 Kg. 24:1ff.). Before the Chaldaean army reached Jerusalem he died (2 Kg. 24:6), leaving Jehoiachin to face the consequences of his policy. The Chronicler says Nebuchadrezzar took him prisoner to Babylon (2 Chr. 36:6). He is condemned by Jeremiah (1) (Jer. 22:18ff.), and he is the king who burned Jeremiah's scroll (Jer. 36:20ff.). He had the prophet Uriah (5) extradited from Egypt and put to death (Jer. 26:20ff.).

2. High Priest to whom the exiles sent gifts for sacrifices (Bar. 1:5ff.).

JEHOIARIB: 1. A priest who returned from exile (1 Chr. 9:10; Neh. 12:6, 19); called Joiarib (3) in Neh. 11:10 (where he is the father of Jedaiah (3), instead of his colleague), 12:6, 19.

2. Head of a priestly course (1 Chr. 24:7); called Joarib in 1 Mac. 2:1, 14:29.

JEHONADAB: Form of the name Jonadab (2) found in 2 Kg. 10:15, 23.

JEHONATHAN: 1. A Levite who expounded the Law in the time of Jehoshaphat (4) (2 Chr. 17:8).

2. A priest in the days of Joiakim (Neh. 12:18).

JEHORAM: 1. Son of Ahab (1) (2 Kg. 3:1). He succeeded his brother Ahaziah (1) as king of Israel and reigned twelve years (2 Kg. 3:1). In his reign Moab rebelled (2 Kg. 3:4ff.) and there was war with Syria (2 Kg. 6:8ff., 7:1ff.). He was wounded in the battle at Ramoth-gilead (2 Kg. 8:28), and killed by Jehu (2) (2 Kg. 9:24). He is frequently called Joram (1).
    2. Son and successor of Jehoshaphat (4), king of Judah (1 Kg. 22:50; 2 Chr. 21:1). He married Athaliah (1) (2 Kg. 8:18, 26) and reigned eight years (2 Kg. 8:17; 2 Chr. 21:5). In his reign Edom revolted (2 Kg. 8:20ff.). He died in great agony (2 Chr. 21:18ff.). He is called Joram (2) in 1 Chr. 3:11; Mt. 1:8.

JEHOSHABEATH: *See* Jehosheba.

JEHOSHAPHAT: 1. Recorder under David and Solomon (2 Sam. 8:16, 20:24; 1 Kg. 4:3).
    2. Solomon's officer in Issachar (1 Kg. 4:17).
    3. Father of Jehu (2) (2 Kg. 9:2, 14).
    4. Son and successor of Asa (1), king of Judah (1 Kg. 22:41; 2 Chr. 17:1). He reigned twenty-five years (1 Kg. 22:42; 2 Chr. 21:31) and made an unsuccessful attempt to create a fleet (1 Kg. 22:47ff.). He made an alliance with Israel, sealed by the marriage of his son with the daughter of Ahab (1) (2 Kg. 8:18, 26; 2 Chr. 18:1), and he fought with Ahab at the battle of Ramoth-gilead (1 Kg. 22; 2 Chr. 18:3ff.) and with Jehoram (1) against Moab (2 Kg. 3:7ff.).

JEHOSHEBA: Daughter of Jehoram (2) (2 Kg. 11:2); called Jehoshabeath in 2 Chr. 22:11. She hid Jehoash (1) when an infant and saved his life (2 Kg. 11:2; 2 Chr. 22:11). She married Jehoiada (3).

JEHOZABAD: 1. One of the assassins of Jehoash (1) (2 Kg. 12:21; 2 Chr. 24:26).
    2. A Levite gatekeeper (1 Chr. 26:4).
    3. A Benjaminite in the time of Jehoshaphat (4) (2 Chr. 17:18).

JEHOZADAK: Father of Joshua (4) (1 Chr. 6:14f.; Hag. 1:1, 12, 14, 2:2, 4; Zech. 6:11); also called Jozadak.

JEHU: 1. A prophet who prophesied against Baasha (1 Kg. 16:1ff.) and who met Jehoshaphat (4) (2 Chr. 19:2f.).
    2. King of Israel, anointed by a disciple of Elisha (2 Kg. 9:1ff.). He seized the throne by violence and murdered the kings of Israel and Judah and all the royal family of Israel, as well as Jezebel (1) (2 Kg. 9:21ff., 10:1ff.; 2 Chr. 22:8f.). He was supported by Jonadab (2) (2 Kg. 10:15ff.) in his wholesale attack on Baal worshippers.
    3. A Jerahmeelite (1 Chr. 2:38).
    4. A Simeonite (1 Chr. 4:35).
    5. A Benjaminite who joined David at Ziklag (1 Chr. 12:3).

JEHUBBAH: An Asherite (1 Chr. 7:34).

JEHUCAL: One sent by the king to Jeremiah (1) to solicit his prayers (Jer. 37:3); called Jucal in Jer. 38:1.

JEHUDI: An officer of Jehoiakim (1) (Jer. 36:14, 21, 23).

JEHUEL: A Levite who helped to cleanse the Temple in the time of Hezekiah (1) (2 Chr. 29:14).

JEIEL: 1. A Reubenite (1 Chr. 5:7).
2. Ancestor of Saul (1) (1 Chr. 8:29, 9:35).
3. One of David's heroes (1 Chr. 11:44).
4. A Levite gatekeeper (1 Chr. 15:18).
5. A Levite musician (1 Chr. 15:21, 16:5). The repetition of the name in 1 Chr. 16:5 may be due to error.
6. Ancestor of Jahaziel (4) (2 Chr. 20:14).
7. A secretary in the time of Uzziah (1) (2 Chr. 26:11).
8. A Levite chief in the time of Josiah (1) (2 Chr. 35:9); called Ochiel in 1 Esd. 1:9.
9. One who married a foreign wife (Ezr. 10:43).

JEKAMEAM: A Levite (1 Chr. 23:19, 24:23).

JEKAMIAH: 1. A Jerahmeelite (1 Chr. 2:41).
2. Son of Jehoiachin (1 Chr. 3:18).

JEKUTHIEL: A Judahite (1 Chr. 4:18).

JEMIMAH: Daughter of Job (Job 42:14).

JEMUEL: Son of Simeon (1) (Gen. 46:10; Exod. 6:15); called Nemuel (1) in Num. 26:12; 1 Chr. 4:24.

JEPHTHAH: One of the Judges (Jg. 11f.), a Gileadite. He was an outlaw (Jg. 11:1ff.) until he was invited to lead against the Ammonites (Jg. 11:4ff.). In fulfilment of a vow he had made before the battle (Jg. 11:29ff.), he sacrificed his daughter when he returned victorious (Jg. 11:34ff.). War with the Ephraimites followed (Jg. 12:1ff.).

JEPHUNNEH: 1. Father of Caleb (Num. 13:6 and often).
2. An Asherite (1 Chr. 7:38).

JERAH: Son of Joktan (Gen. 10:36; 1 Chr. 1:20).

JERAHMEEL: 1. A non-Israelite tribe with which David cultivated relations when he was at Ziklag (1 Chr. 27:10, 30:29), but later reckoned as a part of Judah, when Jerahmeel was reckoned as a son of Hezron (2) (1 Chr. 2:9, 25ff.) and brother of Caleb (1 Chr. 2:42).
2. A Levite, son of Kish (3) (1 Chr. 24:29).
3. One of those sent to arrest Jeremiah (1) (Jer. 36:26).

JERED: A Judahite (1 Chr. 4:18).

JEREMAI: One who married a foreign wife (Ezr. 10:33; 1 Esd. 9:34).

JEREMIAH: 1. The prophet, son of **Hilkiah** (7) of Anathoth (Jer. 1:1), called to be a prophet in the thirteenth year of Josiah (1) (Jer. 1:2ff.). He appears to have supported the reform of Josiah (Jer. 11:1ff.), but in the reign of Jehoiakim (1) he foretold the destruction of the Temple (Jer. 25:1ff.). His scroll of prophecies was burnt by the king (Jer. 36:20ff.), and at one point in Jehoiakim's reign the prophet's life was saved by **Ahikam** (Jer. 26:24). In the reign of Zedekiah (2) Jeremiah was arrested as a traitor (Jer. 37:11ff.), and was rescued from a cistern by an Ethiopian (Jer. 38:5ff.). When the city was taken, he elected to remain in it (Jer. 39:4ff.), but when **Gedaliah** (1) was murdered he was carried to Egypt (Jer. 43:6) and his last prophecies were spoken there (Jer. 44).

2. Maternal grandfather of **Jehoahaz** (2) (2 Kg. 23:31) and of Zedekiah (2) (2 Kg. 24:18; Jer. 52:1).

3. A Manassite (1 Chr. 5:24).

4. A Benjaminite who joined **David** at Ziklag (1 Chr. 12:4).

5. A Gadite who joined **David** in the wilderness (1 Chr. 12:10).

6. Another Gadite who joined **David** in the wilderness (1 Chr. 12:13).

7. A priest who sealed the covenant (Neh. 10:2).

8. A priest who returned with **Zerubbabel** (Neh. 12:1). One of his descendants was priest in the days of **Joiakim** (Neh. 12:12).

9. Father of **Jaazaniah** (2) (Jer. 35:3).

10. One who shared in the dedication of the wall (Neh. 12:34).

JEREMIEL: An archangel (2 Esd. 4:36).

JEREMOTH: 1. A Benjaminite (1 Chr. 7:8).

2. Another Benjaminite (1 Chr. 8:14).

3. A Merarite Levite (1 Chr. 23:23); called **Jerimoth** (3) in 1 Chr. 24:30.

4. A Levite musician (1 Chr. 25:22); called **Jerimoth** (4) in 1 Chr. 25:4.

5. Officer for Naphtali (1 Chr. 27:19).

6. One who married a foreign wife (Ezr. 10:26; 1 Esd. 9:27).

7. Another who married a foreign wife (Ezr. 10:27; 1 Esd. 9:28).

8. A third who married a foreign wife (Ezr. 10:29; 1 Esd. 9:30).

JERIAH: A Levite chief (1 Chr. 23:19, 24:23); called **Jerijah** in 1 Chr. 26:31.

JERIBAI: One of **David's** heroes (1 Chr. 11:46).

JERIEL: A man of Issachar (1 Chr. 7:2).

JERIJAH: A Levite chief (1 Chr. 26:31); called **Jeriah** in 1 Chr. 23:19, 24:23.

JERIMOTH: 1. A Benjaminite (1 Chr. 7:7).

2. A Benjaminite who joined **David** at Ziklag (1 Chr. 12:5).

3. A Merarite Levite (1 Chr. 24:30); called **Jeremoth** (3) in 1 Chr. 23:23.

4. A Levite musician (1 Chr. 25:4); called **Jeremoth** (4) in 1 Chr. 25:22.

5. Rehoboam's father-in-law (2 Chr. 11:18).

6. A Levite in the time of Hezekiah (1) (2 Chr. 31:13).

JERIOTH: Wife of **Caleb** (1 Chr. 2:18).

JEROBOAM: 1. Jeroboam I, first king of Northern Israel (1 Kg. 12:20). In Solomon's reign he was over the corvée (1 Kg. 11:26ff.), and was encouraged to revolt by **Ahijah** (3) (1 Kg. 11:29ff.), and thereafter forced to flee to Egypt (1 Kg. 11:40). He returned to lead the people in their demands of **Rehoboam**, and when they were rejected he became king of the revolting tribes (1 Kg. 12:1ff.). He made the shrines of Bethel and Dan into royal sanctuaries (1 Kg. 12:25ff.), and Ahijah turned against him (1 Kg. 14:2ff.). He reigned twenty-two years (1 Kg. 14:20).

2. Jeroboam II, son and successor of **Jehoash** (2) as king of Israel (2 Kg. 14:23). He reigned forty-one years and in his reign the kingdom prospered (2 Kg. 14:23ff.). The social and religious evils that accompanied this prosperity called forth the sharp condemnation of **Amos** and **Hosea**.

JEROHAM: 1. Grandfather of **Samuel** (1 Sam. 1:1; 1 Chr. 6:27, 34).
2. A Benjaminite (1 Chr. 8:27).
3. Father of a Benjaminite of post-exilic days (1 Chr. 9:8).
4. Father of a priest who returned with **Zerubbabel** (1 Chr. 9:12; Neh. 11:12).
5. Father of two Benjaminites who joined **David** at Ziklag (1 Chr. 12:7).
6. Father of **Azarel** (3) (1 Chr. 27:22).
7. Father of **Azariah** (14) (2 Chr. 23:1).

JERUBBAAL: Name given to **Gideon** (Jg. 6:32, 7:1, 8:29, 35, 9:1f., 5, 16, 19, 24, 28, 57; 1 Sam. 12:11); changed to **Jerubbesheth** in 2 Sam. 11:21.

JERUBBESHETH: *See* **Jerubbaal.**

JERUSHA: Mother of **Jotham** (2) (2 Kg. 15:33); called **Jerushah** in 1 Chr. 27:1.

JERUSHAH: *See* **Jerusha.**

JESHAIAH: 1. A descendant of **Zerubbabel** (1 Chr. 3:21).
2. Son of **Jeduthun** (1 Chr. 25:3, 15).
3. A Levite (1 Chr. 26:25).
4. One who returned with **Ezra** (1) (Ezr. 8:7; 1 Esd. 8:33).
5. A Merarite brought from Casiphia (Ezr. 8:19; 1 Esd. 8:48).
6. A Benjaminite (Neh. 11:7).

JESHARELAH: An Asaphite (1 Chr. 25:14); called **Asharelah** in 1 Chr. 25:2.

JESHEBEAB: Head of a priestly course (1 Chr. 24:13).

JESHER: Son of **Caleb** (1 Chr. 2:18).

JESHISHAI: A Gadite (1 Chr. 5:14).

JESHOHAIAH: A Simeonite (1 Chr. 4:36).

JESHUA: 1. Son of Nun (Neh. 8:17), alternative form of the name of Joshua (1).

2. Head of a priestly course (1 Chr. 24:11).

3. A Levite in the time of Hezekiah (1) (2 Chr. 31:15).

4. Ancestor of some who returned with Zerubbabel (Ezr. 2:6; Neh. 7:11; 1 Esd. 5:11).

5. High Priest contemporary with Zerubbabel (Ezr. 3:2). He is called Jeshua in Ezra and Nehemiah, and Joshua (4) in Haggai and Zechariah. He took a leading part in the building of the Second Temple (Ezr. 3:2ff., 5:2; Hag. 1:1, 12, 14, 2:2, 4). He figures in a symbolic action in Zech. 3:1ff., and is crowned in Zech. 6:11. Some of his descendants married foreign wives (Ezr. 10:18). He is lauded in the Hymn of Praise of the Fathers (Sir. 49:12).

6. Ancestor of a priestly family which returned with Zerubbabel (Ezr. 2:36; Neh. 7:39; 1 Esd. 5:24).

7. Ancestor of some Levites who returned with Zerubbabel (Ezr. 2:40, 3:9; Neh. 7:43; 1 Esd. 5:26; cf. Neh. 12:8, 24).

8. Father of a Levite of the time of Ezra (1) (Ezr. 8:33; 1 Esd. 8:63).

9. Father of Ezer (5) (Neh. 3:19).

10. A Levite who helped to explain the Law (Neh. 8:7, 9:4f.).

11. A Levite who sealed the covenant (Neh. 10:9).

12. A Levite surnamed Emadabun, whose sons shared in the work on the Temple (1 Esd. 5:58).

JESHURUN: A name applied to Israel (Dt. 32:15, 33:5, 26; Isa. 44:2).

JESIMIEL: A Simeonite (1 Chr. 4:36).

JESSE: Father of David (1 Sam. 16:1ff., 18, 17:12). He was a descendant of Boaz and Ruth (Ru. 4:18, 22). When David became an outlaw, he took him to the king of Moab (1 Sam. 22:3f.).

JESUS: 1. Jesus Christ, Son of Mary (1) (Mt. 1:18ff.; Lk. 1:26ff.), but publicly recognized by Joseph (11) as his son (Jn 1:45, 6:42), and hence the genealogy of Jesus is traced through Joseph (Mt. 1:1ff.; Lk. 3:23ff.). He was born in Bethlehem (Mt. 2:1ff.; Lk. 2:1ff.), but brought up in Nazareth (Mt. 2:23; Lk. 2:4, 39). He was taken to the Temple when He was twelve (Lk. 2:41ff.), but nothing further is known of Him until He was about thirty (Lk. 3:23), when He was baptized by John (6) the Baptist (Mt. 3:13ff.; Mk 1:9ff.; Lk. 3:21f.; Jn 1:29ff.) and commenced His ministry. He gathered disciples about Him and taught and healed, mainly in Galilee, but with visits to Jerusalem. He spoke of Himself as the Son of Man, but discouraged the use of the title of Messiah, or Christ, though He accepted the title when Peter used it of Him (Mt. 16:16; Mk 8:29; Lk. 9:20), and claimed it in conversation with the Samaritan woman (Jn 4:25f.) and at His trial (Mt. 26:64). He taught His disciples that His messiahship was through suffering (Mt. 16:21ff.; Mk 8:31ff., 10:45; Lk. 9:22), and not through military conquest (cf. Jn 19:36). At His Last Supper He spoke of His death in terms of redemption and the establishment of a New Covenant (Mt. 26:26ff.; Mk 14:22ff.; Lk. 22:14ff.; 1 C. 11:23ff.). He was arrested (Mt. 26:47ff.; Mk 14:43ff.; Lk. 22:47ff.; Jn 18:1ff.), tried (Mt. 26:57ff., 27:1ff.; Mk 14:53ff., 15:1ff.; Lk. 22:54ff., 23:1ff.; Jn 18:12ff., 19:1ff.) and crucified (Mt. 27:33ff.; Mk 15:22ff.; Lk. 23:33ff.; Jn 19:17ff.), and on the third day rose (Mt. 28:1ff.; Mk 16:1ff.; Lk. 24:1ff.; Jn 20f.). Before His Ascension (Lk. 24:50; Ac. 1:6ff.) He commissioned His disciples to carry His Gospel to the whole world (Mt. 28:19f.).

2. Jesus, the son of Sirach, author of the book of Ecclesiasticus, or the Wisdom of Jesus the Son of Sirach (Sir. 50:27), which was written in Hebrew about 180 B.C. (part of the Hebrew being still extant), and translated into Greek by the grandson of Jesus (*see* Preface) about fifty years later.

3. Jesus Justus, who was a comfort to **Paul** (Col. 4:11).

JETHER: 1. Son of Gideon (Jg. 8:20).

2. Father of **Amasa** (1) (1 Kg. 2:5, 32). He was an Ishmaelite (1 Chr. 2:17). He is called **Ithra** in 2 Sam. 17:25.

3. A Jerahmeelite (1 Chr. 2:32).

4. A Judahite (1 Chr. 4:17).

5. An Asherite (1 Chr. 7:38); called **Ithran** (2) in 1 Chr. 7:37.

JETHETH: An Edomite (Gen. 36:40; 1 Chr. 1:51).

JETHRO: Father-in-law of Moses (Exod. 3:1, 4:18, 18:1ff.); called **Hobab** in Num. 10:29; Jg. 4:11, and **Reuel** (2) in Exod. 2:18, but elsewhere Reuel is the father of Hobab (Num. 10:29). Jethro was a Midianite (Exod. 2:16) or Kenite (Jg. 4:11) priest, who received Moses when he fled from **Pharaoh** and gave him his daughter **Zipporah** (Exod. 2:21). He went to Moses at Sinai (Exod. 18:1ff.), offered sacrifice (Exod. 18:12), and gave advice to Moses (Exod. 18:13ff.).

JETUR: Son of **Ishmael** (1) (Gen. 25:15; 1 Chr. 1:31, 5:19).

JEUEL: 1. A Judahite who returned from exile (1 Chr. 9:6).

2. A Levite in the time of **Hezekiah** (1) (2 Chr. 29:13).

3. One who returned with **Ezra** (1) (Ezr. 8:13).

JEUSH: 1. Son of Esau by **Oholibamah** (1) (Gen. 36:4, 14, 18; 1 Chr. 1:35).

2. A Benjaminite (1 Chr. 7:10).

3. A descendant of **Saul** (1) (1 Chr. 8:39).

4. A Levite in David's time (1 Chr. 23:10f.).

5. Son of **Rehoboam** (2 Chr. 11:19).

JEUZ: A Benjaminite (1 Chr. 8:10).

JEZANIAH: One who came with **Ishmael** (2) to **Gedaliah** (1) (Jer. 40:8) called **Jaazaniah** (1) in 2 Kg. 25:23.

JEZEBEL: 1. Daughter of **Ethbaal**. She married **Ahab** (1) (1 Kg. 16:31), and promoted **Baal** worship in Israel (1 Kg. 16:32, 18:19) and persecuted the prophets of the Lord (1 Kg. 18:4) and sought the life of **Elijah** (1) (1 Kg. 19:2f.). She was responsible for the judicial murder of **Naboth** (1 Kg. 21:5ff.) and her evil influence spread to the southern kingdom through **Athaliah** (1). At the revolution of **Jehu** (2) she was killed (2 Kg. 9:30ff.).

2. Name applied to a false prophetess of Thyatira (Rev. 2:20).

JEZER: Son of **Naphtali** (Gen. 46:24; Num. 26:49; 1 Chr. 7:13).

JEZIEL: A Benjaminite who joined **David** at Ziklag (1 Chr. 12:3).

JEZRAHIAH: Leader of the Temple singers at the dedication of the wall (Neh. 12:42). The same name, borne by a different person, is rendered **Izrahiah** in 1 Chr. 7:3.

JIDLAPH: Son of **Nahor** (2) (Gen. 22:22).

JOAB: 1. Son of **Zeruiah** (2 Sam. 2:18; 1 Chr. 2:16) and **David's** commander-in-chief (2 Sam. 2:13, 8:16, 20:22). He led the forces of David against **Ishbosheth** (2 Sam. 2:12ff.), was the first to enter Jerusalem (1 Chr. 11:6), commanded against the Ammonites and the Syrians (2 Sam. 10:7ff., 11:1ff., 12:26ff.). He led one third of the army against **Absalom** (1) (2 Sam. 18:2), and overthrew the rebellion of **Sheba** (1) (2 Sam. 20:10ff.). In settlement of a blood feud he killed **Abner** (2 Sam. 3:27); he also killed Absalom (2 Sam. 18:14) and **Amasa** (1) (2 Sam. 20:10), and he was ruthless in Edom (1 Kg. 11:16). He supported **Adonijah** (1) for the succession (1 Kg. 1:7), and for this he paid with his life (1 Kg. 2:28ff.).

2. A Judahite (1 Chr. 4:14).

3. Ancestor of some who returned with **Zerubbabel** (Ezr. 2:6; Neh. 7:11; 1 Esd. 5:11) and with **Ezra** (1) (Ezr. 8:9; 1 Esd. 8:35).

JOAH: 1. Recorder under Hezekiah (1) (2 Kg. 18:18, 26, 37; Isa. 36:3, 11, 22).

2. A Gershonite Levite (1 Chr. 6:21), apparently of the time of **Hezekiah** (1) (2 Chr. 29:12).

3. A Levite gatekeeper (1 Chr. 26:4).

4. Recorder under **Josiah** (1) (2 Chr. 34:8).

JOAHAZ: 1. Father of **Joah** (4) (2 Chr. 34:8).

2. King of Israel (2 Kg. 14:1); elsewhere called **Jehoahaz** (1).

JOAKIM: 1. Son of **Zerubbabel** (1 Esd. 5:5).

2. High Priest in the time of **Judith** (2) (Jdt. 4:6, 14).

3. Husband of **Susanna** (1) (Sus. 1:1, 4, 63).

JOANAN: An ancestor of **Jesus** (1) (Lk. 3:27).

JOANNA: Wife of **Chuza**. She provided for **Jesus** (1) of her means (Lk. 8:3). She was one of those who went to the tomb of Jesus (Lk. 24:10).

JOARIB: An ancestor of **Mattathias** (1) (1 Mac. 2:1, 14:29). He was head of a priestly course and is called **Jehoiarib** (2) in 1 Chr. 24:7.

JOASH: 1. King of Judah, *see* **Jehoash** (1).
2. King of Israel, *see* **Jehoash** (2).
3. Father of **Gideon** (Jg. 6:11, 29ff.).
4. Son of **Ahab** (1) (1 Kg. 22:26).
5. A Judahite (1 Chr. 4:22).
6. A Benjaminite (1 Chr. 7:8).
7. A Benjaminite who joined **David** at Ziklag (1 Chr. 12:3).
8. One who was in charge of **David**'s stores of oil (1 Chr. 27:28).

JOB: The central figure in the book of Job. He was a pious and prosperous man (Job 1:1ff.), who was accused by the **Satan** of being pious because it paid (Job 1:9). Permitted to put this to the test, the Satan strikes blow after blow (Job 1:13ff.) and finally afflicts Job with a grievous disease (Job 2:7f.). All this Job bears with patience. When his three friends arrive (Job 2:11ff.) and they enter into dialogue with him, charging him with being the author of his own sufferings, he vigorously replies (Job 3–31). He is then addressed by **Elihu** (5) (Job 32ff.) in a series of speeches to which he makes no reply and which are ignored subsequently and which probably did not belong to the original work. Finally God speaks from the tempest (Job 38ff.) and Job finds peace in the presence of God (Job 42:5f.). He is declared in the right as against the friends (Job 42:7ff.) and, as the sign that the test is over, his prosperity is restored (Job 42:10ff.). He is referred to in Ezek. 14:14, 20; Jas. 5:11.

JOBAB: 1. Son of **Joktan** (Gen. 10:29; 1 Chr. 1:23).
2. King of Edom (Gen. 36:33f.; 1 Chr. 1:44f.).
3. King of Madon and ally of **Jabin** (Jos. 11:1).
4. A Benjaminite (1 Chr. 8:9).
5. Another Benjaminite (1 Chr. 8:18).

JOCHEBED: Daughter of **Levi** (1), born in Egypt (Num. 26:59). She married her nephew **Amram** (1) (Exod. 6:20) and became the mother of **Aaron** and **Moses** (Exod. 6:20; Num. 26:59) and **Miriam** (1) (Num. 26:59).

JODA: 1. Ancestor of some Levites who returned with **Zerubbabel** (1 Esd. 5:58); called **Hodaviah** (4) in Ezr. 2:40, **Judah** (2) in Ezr. 3:9, **Hodevah** in Neh. 7:43, and **Sudias** in 1 Esd. 5:26.
2. An ancestor of **Jesus** (1) (Lk. 3:26).

JODAN: A priest who married a foreign wife (1 Esd. 9:19); called **Gedaliah** (3) in Ezr. 10:18.

JOED: A Benjaminite (Neh. 11:7).

JOEL: 1. A Minor Prophet, son of **Pethuel** (Jl 1:1), of whom nothing is known beyond his book.
2. Son of **Samuel** (1 Sam. 8:2; 1 Chr. 6:28).
3. A Simeonite (1 Chr. 4:35).
4. A Reubenite (1 Chr. 5:4, 8).
5. A Gadite (1 Chr. 5:12).

6. An ancestor of **Samuel** (1 Chr. 6:36); called **Shaul** (3) in 1 Chr. 6:24.

7. A man of Issachar (1 Chr. 7:3).

8. One of **David's** heroes (1 Chr. 11:38); called **Igal** (2) in 2 Sam. 23:26.

9. A Levite who shared in bringing in the Ark (1 Chr. 15:7, 11, 17).

10. A Levite of **David's** time (1 Chr. 23:8) who shared in the care of the Temple treasury (1 Chr. 26:22); possibly the same as 9.

11. **David's** officer over Manasseh (1 Chr. 27:20).

12. A Levite in the time of **Hezekiah** (1) (2 Chr. 29:12).

13. One who married a foreign wife (Ezr. 10:43; 1 Esd. 9:35).

14. A post-exilic Benjaminite overseer (Neh. 11:9).

15. One who married a foreign wife (1 Esd. 9:34); called **Uel** in Ezr. 10:34.

JOELAH: A Benjaminite who joined **David** at Ziklag (1 Chr. 12:7).

JOEZER: A Benjaminite who joined **David** at Ziklag (1 Chr. 12:6).

JOGLI: Father of **Bukki** (1) (Num. 34:22).

JOHA: 1. A Benjaminite (1 Chr. 8:16).

2. One of **David's** heroes (1 Chr. 11:45).

JOHANAN: 1. One who joined **Gedaliah** (1) (2 Kg. 25:23; Jer. 40:8). He wished to slay **Ishmael** (2) to save the life of Gedaliah (Jer. 40:15), and after the murder of Gedaliah he pursued Ishmael and recovered his captives (Jer. 41:11ff.). He carried **Jeremiah** (1) down to Egypt (Jer. 42:1ff.).

2. Son of **Josiah** (1) (1 Chr. 3:15).

3. A descendant of **David** (1 Chr. 3:24).

4. A priest (1 Chr. 6:9f.).

5. A Benjaminite who joined **David** at Ziklag (1 Chr. 12:4).

6. A Gadite who joined **David** in the wilderness (1 Chr. 12:12).

7. Father of **Azariah** (17) (2 Chr. 28:12).

8. One who returned with **Ezra** (1) (Ezr. 8:12; 1 Esd. 8:38).

9. *See* **Jehohanan** (4).

JOHN: 1. Father of **Mattathias** (1) (1 Mac. 2:1).

2. Son of **Mattathias** (1), surnamed **Gaddi** (2) (1 Mac. 2:2). He was killed by the 'sons of **Jambri**' (1 Mac. 9:35f.). He is perhaps called **Joseph** (8) in 2 Mac. 8:22, 10:19.

3. Father of **Eupolemus** (1 Mac. 8:17; 2 Mac. 4:11).

4. A Jewish envoy sent to **Lysias** (1) (2 Mac. 11:17).

5. Son of **Simon** (3) (1 Mac. 16:2). He is known as John Hyrcanus and he succeeded **Jonathan** (3) as the ruler and High Priest of the Jews.

6. John the Baptist, son of **Zechariah** (34) and **Elizabeth** (Lk. 1:5ff.), who called people to repentance in preparation for the Kingdom of God and baptism as its sign (Mt. 3:1ff.; Mk 1:4ff.; Lk. 3:2ff.; Jn 1:24ff.). He baptized **Jesus** (1) (Mt. 3:13ff.; Mk 1:9ff.; Lk. 3:21f.; Jn 1:29ff.), to whom he later sent messengers to ask if He were the expected One (Mt. 11:2ff.; Lk. 7:19ff.),

though the Fourth Gospel records that he already knew this (Jn 1:15, 29ff.). He rebuked Herod (3) for his marriage with Herodias (Mt. 14:3f.; Mk 6:16ff.; Lk. 3:19f.), for which he was imprisoned and beheaded (Mt. 14:6ff.; Mk 6:16ff.). His followers continued after his death (Ac. 19:1ff.).

7. Son of Zebedee and brother of James (1) (Mt. 4:21, 10:2; Mk 1:9, 3:17; Lk. 5:10). He was one of the twelve Apostles (Mt. 10:2; Mk 3:17; Lk. 6:14; Ac. 1:13) and he belonged to the inner group of three (Mt. 17:1, 26:37; Mk 5:37, 9:2, 14:33; Lk. 8:51, 9:28). He and James asked Jesus (1) to promise them special positions in His Kingdom (Mk 10:35ff.; cf. Mt. 20:20ff.), and they were called Boanerges (Mk 3:17). They were fishermen before they became disciples (Mt. 4:21f.; Mk 1:19f.; Lk. 5:10f.), and after the Crucifixion they returned to that occupation (Jn 21:2f.). In the Early Church John appears with Peter in the incident of the healing of the lame man (Ac. 3:1ff.) and before the Council (Ac. 4:5ff.), and these two were sent to Samaria (Ac. 8:14ff.). The disciple whom Jesus loved can scarcely be any other than John. At the Last Supper he lay close to the breast of Jesus (Jn 13:23) and was almost certainly one of the inner circle. Here and in Jn 20:2, 21:7, 20 he is associated with Peter, and in Jn 21:24 he is declared to be the author of the Gospel. Though this has been much contested in modern times, many scholars still accept his authorship of the Gospel and the First Letter of John. Far fewer accept the traditional ascription of the other two Letters and Revelation.

8. The father of Peter (Jn 1:42, 21:15ff.); cf. Bar-Jona (Mt. 16:17).

9. A member of the high priestly family (Ac. 4:6).

10. John Mark (Ac. 12:12, 25, 15:37), see Mark.

JOIADA: 1. One who repaired the Old Gate (Neh. 3:6).

2. High Priest, son of Eliashib (7) (Neh. 12:10, 13:28) and father of Jehohanan (4) (Neh. 12:11, 22; see Jonathan, 11). His son married the daughter of Sanballat (Neh. 13:28).

JOIAKIM: High Priest, son of Jeshua (5) (Neh. 12:10, 26).

JOIARIB: 1. One sent for by Ezra (1) from Ahava (Ezr. 8:16).

2. Ancestor of Maaseiah (9) (Neh. 11:5).

3. A priest (Neh. 11:10, 12:6, 19). See Jehoiarib (1).

JOKIM: A Judahite (1 Chr. 4:22).

JOKSHAN: Son of Abraham and Keturah (Gen. 25:2; 1 Chr. 1:32).

JOKTAN: Son of Eber (1) (Gen. 10:25ff.; 1 Chr. 1:19ff.) and progenitor of Arabian tribes.

JONADAB: 1. David's nephew, who aided Amnon (1) in his plan to rape Tamar (2) (2 Sam. 13:3ff.) and calmed the king after the murder of Amnon (2 Sam. 13:32f.).

2. Son of Rechab (2) (Jer. 35:6ff.), a Kenite (1 Chr. 2:55). He supported Jehu (2) (2 Kg. 10:15ff.) and forbade his descendants to drink wine or build

houses or to engage in agriculture or viticulture (Jer. 35:6f.). He is called Jehonadab in 2 Kg. 10:15, 23.

JONAH: 1. A prophet, son of **Amittai** (2 Kg. 14:25), to whom the book of Jonah is ascribed (Jon. 1:1). This tells how he was sent to Nineveh (Jon. 1:2), but fled to Tarshish (Jon. 1:3) and was shipwrecked (Jon. 1:4ff.) and rescued by a fish (Jon. 1:17, 2:10), after which he went to Nineveh and converted the city (Jon. 3).

2. A Levite who married a foreign wife (1 Esd. 9:23); called **Eliezer** (10) in Ezr. 10:23.

JONAM: An ancestor of **Jesus** (1) (Lk. 3:30).

JONATHAN: 1. Priest of Dan and grandson of **Moses** (Jg. 18:30).

2. Son of **Saul** (1), who defeated the Philistine garrison at Geba (1 Sam. 13:3) and opened the attack at the battle of Michmash (1 Sam. 14). For breaking a taboo of which he was ignorant he almost lost his life (1 Sam. 14:27ff., 43ff.). He became the close friend of **David** (1 Sam. 18:1ff., 19:1ff., 20:1ff.), and when he was killed at the battle of Gilboa (2 Sam. 31:2), David wrote a noble elegy on him and Saul (2 Sam. 1:19ff.).

3. Nephew of **David** (2 Sam. 21:21; 1 Chr. 20:7), who killed a Philistine giant.

4. Uncle of **David**, renowned for his wisdom (1 Chr. 27:32); sometimes identified with 3.

5. Son of **Abiathar** (2 Sam. 15:27ff., 17:17, 20; 1 Kg. 1:42f.).

6. One of David's heroes (2 Sam. 23:32; 1 Chr. 11:34).

7. A Jerahmeelite (1 Chr. 2:32f.).

8. One of David's treasurers (1 Chr. 27:25).

9. Father of **Ebed** (2) (Ezr. 8:6).

10. One who opposed the policy of **Ezra** (1) on mixed marriages (Ezr. 10:15; cf. 1 Esd. 9:14, where he and **Jahzeiah** are represented as supporting Ezra).

11. High Priest (Neh. 12:11). *See* **Jehohanan** (4).

12. A priest in the days of **Joiakim** (Neh. 12:14).

13. Father of **Zechariah** (29) (Neh. 12:35).

14. A secretary in whose house **Jeremiah** (1) was imprisoned (Jer. 37:15, 20, 38:26).

15. Son of **Mattathias** (1) and surnamed **Apphus** (1 Mac. 2:5). He succeeded **Judas** (1) in the leadership of the Jews (1 Mac. 9:29ff.). By his skill in playing off the rivals for the Syrian throne against one another he furthered the fortunes of the Jews (1 Mac. 10ff.) until being killed by **Trypho** (1 Mac. 12:46ff.). He was appointed to the high priestly office (1 Mac. 10:20).

16. Son of **Absalom** (2) (1 Mac. 13:11), sent with an army to Joppa.

17. A priest who led the prayer in the time of **Nehemiah** (2 Mac. 1:23).

JORAH: Ancestor of some who returned with **Zerubbabel** (Ezr. 2:18; 1 Esd. 5:16); called **Hariph** (1) in Neh. 7:24.

JORAI: A Gadite (1 Chr. 5:13).

JORAM: 1. King of Israel, *see* **Jehoram** (1).

2. King of Judah, *see* **Jehoram** (2).

3. Son of **Tou** (2 Sam. 8:10). He was sent to congratulate **David**. He is called Hadoram (2) in 1 Chr. 18:10.

4. A Levite (1 Chr. 26:25).

5. A Levite chief in the time of **Josiah** (1) (1 Esd. 1:9); called **Jozabad** (5) in 2 Chr. 35:9.

JORIM: An ancestor of **Jesus** (1) (Lk. 3:29).

JORKEAM: A Calebite (1 Chr. 2:44).

JOSECH: An ancestor of **Jesus** (1) (Lk. 3:26).

JOSEPH: 1. Son of **Jacob** (1) and **Rachel** (Gen. 30:24, 35:24), and the favourite son of his father (Gen. 37:3f.). By his dreams he aroused the hatred of his brothers (Gen. 37:5ff.), who plotted against him (Gen. 37:12ff.) and caused him to be taken as a slave to Egypt (Gen. 37:25ff.), deceiving their father into thinking he had been killed (Gen. 37:31ff.). In Egypt Joseph prospered (Gen. 39:1ff.) until he was cast into prison for resisting the advances of his master's wife (Gen. 39:6ff.). Through his interpretation of the dreams of his fellow prisoners (Gen. 40) he was introduced to **Pharaoh** to interpret his dreams (Gen. 41:1ff.), and this led to his advancement to high office in Egypt (Gen. 41:37ff.) and his preparation for years of famine. When his brothers came without **Benjamin** (1) to seek corn (Gen. 42:1ff.), he kept one as a hostage until Benjamin should be brought (Gen. 42:24). When Benjamin was brought (Gen. 43), he first alarmed them (Gen. 44) and then magnanimously forgave them (Gen. 45) and brought his whole family into Egypt (Gen. 46f.). Joseph died at the age of 110 (Gen. 50:26), and his body was taken by **Moses** to Palestine at the Exodus (Exod. 13:19) and buried at Shechem (Jos. 24:32).

2. Father of **Igal** (1) (Num. 13:7).

3. A Levite in the time of **David** (1 Chr. 25:2).

4. One who married a foreign wife (Ezr. 10:42; 1 Esd. 9:34).

5. A priest in the days of **Joiakim** (Neh. 12:14).

6. An ancestor of **Judith** (2) (Jdt. 8:1).

7. An officer under **Judas** (1) (1 Mac. 5:18) who was routed by **Gorgias** (1 Mac. 5:55ff.).

8. *See* **John** (2).

9. An ancestor of **Jesus** (1) (Lk. 3:24).

10. Another ancestor of **Jesus** (1) (Lk. 3:30).

11. Husband of **Mary** (1) (Mt. 1:18ff.; Lk. 1:27, 2:4ff.), who brought **Jesus** (1) up as his own child (Lk. 2:33, 41ff.) and hence was regarded as His father by other people (Mt. 13:55; Jn 1:45, 6:42). The genealogy of Joseph, who was of Davidic descent (Mt. 1:20; Lk. 2:4), is therefore legally the genealogy of Jesus (Mt. 1:1ff.; Lk. 3:23ff.). Joseph went to Bethlehem to be

enrolled (Lk. 2:4), and there Jesus was born. Being warned in a dream to go to Egypt, Joseph took Jesus there until he heard that Herod (1) had died (Mt. 2:13ff.), when he returned to Nazareth (Mt. 2:23). He was a carpenter (Mt. 13:55) and his early disappearance from the Gospels is generally thought to indicate that he died before the ministry of Jesus began, the last reference to him in the NT being in connexion with the visit of Jesus to the Temple when He was twelve years old (Lk. 2:41ff.).

12. Brother of Jesus (1) (Mt. 13:55); called Joses in Mk 6:3.

13. Son of Mary (2) (Mt. 27:56); called Joses in Mk 15:40, 47. He is the brother of James (5).

14. Joseph of Arimathea, a member of the Council (Mk 15:43; Lk. 23:50) and a disciple of Jesus (1) (Mt. 27:57; Jn 19:38), who buried the body of Jesus in his own tomb (Mt. 27:57ff.; Mk 15:43ff.; Lk. 23:50ff.; Jn 19:38ff.).

15. Joseph Barsabbas, one of the two put forward to fill the place of Judas (5) (Ac. 1:23), but not chosen.

16. *See* Barnabas.

JOSES: 1. Brother of Jesus (1) (Mk 6:3); called Joseph (12) in Mt. 13:55.

2. Son of Mary (2) (Mk 15:40, 47); called Joseph (13) in Mt. 27:56.

JOSHAH: A Simeonite (1 Chr. 4:34).

JOSHAPHAT: 1. One of David's heroes (1 Chr. 11:43).

2. A priest who accompanied the Ark (1 Chr. 15:24).

JOSHAVIAH: One of David's heroes (1 Chr. 11:46).

JOSHBEKASHAH: A Levite musician (1 Chr. 25:4, 24).

JOSHEB-BASSHEBETH: One of David's heroes (2 Sam. 23:8). In the parallel 1 Chr. 11:11 the name Jashobeam stands.

JOSHIBIAH: A Simeonite (1 Chr. 4:35).

JOSHUA: 1. Son of Nun (Exod. 33:11; Num. 11:28), successor to Moses (Num. 27:18ff.; Dt. 34:9; Jos. 1:1ff.). He commanded the army in the fight with the Amalekites (Exod. 17:9ff.), accompanied Moses to the sacred mountain (Exod. 24:13, 32:17), and was the custodian of the Tent of Meeting (Exod. 33:11). He wanted Moses to forbid Eldad and Medad to prophesy (Num. 11:28). He was one of the spies (Num. 13:8, 16, 14:6) and was promised entrance into the land (Num. 14:30, 38). He led the Israelites into Canaan and conquered Jericho (Jos. 1ff.) and then conquered the rest of the land (Jos. 7ff.) and divided it among the tribes (Jos. 14ff.). He convened the tribes at Shechem for a farewell address (Jos. 24:1ff.) and died at the age of 110 (Jos. 24:29). He is called Hoshea (1) in Num. 13:8, 16.

2. The man of Beth-shemesh in whose field the Ark stopped when it returned from the Philistines (1 Sam. 6:14, 18).

3. Governor of Jerusalem in the time of Josiah (1) (2 Kg. 23:8).

4. *See* Jeshua (5).

5. An ancestor of Jesus (1) (Lk. 3:29).

JOSIAH: 1. Son and successor of Amon (1), king of Judah (2 Kg. 21:24). He was eight years old when he succeeded and he reigned thirty-one years (2 Kg. 22:1; 2 Chr. 34:1). He reformed religion and repaired the Temple. The Chronicler dates the beginning of the reform in the twelfth year of his reign (2 Chr. 34:3). In the eighteenth year of his reign the book of the Law was found in the Temple (2 Kg. 22:8ff.; 2 Chr. 34:14ff.) and this was now made the basis of the reform (2 Kg. 23:1ff.; 2 Chr. 34:29ff., 35:1ff.). In his reign the Assyrian empire was collapsing and when **Pharaoh Neco** went to the support of Assyria Josiah opposed him and was slain at Megiddo (2 Kg. 23:29f.; 2 Chr. 35:20ff.).

2. Son of Zephaniah (4) (Zech. 6:10). From his household gold and silver were to be taken to make a crown for **Jeshua** (5).

JOSIPHIAH: Father of Shelomith (5) (Ezr. 8:10; 1 Esd. 8:36).

JOTHAM: 1. Youngest son of Gideon (Jg. 9:5). He escaped the massacre by **Abimelech** (2) and told 'Jotham's Parable' (Jg. 9:7ff.).

2. Regent in the reign of **Uzziah** (1) (2 Kg. 15:5; 2 Chr. 27:21) and then his successor as king of Judah (2 Kg. 15:32; 2 Chr. 28:1), but little is known of his reign.

3. A Calebite (1 Chr. 2:47).

JOZABAD: 1. A Benjaminite who joined **David** at Ziklag (1 Chr. 12:4).

2. A Manassite who joined **David** at Ziklag (1 Chr. 12:20).

3. Another Manassite who joined **David** (1 Chr. 12:20).

4. A Levite overseer under **Hezekiah** (1) (2 Chr. 31:13).

5. A Levite chief under **Josiah** (1) (2 Chr. 35:9); called **Joram** (5) in 1 Esd. 1:9.

6. A Levite who received the treasure in the Temple (Ezr. 8:33; 1 Esd. 8:63).

7. A priest who married a foreign wife (Ezr. 10:22); called **Gedaliah** (5) in 1 Esd. 9:22.

8. A Levite who married a foreign wife (Ezr. 10:23; 1 Esd. 9:23).

9. A Levite who expounded the Law (Neh. 8:7; 1 Esd. 9:48).

10. A Levite chief in Jerusalem (Neh. 11:16); possibly the same as 9.

JOZACAR: One of the assassins of **Jehoash** (1) (2 Kg. 12:21); called **Zabad** (4) in 2 Chr. 24:26.

JOZADAK: Father of **Joshua** (4) (Ezr. 3:2, 8, 5:2, 10:18; Neh. 12:26); elsewhere called **Jehozadak.**

JUBAL: Son of **Lamech** (1) and **Adah** (1) (Gen. 4:21). He was the first musician.

JUCAL: One who urged **Zedekiah** (2) to put **Jeremiah** (1) to death (Jer. 38:1ff.); called **Jehucal** in Jer. 37:3.

JUDAH: 1. Son of Jacob (1) by Leah (Gen. 29:35, 35:23). He gave his name to one of the twelve tribes of Israel. He proposed to sell Joseph (1) (Gen. 37:26f.), and was the spokesmen of the brethren to Jacob (Gen. 43:3) and to Joseph on their second visit to Egypt (Gen. 44:14ff.). He married Bathshua (1) (1 Chr. 2:3; cf. Gen. 38:2) and his line almost became extinct (Gen. 38). This story is referred to in Ru. 4:12.

    2. Ancestor of some Levites who returned with Zerubbabel (Ezr. 3:9); called Joda (1) in 1 Esd. 5:58.

    3. A Levite who married a foreign wife (Ezr. 10:23; 1 Esd. 9:23).

    4. A Benjaminite overseer (Neh. 11:9).

    5. A Levite who returned with Zerubbabel (Neh. 12:8).

    6. One who shared in the dedication of the wall (Neh. 12:34).

    7. A priestly musician who shared in the dedication of the wall (Neh. 12:36).

    8. An ancestor of Jesus (1) (Lk. 3:30).

JUDAS: 1. Son of Mattathias (1) and surnamed Maccabeus (1 Mac. 2:4). He commanded the army against the army of Antiochus (4) (1 Mac. 2:66), and his battles are recorded in 1 Mac. 3:1–9:17; 2 Mac. 8:5–15:36. He was killed in the battle of Elasa (1 Mac. 9:18).

    2. An army commander (1 Mac. 11:70).

    3. Son of Simon (3) (1 Mac. 16:2). He was murdered by Ptolemy (9) (1 Mac. 16:11ff.).

    4. A leading Jew in Jerusalem (2 Mac. 1:10).

    5. Son of Simon (10) (Jn 13:2; cf. 6:71, 13:26) and surnamed Iscariot (Mt. 10:4). He was one of the twelve disciples of Jesus (1) (Mt. 10:4, 26:14; Mk 3:19, 14:10; Lk. 6:16, 22:3) and their treasurer (Jn 12:6, 13:29). He betrayed his Master for thirty pieces of silver (Mt. 26:15) with a kiss (Lk. 22:47f.), and afterwards in remorse hanged himself (Mt. 27:3ff.; cf. Ac. 1:18f.).

    6. Son of James (4) and one of the twelve Apostles (Lk. 6:16; Ac. 1:13); called Thaddaeus in Mt. 10:3; Mk 3:18.

    7. Brother of Jesus (1) (Mt. 13:55; Mk 6:3). The Letter of Jude bears his name in a shortened form.

    8. The Galilean (Ac. 5:37), a Jewish insurrectionary who raised a revolt in A.D. 6, and whose followers became known as the Zealots.

    9. A Damascus Jew with whom Paul was staying when Ananias (2) came to see him (Ac. 9:11).

    10. Judas Barsabbas (Ac. 15:22), one who was sent from the Jerusalem church to Antioch to report the decisions of the Jerusalem Council (Ac. 15:22ff.).

JUDE: Author of the Letter of Jude (Jude 1); *see* **Judas (7).**

JUDITH: 1. Daughter of Esau by Beeri (1) (Gen. 26:34).

    2. Heroine of the book of Judith, who outwitted and beheaded Holofernes (Jdt. 13:8).

JULIA: A Roman Christian lady greeted by **Paul** (Rom. 16:15).

JULIUS: A Roman centurion in whose charge **Paul** was sent to Rome (Ac. 27:1).

JUNIAS: A Roman Christian greeted by **Paul** (Rom. 16:7).

JUSHAB-HESED: Son of **Zerubbabel** (1 Chr. 3:20).

JUSTUS: 1. Surname of **Joseph** (15) Barsabbas (Ac. 1:23).

2. Titius Justus (Ac. 18:7), a Corinthian with whom **Paul** lodged.

3. Surname of **Jesus** (3), who was a comfort to **Paul** in his imprisonment (Col. 4:11).

K

KADMIEL: 1. A Levite who returned with **Zerubbabel** (Neh. 12:8; 1 Esd. 5:58). His sons are also mentioned (Ezr. 2:40; Neh. 7:43, 12:24; 1 Esd. 5:26), and he and his sons shared in rebuilding the Temple (Ezr. 3:9).

2. A Levite in the time of **Ezra** (1) (Neh. 9:4f.).

3. A Levite who sealed the covenant (Neh. 10:4); perhaps the same as 2.

KAIWAN: A star-god (Am. 5:26); called **Rephan** in Ac. 7:43. He is commonly identified with Kaiwanu, the Akkadian name for the planet Saturn. *See* **Sakkuth.**

KALLAI: A priest in the days of **Joiakim** (Neh. 12:20).

KAREAH: Father of **Johanan** (1) (2 Kg. 25:23; Jer. 40:8, 41:11, 42:1, 43:2).

KEDAR: Son of **Ishmael** (1) (Gen. 25:13; 1 Chr. 1:29) and progenitor of an Arab tribe.

KEDEMAH: Son of **Ishmael** (1) (Gen. 25:15; 1 Chr. 1:31).

KELAIAH: A Levite who married a foreign wife (Ezr. 10:23; 1 Esd. 9:23); also called **Kelita** (1).

KELITA: 1. Alternative name of **Kelaiah** (Ezr. 10:23; 1 Esd. 9:23).

2. One who expounded the Law (Neh. 8:7; 1 Esd. 9:48); perhaps the **Kelita** who sealed the covenant (Neh. 10:10).

KEMUEL: 1. Father of **Aram** (2) (Gen. 22:21).

2. Ephraimite representative for the division of the land (Num. 34:24).

3. Father of **Hashabiah** (5) (1 Chr. 27:17).

KENAN: Son of **Enosh** (Gen. 5:9, 12; 1 Chr. 1:2).

KENAZ: 1. Grandson of **Esau** (Gen. 36:11; 1 Chr. 1:36) and an Edomite chief (Gen. 36:15, 42; 1 Chr. 1:53); he was the eponymous ancestor of the Kenizzites.

2. Father of **Othniel** (Jos. 15:17; Jg. 1:13, 3:9, 11) and **Seraiah (4)** (1 Chr. 4:13), and nephew of **Caleb** (Jos. 15:17; Jg. 1:13).

3. Son of **Elah (4)** and grandson of **Caleb** (1 Chr. 4:15).

KEREN-HAPPUCH: Daughter of **Job** (Job 42:14).

KEROS: Ancestor of some who returned with **Zerubbabel** (Ezr. 2:44; Neh. 7:47; 1 Esd. 5:29).

KETAB: Ancestor of some who returned with **Zerubbabel** (1 Esd. 5:30).

KETURAH: Wife (Gen. 25:1ff.) or concubine (1 Chr. 1:32f.) of **Abraham.**

KEZIAH: Daughter of **Job** (Job 42:14).

KILAN: Ancestor of some who returned with **Zerubbabel** (1 Esd. 5:15).

KISH: 1. Father of **Saul (1)** (1 Sam. 9:1, 10:11, 21, 14:51; Ac. 13:21).

2. Son of **Jeiel (2)** (1 Chr. 8:30, 9:36).

3. A Merarite Levite (1 Chr. 23:21, 24:29).

4. A Merarite Levite in the time of **Hezekiah (1)** (2 Chr. 29:12).

5. An ancestor of **Mordecai (2)** (Est. 2:5; Ad. Est. 11:2).

KISHI: A Levite musician (1 Chr. 6:44); called **Kushaiah** in 1 Chr. 15:17.

KOHATH: Son of **Levi (1)** (Gen. 46:11; Exod. 6:16; Num. 3:17; 1 Chr. 6:1, 16, 23:6), who gave his name to a section of the Levites.

KOLAIAH: 1. Father of **Ahab (2)** (Jer. 29:21).

2. A Benjaminite (Neh. 11:7).

KORAH: 1. Son of **Esau** by **Oholibamah (1)** (Gen. 36:5, 14, 18).

2. A Kohathite Levite, son of **Izhar (1)**, who led a revolt against the priestly privilege of **Aaron** and perished (Num. 16:1ff.). The same Korah (Exod. 6:21, 24) is described as the father of the Korahites, who formed a guild of Temple singers (2 Chr. 20:19), to whom some psalms are ascribed (Pss. 42–49, 84f., 87f.).

3. A Calebite (1 Chr. 2:43).

KORE: 1. A Korahite gatekeeper (1 Chr. 9:19, 26:1).

2. A Levite in charge of freewill offerings in the time of **Hezekiah (1)** (2 Chr. 31:14).

KOZ: A Judahite (1 Chr. 4:8).

KUSHAIAH: A Levite musician (1 Chr. 15:17); called **Kishi** in 1 Chr. 6:44.

L

LAADAH: A Judahite (1 Chr. 4:21).

LABAN: Brother of Rebekah (Gen. 24:29) and father of **Leah** and **Rachel** (Gen. 29:16), with whom **Jacob** (1) lived at Haran (Gen. 29ff.). When Jacob escaped he pursued him to Gilead and made a covenant with him (Gen. 31:25ff.).

LACCUNUS: One who married a foreign wife (1 Esd. 9:31).

LADAN: 1. An ancestor of **Joshua** (1) (1 Chr. 7:26).
   2. A Levite and son of **Gershom** (2) (1 Chr. 23:7, 26:21); called **Libni** (1) in Exod. 6:17; Num. 3:18; 1 Chr. 6:17, 20.

LAEL: A Gershonite Levite (Num. 3:24).

LAHAD: A Judahite (1 Chr. 4:2).

LAHMI: Brother of **Goliath** (1 Chr. 20:5); but *see* **El-hanan** (1).

LAISH: Father of **Palti** (2) (1 Sam. 25:44) or **Paltiel** (2) (2 Sam. 3:15).

LAMECH: 1. Son of **Methushael** and descendant of **Cain** (Gen. 4:18). To him is ascribed the vengeful song of Gen. 4:23f.
   2. Son of **Methuselah** and descendant of **Seth** (Gen. 5:26).

LAPPIDOTH: Husband of **Deborah** (2) (Jg. 4:4).

LASTHENES: Officer of **Demetrius** (2) (1 Mac. 11:31).

LAZARUS: 1. Brother of **Martha** and **Mary** (3) (Jn 11:5). He was raised from the dead by **Jesus** (1) (Jn 11:43f.), and was present at the supper in his house (Jn 12:2).
   2. The poor man in one of the parables of **Jesus** (1) (Lk. 16:19ff.).

LEAH: Elder daughter of **Laban** (Gen. 29:16). She was given in marriage to **Jacob** (1) instead of her sister (Gen. 29:23). She was the mother of six sons and a daughter (Gen. 29:31ff., 30:17ff.). When she died, she was buried in the cave of Machpelah (Gen. 49:31).

LEBANA: Ancestor of some Temple servants who returned with **Zerubbabel** (Neh. 7:48); called **Lebanah** in Ezr. 2:45; 1 Esd. 5:29.

LEBANAH: *See* **Lebana.**

LECAH: A Judahite (1 Chr. 4:21).

LEMUEL: An otherwise unknown king to whose mother the passage Prov. 31:1–9 is ascribed.

LEVI: 1. Son of Jacob (1) and **Leah** (Gen. 29:34). He gave his name to one of the tribes of Israel. He joined **Simeon** (1) in avenging the dishonour of **Dinah** (Gen. 34:25ff.) and was cursed by Jacob (Gen. 49:5ff.).
   2. A contemporary of **Ezra** (1) (1 Esd. 9:14).
   3. A tax collector who became a disciple of **Jesus** (1) and made a feast in his house (Mk 2:14ff.; Lk. 5:27ff.); called **Matthew** in Mt. 9:9ff.
   4. An ancestor of **Jesus** (1) (Lk. 3:24).
   5. Another ancestor of **Jesus** (1) (Lk. 3:29).

LIBNI: 1. A Levite, son of **Gershon** (Exod. 6:17; Num. 3:18; 1 Chr. 6:17, 20); called **Ladan** in 1 Chr. 23:7, 26:21.
   2. A Merarite Levite (1 Chr. 7:19).

LIKHI: A Manassite (1 Chr. 7:19).

LINUS: A Christian who sent greetings to **Timothy** (2) (2 Tim. 4:21).

LOIS: Grandmother of **Timothy** (2) (2 Tim. 1:5).

LOT: Nephew of **Abraham** (Gen. 11:27), who accompanied his uncle when he migrated (Gen. 11:31, 12:4, 13:1). He separated from Abraham and went to Sodom (Gen. 13:8ff.), and when he was captured by **Chedorlaomer** and his allies, Abraham rescued him (Gen. 14:12ff.). He escaped from Sodom before its destruction (Gen. 19:1ff.), but his wife looked back and became a pillar of salt (Gen. 19:26). By incestuous unions with his daughters he became the father of **Ben-ammi** and **Moab** (Gen. 19:30ff.).

LOTAN: A Horite (Gen. 36:20, 22, 29; 1 Chr. 1:38f.).

LOTHASUBUS: One who stood on the left hand of **Ezra** (1) at the reading of the Law (1 Esd. 9:44); called **Hashum** (2) in Neh. 8:4.

LOZON: One whose sons returned with **Zerubbabel** (1 Esd. 5:33); called **Darkon** in Ezr. 2:56; Neh. 7:58.

LUCIUS: 1. A Roman consul, who made known the decree of the Senate about the Jews (1 Mac. 15:16ff.).
   2. Lucius of Cyrene, a Christian of Antioch (Ac. 13:1).
   3. A Christian who sent greetings to the Roman Church (Rom. 16:21).

LUD: Son of **Shem** (Gen. 10:22; 1 Chr. 1:17).

LUKE: Paul's companion (Col. 4:14; 2 Tim. 4:11; Phm. 24) and a physician (Col. 4:14); he is generally accepted as the author of the Third Gospel and Acts.

LYDIA: A woman from Thyatira who sold purple goods in Philippi and who became a convert of **Paul's** (Ac. 16:14f., 40).

LYSANIAN: Tetrarch of Abilene (Lk. 3:1).

LYSIAS: 1. General of **Antiochus** (4) who fought against **Judas** (1) (1 Mac. 3:32ff., 4:34ff.). After the death of Antiochus he supported **Antiochus** (5)

(1 Mac. 6:17; 2 Mac. 10:11ff., 11:1ff.) until his death at the hands of the army of **Demetrius (1)** (1 Mac. 7:3f.).

2. Claudius Lysias, a Roman officer (Ac. 23:26) who arrested **Paul** in the Temple (Ac. 21:32ff.) and later sent him to Caesarea (Ac. 23:26ff.).

LYSIMACHUS: 1. Translator of the Letter of Purim (Ad. Est. 11:1).

2. Brother of **Menelaus** (2 Mac. 4:29). He committed many acts of sacrilege (2 Mac. 4:39) and was killed close by the treasury (2 Mac. 4:42).

M

MAACAH: 1. Son of **Nahor (2)** by **Milcah (1)** (Gen. 22:24).

2. Wife of **David** and mother of **Absalom (1)** (2 Sam. 3:3; 1 Chr. 3:2).

3. Father of **Achish (2)** (1 Kg. 2:39). If **Achish (1)** and (2) are identified, then Maacah is the same as **Maoch** (1 Sam. 27:2).

4. Wife of **Rehoboam** and mother of **Abijah (1)** (1 Kg. 15:2; 2 Chr. 11:20). She is also said to be the wife of **Abijam** (i.e. **Abijah**, 1) and mother of **Asa (1)** (1 Kg. 14:10), but grandmother is probably meant. It is also probable that she was the granddaughter of **Absalom (1)** rather than the daughter, as the above passages state, since 2 Chr. 13:2 says that Abijah married **Micaiah (3)**, the daughter of **Uriel (2)**, who may have married **Tamar (3)**, Absalom's only known daughter (2 Sam. 14:27). Maacah was deposed by Asa from her position for her idolatry (1 Kg. 15:13; 2 Chr. 15:16).

5. A concubine of **Caleb** (1 Chr. 2:48).

6. Wife of **Machir (1)** (1 Chr. 7:16); in 1 Chr. 7:15 she is called his sister.

7. Wife of **Jeiel (2)** (1 Chr. 8:29, 9:35).

8. One of **David's** heroes (1 Chr. 11:43).

9. Father of **Shephatiah (4)** (1 Chr. 27:16).

MAADAI: One who married a foreign wife (Ezr. 10:34; 1 Esd. 9:34).

MAADIAH: A priest who returned with **Zerubbabel** (Neh. 12:5); possibly the same as **Moadiah** in Neh. 12:17.

MAAI: One who shared in the dedication of the wall (Neh. 12:36).

MAASAI: A priest in post-exilic times (1 Chr. 9:12).

MAASEIAH: 1. A Levite musician (1 Chr. 15:18, 20).

2. One of the commanders who helped to make **Jehoash (1)** king (2 Chr. 23:1).

3. An officer under **Uzziah (1)** (2 Chr. 26:11).

4. Son of **Ahaz (1)**, slain by **Zichri (10)** (2 Chr. 28:7).

5. Governor of Jerusalem under **Josiah (1)** (2 Chr. 34:8).

6. A priest who married a foreign wife (Ezr. 10:18; 1 Esd. 9:19).

7. Another priest who married a foreign wife (Ezr. 10:21; 1 Esd. 9:21).
8. A third priest who married a foreign wife (Ezr. 10:22; 1 Esd. 9:22).
9. A layman who married a foreign wife (Ezr. 10:30).
10. Father of **Azariah** (21) (Neh. 3:23).
11. One who stood on the right of **Ezra** (1) at the reading of the Law (Neh. 8:4); called **Baalsamus** in 1 Esd. 9:43.
12. A Levite who expounded the Law (Neh. 8:7; 1 Esd. 9:48); possibly the same as 10.
13. One who sealed the covenant (Neh. 10:25).
14. A Judahite (Neh. 11:5).
15. A Benjaminite (Neh. 11:7).
16. A priest who shared in the dedication of the wall (Neh. 12:41).
17. Another priest who shared in the dedication of the wall (Neh. 12:42).
18. Father of **Zephaniah** (2) (Jer. 21:1, 29:25, 37:3).
19. Father of **Zedekiah** (4) (Jer. 29:21).
20. Keeper of the threshold in the time of **Jeremiah** (1) (Jer. 35:4); possibly the same as 18.

MAASMAS: One of those sent to **Iddo** (6) (1 Esd. 8:43); possibly a duplicate of **Shemaiah** (15) (1 Esd. 8:44; cf. Ezr. 8:16).

MAATH: An ancestor of **Jesus** (1) (Lk. 3:26).

MAAZ: A Jerahmeelite (1 Chr. 2:27).

MAAZIAH: 1. Head of a priestly course (1 Chr. 24:18).
2. One who sealed the covenant (Neh. 10:8).

MACCABEUS: Surname of **Judas** (1) (1 Mac. 2:4).

MACHBANNAI: A Gadite who joined **David** in the wilderness (1 Chr. 12:13).

MACHBENAH: A Calebite (1 Chr. 2:49).

MACHI: Father of **Geuel** (Num. 13:15).

MACHIR: 1. Son of **Manasseh** (1) (Num. 26:29; Jos. 17:1).
2. One who sheltered **Mephibosheth** (1) (2 Sam. 9:4f.) and met **David** with supplies when he fled before **Absalom** (1) (2 Sam. 17:27ff.).

MACHNADEBAI: One who married a foreign wife (Ezr. 10:40; 1 Esd. 9:34).

MACRON: Surname of **Ptolemy** (8) (2 Mac. 10:12).

MADAI: Son of **Japheth** (Gen. 10:2; 1 Chr. 1:5), and eponymous ancestor of the Medes.

MAGBISH: Ancestor of some who returned with **Zerubbabel** (Ezr. 2:30; 1 Esd. 5:21).

MAGDALENE: *See* **Mary** (4).

MAGDIEL: An Edomite chief (Gen. 36:43; 1 Chr. 1:54).

MAGOG: Son of Japheth (Gen. 10:2; 1 Chr. 1:5), who gave his name to a land or people far north of Palestine (Ezek. 38:2, 39:6; cf. 39:2). In Rev. 20:8 Gog and Magog are equated with the nations which Satan will lead.

MAGPIASH: One who sealed the covenant (Neh. 10:20).

MAHALALEEL: *See* Mahalalel (1).

MAHALALEL: 1. Great-grandson of Seth (Gen. 5:12f., 15ff.; 1 Chr. 1:2); called Mahalaleel in Lk. 3:37. He was the father of Jared (Gen. 5:15).
  2. A Judahite (Neh. 11:4).

MAHALATH: 1. Daughter of Ishmael (1) and wife of Esau (Gen. 28:9); called Basemath (2) in Gen. 36:3.
  2. First wife of Rehoboam (2 Chr. 11:18).

MAHARAI: One of David's heroes (2 Sam. 23:28; 1 Chr. 11:30). He was one of David's monthly commanders (1 Chr. 27:13).

MAHATH: 1. A Kohathite Levite in the time of David (1 Chr. 6:35).
  2. A Levite in the time of Hezekiah (1) (2 Chr. 29:12, 31:13).

MAHAZIOTH: A Hemanite who led one of the divisions of Levites (1 Chr. 25:4, 30).

MAHER-SHALAL-HASH-BAZ: Symbolic name given to a son of Isaiah (Isa. 8:1f.).

MAHLAH: 1. Daughter of Zelophehad (Num. 26:33, 27:1, 36:11; Jos. 17:3).
  2. Son of Hammolecheth (1 Chr. 7:18).

MAHLI: 1. A Levite, son of Merari (1) and brother of Mushi (Exod. 6:19; Num. 3:20; 1 Chr. 6:19, 29).
  2. A Levite, son of Mushi (1 Chr. 6:47, 23:23, 24:30); nephew of 1.

MAHLON: Son of Elimelech and Naomi (Ru. 1:2) and husband of Ruth (Ru. 1:4, 4:10).

MAHOL: Father of Ethan (1) (1 Kg. 4:31).

MAHSEIAH: Grandfather of Baruch (1) (Jer. 32:12, 51:59; Bar. 1:1).

MALACHI: Apparent author of the last book of the OT, of whom nothing is known beyond this book. It is probable that this is not a personal name, but means 'My messenger' (cf. Mal. 3:1).

MALCAM: A Benjaminite (1 Chr. 8:9).

MALCHIAH: 1. Father of Pashhur (5) (Jer. 21:1, 38:1); called Malchijah (2) in 1 Chr. 9:12; Neh. 11:12.
  2. One in whose cistern Jeremiah (1) was imprisoned (Jer. 38:6).

MALCHIEL: An Asherite (Gen. 46:17; Num. 26:45; 1 Chr. 7:31).

MALCHIJAH: 1. Father of **Baaseiah** (1 Chr. 6:40).

  2. Father of **Pashhur** (1) (1 Chr. 9:12; Neh. 11:12); called **Malchiah** (1) in Jer. 21:1, 38:1.

  3. Head of a priestly course (1 Chr. 24:9).

  4. One who married a foreign wife (Ezr. 10:25; 1 Esd. 9:26).

  5. Another who married a foreign wife (Ezr. 10:31); called **Melchias** in 1 Esd. 9:32.

  6. One who helped to repair the wall (Neh. 3:11).

  7. One who repaired the Dung Gate (Neh. 3:14).

  8. A goldsmith who helped to repair the wall (Neh. 3:31).

  9. One who stood on the left hand of **Ezra** (1) at the reading of the Law (Neh. 8:4; 1 Esd. 9:44).

  10. A priest who sealed the covenant (Neh. 10:3); possibly the same as 9.

  11. A priest who shared in dedicating the wall (Neh. 12:42).

MALCHIRAM: Son of **Jehoiachin** (1 Chr. 3:18).

MALCHISHUA: Son of **Saul** (1) (1 Sam. 14:49). He died in the battle of Gilboa (1 Sam. 31:2; 1 Chr. 10:2).

MALCHUS: The High Priest's slave whose ear **Peter** cut off in Gethsemane (Jn 18:10).

MALLOTHI: A Levite musician (1 Chr. 25:4, 26).

MALLUCH: 1. A Levite (1 Chr. 6:44).

  2. One who married a foreign wife (Ezr. 10:29; 1 Esd. 9:30).

  3. Another who married a foreign wife (Ezr. 10:32).

  4. A priest who sealed the covenant (Neh. 10:4).

  5. A chief of the people who sealed the covenant (Neh. 10:27).

  6. One who returned with **Zerubbabel** (Neh. 12:2).

MALLUCHI: A priestly family head (Neh. 12:14).

MAMDAI: One who married a foreign wife (1 Esd. 9:34); perhaps the same as **Benaiah** (10) in Ezr. 10:35.

MAMMON: A personification of riches (Mt. 6:24; Lk. 16:13).

MANAEN: A Christian of Antioch (Ac. 13:1).

MANAHATH: A Horite (Gen. 36:23; 1 Chr. 1:40), ancestor of an Edomite clan.

MANASSEH: 1. Son of **Joseph** (1) (Gen. 41:51, 46:20, 48:1); he gave his name to one of the tribes of Israel.

  2. Son and successor of **Hezekiah** (1), king of Judah (2 Kg. 20:21; 2 Chr. 32:33). He reigned fifty-five years (2 Kg. 21:1; 2 Chr. 33:1) and shed much innocent blood (2 Kg. 21:16). The Chronicler records that he was taken prisoner to Babylon and repented of his sins (2 Chr. 33:10ff.).

MANIUS: Titus Manius, one of two Roman envoys who wrote to the Jews (2 Mac. 11:34).

MANOAH: Father of **Samson** (Jg. 13:24). His wife was promised the birth of a son (Jg. 13:3ff.) and the promise was repeated to him (Jg. 13:8ff.). He disapproved of Samson's marriage to a Philistine woman (Jg. 14:3).

MAOCH: Father of **Achish** (1) (1 Sam. 27:2); *see* **Maacah** (3).

MARA: The name which **Naomi** thought appropriate for herself (Ru. 1:20). It means 'bitter'.

MARESHAH: 1. A Calebite (1 Chr. 2:42).
    2. A Judahite (1 Chr. 4:21).

MARK: Surname of **John** (10) (Ac. 12:12, 25, 15:37). He was the son of **Mary** (5), a woman in Jerusalem, in whose house the Christians were gathered when **Peter** was freed from prison (Ac. 12:12ff.). He was a companion of **Paul** and **Barnabas**, who was his cousin (Col. 4:10), on their first missionary journey (Ac. 12:25, 13:4), but at Perga he left them and returned to Jerusalem (Ac. 13:13). Paul refused to take him on his second journey (Ac. 15:38), and he went with Barnabas to Cyprus (Ac. 15:39). Later Paul speaks of him as his fellow worker (Col. 4:11; Phm. 24) and useful in serving him (2 Tim. 4:11). Peter speaks of him as his 'son' (1 Pet. 5:13). He is generally accepted as the author of the Second Gospel.

MARSENA: One of the seven princes of **Ahasuerus** (1) (Est. 1:14).

MARTHA: Sister of **Mary** (3) (Lk. 10:38) and **Lazarus** (1) (Jn 11:2). She was more active than contemplative (Lk. 10:40ff.) and when **Jesus** (1) went to raise Lazarus she went out to meet Him (Jn 11:20).

MARY: 1. The Virgin, mother of **Jesus** (1) (Mt. 1:18ff.; Lk. 2:6). The birth of Jesus was announced to her by the angel **Gabriel** (Lk. 1:26ff.), and to her is ascribed the Magnificat (Lk. 1:46ff.). She accompanied Jesus when He went to the Passover (Lk. 2:41ff.) and she was present at the marriage in Cana (Jn 2:1). Once she sought to approach Jesus (Mt. 12:46ff.; Mk 3:31ff.; Lk. 8:19ff.), and she was present at the Crucifixion (Jn 19:25), when He commended her to the care of the Fourth Evangelist (Jn 19:26f.; cf. Jn 21:24).
    2. Mother of **James** (5) and **Joses** (2) (Mt. 27:56; Mk 15:40, 47). She was present at the Crucifixion and at the burial of **Jesus** (1) (Mt. 27:61; Mk 15:47; Lk. 23:55), as well as on the Resurrection morning (Mt. 28:1; Mk 16:1; Lk. 24:10). She would appear to be the same as Mary the wife of **Clopas** (Jn 19:25).
    3. Sister of **Martha** (Lk. 10:38f.) and **Lazarus** (1) (Jn 11:2). She listened to **Jesus** (1) while Martha served (Lk. 10:39f.), and when Jesus went to raise Lazarus she remained at home until He was near (Jn 11:20), and when she met Him she fell at His feet (Jn 11:32). At the subsequent feast she anointed His feet (Jn 12:3).

4. Mary Magdalene, out of whom seven devils had been cast and who ministered to Jesus (1) of her substance (Lk. 8:2). She was present at the Crucifixion (Mt. 27:56; Mk 15:40; Jn 19:25) and at the burial of Jesus (Mt. 27:61; Mk 15:47), and she came to the tomb on the Resurrection morning (Mt. 28:1; Mk 16:1; Lk. 24:10; Jn 20:1, 18).

5. Mother of Mark (Ac. 12:12).

6. Roman Christian greeted by Paul (Rom. 16:6).

MASH: Son of Aram (1) (Gen. 10:23).

MASIAH: Father of some of Solomon's servants (1 Esd. 5:34).

MASSA: Son of Ishmael (1) (Gen. 25:14; 1 Chr. 1:30).

MATRED: Mother-in-law of Hadar (Gen. 36:39) or Hadad (4) (1 Chr. 1:50).

MATTAN: 1. Priest of Baal (1) in the time of Athaliah (1) (2 Kg. 11:18). He was slain.

2. Father of Shephatiah (9) (Jer. 38:1).

MATTANIAH: 1. Original name of Zedekiah (2) (2 Kg. 24:17).

2. A Levite (1 Chr. 9:15).

3. A Levite in the time of David (1 Chr. 25:4, 16).

4. Levite ancestor of Jahaziel (4) (2 Chr. 20:14); perhaps the same as 3.

5. A Levite in the time of Hezekiah (1) (2 Chr. 29:13).

6. One who married a foreign wife (Ezr. 10:26; 1 Esd. 9:27).

7. Another who married a foreign wife (Ezr. 10:27); called Othoniah in 1 Esd. 9:28.

8. A third who married a foreign wife (Ezr. 10:30); called Bescaspasmys in 1 Esd. 9:31.

9. A fourth who married a foreign wife (Ezr. 10:37).

10. A Levite in the post-exilic period (Neh. 11:17, 22).

11. A Levite musician who returned with Zerubbabel (Neh. 12:8); possibly the same as 10.

12. A Levite gatekeeper in the days of Joiakim (Neh. 12:25).

13. Ancestor of a priest who shared in the dedication of the wall (Neh. 12:35).

14. Ancestor of a storekeeper of the days of Nehemiah (2) (Neh. 13:13).

MATTATHA: An ancestor of Jesus (1) (Lk. 3:31).

MATTATHIAH: One who stood on the right of Ezra (1) at the reading of the Law (1 Esd. 9:43); called Mattithiah (5) in Neh. 8:4.

MATTATHIAS: 1. A priest of Modein (1 Mac. 2:1), who refused to offer idolatrous sacrifice (1 Mac. 2:15ff.) and killed a renegade Jew (1 Mac. 2:24). He fled with his sons to the mountains (1 Mac. 2:28), and they began the Maccabean rising.

2. An army commander (1 Mac. 11:70).

3. Son of **Simon** (3) (1 Mac. 16:14ff.). He was murdered by **Ptolemy** (9).

4. Envoy of **Nicanor** (1) (2 Mac. 14:19).

5. An ancestor of Jesus (1) (Lk. 3:25).

6. Another ancestor of Jesus (1) (Lk. 3:26).

MATTATTAH: One who married a foreign wife (Ezr. 10:33; 1 Esd. 9:33).

MATTENAI: 1. One who married a foreign wife (Ezr. 10:33; 1 Esd. 9:33).

2. Another who married a foreign wife (Ezr. 10:37).

3. A priest in the days of **Joiakim** (Neh. 12:19).

MATTHAN: An ancestor of Jesus (1) (Mt. 1:15).

MATTHAT: 1. An ancestor of Jesus (1) (Lk. 3:24); apparently the same as **Matthan.**

2. Another ancestor of Jesus (1) (Lk. 3:29).

MATTHEW: A tax collector who became a disciple of Jesus (1) and made a feast in his house (Mt. 9:9ff.); called **Levi** (3) in Mk 2:14ff.; Lk. 5:27ff. He became one of the twelve Apostles (Mt. 10:3; Mk 3:18; Lk. 6:15; Ac. 1:13). He is traditionally the author of the First Gospel.

MATTHIAS: The disciple chosen by lot to replace **Judas** (5) (Ac. 1:24ff.).

MATTITHIAH: 1. A Kohathite Levite who made flat cakes (1 Chr. 9:31).

2. A Levite musician in the time of **David** (1 Chr. 15:18, 21, 25:3, 21).

3. An Asaphite Levite (1 Chr. 16:5).

4. One who married a foreign wife (Ezr. 10:43; 1 Esd. 9:35).

5. One who stood on the right of **Ezra** (1) at the reading of the Law (Neh. 8:4); called **Mattathiah** in 1 Esd. 9:43.

MEBUNNAI: One of **David's** heroes (2 Sam. 23:27); called **Sibbecai** in 2 Sam. 21:18; 1 Chr. 11:29, 20:4, 27:11).

MEDAD: One who prophesied in the camp in the wilderness (Num. 11:26ff.).

MEDAN: Son of **Abraham** and **Keturah** (Gen. 25:2; 1 Chr. 1:32).

MEHETABEL: 1. Grandfather of **Shemaiah** (19) (Neh. 6:10).

2. Wife of **Hadar** (Gen. 36:39) or **Hadad** (4) (1 Chr. 1:50).

MEHIDA: Ancestor of some Temple servants who returned with **Zerubbabel** (Ezr. 2:52; Neh. 7:54; 1 Esd. 5:32).

MEHIR: A Judahite (1 Chr. 4:11).

MEHUJAEL: Descendant of **Cain** (Gen. 4:18).

MEHUMAN: One of the seven eunuchs of **Ahasuerus** (1) (Est. 1:10).

MELATIAH: One who helped to repair the wall (Neh. 3:7).

MELCHI: 1. An ancestor of Jesus (1) (Lk. 3:24).

2. Another ancestor of Jesus (1) (Lk. 3:28).

MELCHIAS: One who married a foreign wife (1 Esd. 9:32); called Malchijah (5) in Ezr. 10:31.

MELCHIEL: Father of Charmis (Jdt. 6:15).

MELCHIZEDEK: King of Salem and priest of God Most High (Gen. 14:18), to whom Abraham gave tithes of the spoil he had taken (Gen. 14:20) and who blessed Abraham (Gen. 14:19). A priesthood after the order of Melchizedek is referred to in Ps. 110:4 and in Heb. 5:6, 10, 6:20, 7:11, 17.

MELEA: An ancestor of Jesus (1) (Lk. 3:31).

MELECH: A descendant of Jonathan (2) (1 Chr. 8:35, 9:41).

MEMMIUS: Quintus Memmius, one of two Roman envoys who wrote to the Jews (2 Mac. 11:34).

MEMUCAN: One of the seven princes of Ahasuerus (1) (Est. 1:14, 16, 21).

MENAHEM: King of Israel, who became king by assassinating Shallum (1) (2 Kg. 15:14) and reigned ten years (2 Kg. 15:17). He bought off Assyria by the payment of tribute, for which he had to impose heavy taxation (2 Kg. 15:19ff.).

MENELAUS: A Benjaminite (cf. 2 Mac. 3:4 and 4:23), who bought the office of High Priest (2 Mac. 4:24) but had to rob the Temple in order to pay for it (2 Mac. 4:23). He brought about the death of Onias (3) (2 Mac. 4:34ff.).

MENESTHEUS: Father of Apollonius (2) (2 Mac. 4:21).

MENNA: An ancestor of Jesus (1) (Lk. 3:31).

MEONOTHAI: Son of Othniel (1 Chr. 4:13f.).

MEPHIBOSHETH: 1. Son of Jonathan (2) (2 Sam. 4:4); called Meribbaal in 1 Chr. 8:34, 9:40. He was a child when his father died (2 Sam. 4:4) and was cared for by Machir (2) (2 Sam. 9:4f.) until David provided for him (2 Sam. 9:9ff.). His loyalty to David was impugned at the time of the rebellion of Absalom (1) (2 Sam. 16:1ff.) and David revoked his provision, but restored half on his return to Jerusalem (2 Sam. 19:24ff.). When the other descendants of Saul (1) were killed (2 Sam. 21:1ff.), Mephibosheth was spared (2 Sam. 21:7).

2. Son of Rizpah, the concubine of Saul (1) (2 Sam. 21:8). He was killed to appease the Gibeonites (2 Sam. 21:9).

MERAB: Elder daughter of Saul (1) (1 Sam. 14:49). She was promised in marriage to the slayer of Goliath (1 Sam. 17:25, 18:17), but then given to another instead of to David (1 Sam. 18:19). Her sons were killed to appease the Gibeonites (2 Sam. 21:8).

MERAIAH: A priest in the days of Joiakim (Neh. 12:12).

MERAIOTH: 1. A priest (1 Chr. 6:6f.); he was an ancestor of **Ezra (1)** (Ezr. 7:3; 2 Esd. 1:2).

2. A priest, son of **Ahitub (2)** (1 Chr. 9:11; Neh. 11:11).

3. Head of a priestly house (Neh. 12:15); called **Meremoth (4)** in Neh. 12:3.

MERARI: 1. Son of **Levi (1)** (Gen. 46:11; Exod. 6:16; Num. 3:17; 1 Chr. 6:1, 16, 23:6). He gave his name to a division of the Levites.

2. A Levite whose sons were brought to **Ezra (1)** (Ezr. 8:19); called **Hananiah (16)** in 1 Esd. 8:48.

3. Father of **Judith (2)** (Jdt. 8:1, 16:7).

MERED: A Judahite (1 Chr. 4:17).

MEREMOTH: 1. A priest who acted as treasurer of the Temple (Ezr. 8:33; 1 Esd. 8:62). He shared in building the wall (Neh. 3:4, 21).

2. One who married a foreign wife (Ezr. 10:36); called **Carabasion** in 1 Esd. 9:34.

3. One who sealed the covenant (Neh. 10:5).

4. Head of a priestly house (Neh. 12:3); called **Meraioth (3)** in Neh. 12:15.

MERES: One of the seven princes of **Ahasuerus (1)** (Est. 1:14).

MERIBBAAL: Son of **Jonathan (2)** (1 Chr. 8:34, 9:40). *See* **Mephibosheth (1)**.

MERODACH: God of Babylon (Jer. 50:2), also called **Bel**.

MERODACH-BALADAN: A rebel against Assyria who made himself king of Babylon. He sent an embassy to **Hezekiah (1)** to congratulate him on his recovery from illness (2 Kg. 20:12; Isa. 39:1). His purpose was probably to encourage Hezekiah to rebel, as is indicated by Hezekiah's showing him his resources and by Isaiah's condemnation (2 Kg. 20:13ff.; Isa. 39:2ff.).

MESHA: 1. King of Moab, who rebelled against **Jehoram (1)** (2 Kg. 3:5). In a crisis of the war that followed he sacrificed his son to his god (2 Kg. 3:27), and he was ultimately victorious. His account of the revolt is on the Moabite Stone.

2. A Benjaminite (1 Chr. 8:9).

MESHACH: One of the companions of **Daniel (5)** (Dan. 1:7). He was cast into the fire for refusing to worship the image of **Nebuchadnezzar** (Dan. 3:20ff.), and praised God (S 3 Ch. 28ff.). His Hebrew name was **Mishael (3)** (Dan. 1:6f.).

MESHECH: 1. Son of **Shem** (1 Chr. 1:17).

2. Son of **Japheth** (Gen. 10:2; 1 Chr. 1:5).

MESHELEMIAH: Father of **Zechariah (4)** (1 Chr. 9:21, 26:1f., 9); called **Shelemiah (1)** in 1 Chr. 26:14. He is perhaps the same as **Shallum (9)** in 1 Chr. 9:17, 19, 31.

MESHEZABEL: 1. Ancestor of one who helped to repair the wall (Neh. 3:4).
  2. One who sealed the covenant (Neh. 10:21).
  3. Father of Pethahiah (4) (Neh. 11:24).

MESHILLEMITH: A priest (1 Chr. 9:12); called Meshillemoth (2) in Neh. 11:13.

MESHILLEMOTH: 1. An Ephraimite (1 Chr. 9:12).
  2. *See* Meshillemith.

MESHOBAB: A Simeonite (1 Chr. 4:34).

MESHULLAM: 1. Grandfather of Shaphan (1) (2 Kg. 22:3).
  2. Son of Zerubbabel (1 Chr. 3:19).
  3. A Gadite (1 Chr. 5:13).
  4. A Benjaminite (1 Chr. 8:17).
  5. Another Benjaminite (1 Chr. 9:7).
  6. A third Benjaminite (1 Chr. 9:8).
  7. A priest, father of Hilkiah (2) (1 Chr. 9:11; Neh. 11:11).
  8. A priest, son of Meshillemith (1 Chr. 9:12).
  9. A Kohathite who shared the oversight of the repair of the Temple in the time of Josiah (1) (2 Chr. 34:12).
  10. One of those sent by Ezra (1) to Iddo (6) (Ezr. 8:16; 1 Esd. 8:44).
  11. One who opposed Ezra (1) on mixed marriages (Ezr. 10:15; cf. 1 Esd. 9:14).
  12. One who married a foreign wife (Ezr. 10:29; 1 Esd. 9:30).
  13. One who helped to repair the wall (Neh. 3:4, 30). His daughter married Tobiah (2) (Neh. 6:18).
  14. One who repaired the Old Gate (Neh. 3:6).
  15. One of those who stood on the left hand of Ezra (1) at the reading of the Law (Neh. 8:4).
  16. A priest who sealed the covenant (Neh. 10:7).
  17. A chief of the people who sealed the covenant (Neh. 10:20).
  18. A priest in the days of Joiakim (Neh. 12:13).
  19. Another priest in the days of Joiakim (Neh. 12:16).
  20. A gatekeeper in the days of Joiakim (Neh. 12:25).
  21. One who shared in the dedication of the wall (Neh. 12:33).

MESHULLEMETH: Wife of Manasseh (2) (2 Kg. 21:19).

METHUSELAH: A descendant of Seth and father of Lamech (2) (Gen. 5:21f., 25ff.; 1 Chr. 1:3; Lk. 3:37). He lived longer than anyone else mentioned in the Bible.

METHUSHAEL: A descendant of Cain and father of Lamech (1) (Gen. 4:18).

MEUNIM: Ancestor of some Temple servants who returned with Zerubbabel (Ezr. 2:50; Neh. 7:52); called Meunites in 1 Esd. 5:31.

ME-ZAHAB: Father of **Matred** (Gen. 36:39; 1 Chr. 1:50).

MIBHAR: One of David's heroes (1 Chr. 11:38; cf. the parallel 2 Sam. 23:26).

MIBSAM: 1. Son of **Ishmael** (1) (Gen. 25:13; 1 Chr. 1:29).
2. A Simeonite (1 Chr. 4:25).

MIBZAR: An Edomite chief (Gen. 36:42; 1 Chr. 1:53).

MICA: 1. Son of **Mephibosheth** (1) (2 Sam. 9:12); called **Micah** (3) in 1 Chr. 8:34f., 9:40f.
2. A Levite (1 Chr. 9:15; Neh. 11:17, 22); called **Micaiah** (5) in Neh. 12:35.
3. One who sealed the covenant (Neh. 10:11).

MICAH: 1. An Ephraimite who stole silver from his mother, who devoted it to the making of an image when he returned it, and this image Micah set up in his house (Jg. 17:1ff.). Later he installed **Jonathan** (1) (Jg. 18:30) as his priest (Jg. 17:7ff.), until the migrating Danites took the image and the priest to Dan (Jg. 18).
2. A Reubenite (1 Chr. 5:5).
3. Son of **Mephibosheth** (1) (1 Chr. 8:34f., 9:40f.); called **Mica** (1) in 2 Sam. 9:12.
4. A Levite of **David's** time (1 Chr. 23:20, 24:24f.).
5. Father of **Abdon** (4) (2 Chr. 34:20); called **Micaiah** (2) in 2 Kg. 22:12.
6. A Minor Prophet, a man of Moresheth (Jer. 26:18; Mic. 1:1), of whom nothing is known beyond what stands in his book, save that when **Jeremiah** (1) prophesied the destruction of the Temple and there was clamour for his execution, it was remembered that in the time of **Hezekiah** (1) Micah had prophesied similarly (Mic. 3:12) and had not been executed (Jer. 26:16ff.).
7. Father of **Uzziah** (6) (Jdt. 6:15).

MICAIAH: 1. Son of **Imlah** (1 Kg. 22:8; 2 Chr. 18:7), who alone of the prophets foretold disaster for **Ahab** (1) at the battle of Ramoth-gilead, and was imprisoned until the king should return in peace (1 Kg. 22:13ff.; 2 Chr. 18:12ff.).
2. Father of **Achbor** (2) (2 Kg. 22:12); called **Micah** (5) in 2 Chr. 34:20.
3. Mother of **Abijah** (1) and daughter of **Uriel** (2) (2 Chr. 13:2). *See* **Maacah** (4).
4. One of those sent by **Jehoshaphat** (4) to teach in the cities of Judah (2 Chr. 17:7).
5. A Levite (Neh. 12:35); called **Mica** (2) in 1 Chr. 9:15; Neh. 11:17, 22.
6. One who shared in dedicating the walls (Neh. 12:41).
7. Son of **Gemariah** (1) (Jer. 36:11). He heard **Baruch** (1) reading the scroll of **Jeremiah** (1) and reported on it to the princes (Jer. 36:11ff.).

MICHAEL: 1. Father of **Sethur** (Num. 13:13).
2. A Gadite (1 Chr. 5:13).

3. Another Gadite (1 Chr. 5:14).
4. A Levite (1 Chr. 6:40).
5. A man of Issachar (1 Chr. 7:3, 27).
6. A Benjaminite (1 Chr. 8:16).
7. A Manassite who joined David at Ziklag (1 Chr. 12:20).
8. Father of Omri (4) (1 Chr. 27:18).
9. Son of Jehoshaphat (4) (2 Chr. 21:2). He was killed by Jehoram (2) (2 Chr. 21:4).
10. Father of Zebadiah (8) (Ezr. 8:8) or Zeraiah (1 Esd. 8:34).
11. One of the archangels, mentioned in the book of Daniel (Dan. 10:13, 21, 12:1) and in the NT (Jude 1:9; Rev. 12:7), usually as fighting.

MICHAL: Younger daughter of Saul (1) (1 Sam. 14:49). David married her at the price of a hundred Philistine lives (1 Sam. 18:20). She saved David's life by placing an image in his bed (1 Sam. 19:11ff.), but was then married to Palti (2) (1 Sam. 25:44). David demanded her return after Saul's death (2 Sam. 3:13ff.), but when she chided him for his dance before the Ark they became estranged (2 Sam. 6:16, 20ff.).

MICHRI: A Benjaminite (1 Chr. 9:8).

MIDIAN: Son of Abraham by Keturah (Gen. 25:2; 1 Chr. 1:32) and ancestor of the Midianites.

MIJAMIN: 1. Head of a priestly course (1 Chr. 24:9).
2. One who married a foreign wife (Ezr. 10:25; 1 Esd. 9:26).
3. A priest who sealed the covenant (Neh. 10:7).
4. A priest who returned with Zerubbabel (Neh. 12:5).

MIKLOTH: A Benjaminite (1 Chr. 8:32, 9:37f.).

MIKNEIAH: A Levite musician (1 Chr. 15:18, 21).

MILALAI: One who shared in the dedication of the wall (Neh. 12:36).

MILCAH: 1. Daughter of Haran (1) and wife of Nahor (2) (Gen. 11:29). Rebekah was her granddaughter (Gen. 24:15, 24, 47).
2. Daughter of Zelophehad (Num. 26:33, 27:1, 36:11; Jos. 17:3).

MILCOM: The god of the Ammonites (1 Kg. 11:5, 33; 2 Kg. 23:13; Jer. 49:1, 3; Zeph. 1:5). *See* Molech.

MINIAMIN: 1. A Levite in the time of Hezekiah (1) (2 Chr. 31:15).
2. Head of a priestly house (Neh. 12:17).
3. A priest who shared in the dedication of the wall (Neh. 12:41).

MIRIAM: 1. Sister of Moses and Aaron (Num. 26:59; 1 Chr. 6:3); called a prophetess in Exod. 15:20. She watched Moses in the bulrushes (Exod. 2:4ff.) and led the women in celebrating the crossing of the Red Sea (Exod. 15:20f.). She and Aaron complained against Moses and she was struck with leprosy until Moses interceded for her (Num. 12:1ff.). She died at Kadesh (Num. 20:1).
2. A Calebite man or woman (1 Chr. 4:17).

MIRMAH: A Benjaminite (1 Chr. 8:10).

MISHAEL: 1. A Levite (Exod. 6:22) who helped to bury Nadab (1) and Abihu (Lev. 10:4).
   2. One who stood at the left hand of Ezra (1) at the reading of the Law (Neh. 8:4; 1 Esd. 9:44).
   3. The Hebrew name of Meshach (Dan. 1:6f.).

MISHAM: A Benjaminite (1 Chr. 8:12).

MISHMA: 1. Son of Ishmael (1) (Gen. 25:14; 1 Chr. 1:30).
   2. A Simeonite (1 Chr. 4:25f.).

MISHMANNAH: A Gadite who joined David in the wilderness (1 Chr. 12:10).

MISPAR: One who returned with Zerubbabel (Ezr. 2:2; 1 Esd. 5:8); called Mispereth in Neh. 7:7.

MISPERETH: *See* Mispar.

MITHREDATH: 1. A Persian treasurer who delivered the sacred vessels to Sheshbazzar (Ezr. 1:8); called Mithridates in 1 Esd. 2:11.
   2. A Persian officer who sought to stop the rebuilding of the walls of Jerusalem (Ezr. 4:7); called Mithridates in 1 Esd. 2:16.

MITHRIDATES: *See* Mithredath (1) and (2).

MIZZAH: An Edomite (Gen. 36:13, 17; 1 Chr. 1:37).

MNASON: A Christian from Cyprus with whom Paul lodged (Ac. 21:16).

MOAB: Son of Lot by an incestuous union (Gen. 19:37) and eponymous ancestor of the Moabites.

MOADIAH: *See* Maadiah.

MOETH: A Levite who shared in the care of the Temple treasure (1 Esd. 8:63); called Noadiah (1) in Ezr. 8:33.

MOLECH: A god to whom child sacrifices were made (Lev. 18:21, 20:2ff.; 2 Kg. 23:10; Isa. 30:33; Jer. 32:35), especially in the Valley of Hinnom. In 1 Kg. 11:7 he is called the god of the Ammonites, whose name was Milcom. Many scholars think Molech was not the name of a god but the designation of a particular type of sacrifice.

MOLID: A Jerahmeelite (1 Chr. 2:29).

MOLOCH: Apparently the name of a god in Ac. 7:43, in a citation from Am. 5:26, where 'Sakkuth your king' stands instead of 'the tent of Moloch'.

MORDECAI: 1. One who returned with Zerubbabel (Ezr. 2:2; Neh. 7:7; 1 Esd. 5:8).
   2. Cousin of Esther (Est. 2:7). He saved the life of Ahasuerus (1) (Est. 2:21ff.) and thwarted the plot of Haman against the Jews (Est. 4ff.).

MOSES: A Levite, son of **Amram** (1) and **Jochebed** (Exod. 6:20). He was saved from death at birth (Exod. 2:1ff.) and brought up by **Pharaoh's** daughter (Exod. 2:5ff.). When he grew up, he killed an Egyptian (Exod. 2:11ff.) and fled to Midian, where he stayed with **Jethro** (Exod. 2:15ff., 3:1ff.) and married his daughter **Zipporah** (Exod. 2:21). Called of God to bring the Israelites out of Egypt (Exod. 3f.), he went to Egypt and after a lengthy contest with Pharaoh involving the ten plagues of Egypt (Exod. 5ff.) he led the Israelites out (Exod. 12:50). When Pharaoh pursued, Moses led the Israelites safely across the Red Sea (Exod. 14:5ff.), and then to the sacred mountain where the Covenant between God and Israel was made and the commands of God were received (Exod. 19ff.). Moses sent spies into Canaan (Num. 13), but the response to their report brought divine punishment upon the people (Num. 14), with the result that forty years were spent in the wilderness (Exod. 16:35; Num. 14:33f., 32:13; Dt. 8:2; Ps. 95:10). Under the leadership of Moses the Amorites and Bashan (Num. 21:21ff.; Dt. 1:4, 2:26ff., 3:1ff., 29:7; Jos. 2:10, 9:10; Ps. 135:11) were conquered and part of the tribes were settled in Transjordan (Num. 32; Dt. 3:12ff.; Jos. 13:15ff.), and then Moses died on Mt Nebo (Dt. 34).

MOZA: 1. Son of **Caleb** (1 Chr. 2:46).
2. A descendant of **Saul** (1) (1 Sam. 8:36f., 9:42f.).

MUPPIM: Son of **Benjamin** (1) (Gen. 46:21); called **Shuppim** (1) in 1 Chr. 7:12, Shephupham in Num. 26:39, and **Shephuphan** in 1 Chr. 8:5.

MUSHI: Son of **Merari** (1) (Exod. 6:19; Num. 3:30; 1 Chr. 6:19, 47, 23:21, 23, 24:26, 30).

N

NAAM: Son of **Caleb** (1 Chr. 4:15).

NAAMAH: 1. Sister of **Tubal-cain** (Gen. 4:22).
2. Mother of **Rehoboam** (1 Kg. 14:21, 31; 2 Chr. 12:13).

NAAMAN: 1. Son of **Benjamin** (1) (Gen. 46:21); probably the same as **2**.
2. Grandson of **Benjamin** (1) (Num. 26:40; 1 Chr. 8:4).
3. Son of **Ehud** (2) and great-grandson of **Benjamin** (1) (1 Chr. 8:7).
4. A Syrian general who was cured of leprosy by **Elisha** (2 Kg. 5).

NAARAH: One of the wives of **Ashhur** (1 Chr. 4:5f.).

NAARAI: One of **David's** heroes (1 Chr. 11:37); called **Paarai** in 2 Sam. 23:35.

NAATHUS: One who married a foreign wife (1 Esd. 9:31); perhaps the same as **Adna** (1) in Ezr. 10:30.

NABAL: A wealthy Calebite sheep-farmer (1 Sam. 25:2), who answered David's request for a gift rudely and would have brought disaster on himself but for the address of his wife, **Abigail** (1) (1 Sam. 25:4ff.). When he learned what had happened, he collapsed and did not recover (1 Sam. 25:36ff.). David thereupon married Abigail (1 Sam. 25:39ff.).

NABARIAH: One who stood on the left hand of **Ezra** (1) at the reading of the Law (1 Esd. 9:44); called **Hashbaddanah** in Neh. 8:4.

NABOTH: Owner of a vineyard at Jezreel adjoining the palace of **Ahab** (1) (1 Kg. 21:1). **Jezebel** (1) brought about the death of Naboth, when he refused to sell his vineyard to the king (1 Kg. 21:2ff.) and the estate was seized by the crown. Elijah (1) rebuked the king for this (1 Kg. 21:17ff.), and retribution came in the death of **Jehoram** (1) and of Jezebel (2 Kg. 9:21ff.).

NACON: Owner of the threshing floor where **Uzzah** died (2 Sam. 6:6); called **Chidon** in 1 Chr. 13:9.

NADAB: 1. Son of Aaron (Exod. 6:23; Num. 3:2, 26:60; 1 Chr. 6:3, 24:1), who accompanied **Moses** and Aaron to the sacred mountain (Exod. 24:1, 9). He became a priest (Exod. 28:1), but offered unholy fire and was consumed by divine fire (Lev. 10:1f.; Num. 3:4, 26:61).

2. Son and successor of **Jeroboam** (1), king of Israel (1 Kg. 14:20). He reigned two years and was assassinated by **Baasha** (1 Kg. 15:25ff.).

3. A Jerahmeelite (1 Chr. 2:28, 30).

4. A Benjaminite (1 Chr. 8:30, 9:36).

5. Nephew (Tob. 11:19) and foster son (Tob. 14:10) of **Ahikar**, who fell into the trap he had ungratefully set for Ahikar (Tob. 14:10).

NAGGAI: An ancestor of **Jesus** (1) (Lk. 3:25).

NAHAM: The brother-in-law of **Hodiah** (1) (1 Chr. 4:19).

NAHAMANI: One who returned with **Zerubbabel** (Neh. 7:7).

NAHARAI: One of David's heroes (2 Sam. 23:37; 1 Chr. 11:39).

NAHASH: 1. King of the Ammonites, from whom **Saul** (1) delivered Jabesh-gilead (1 Sam. 11:1ff.). He dealt loyally with **David** (2 Sam. 10:2) and his son, **Shobi**, brought supplies to David when he fled from **Absalom** (1) (2 Sam. 17:27ff.).

2. Father of Abigal (2 Sam. 17:25).

NAHATH: 1. An Edomite chief (Gen. 36:13, 17; 1 Chr. 1:37).

2. A Levite (1 Chr. 6:26); perhaps the same as **Toah** in 1 Chr. 6:34, and **Tohu** in 1 Sam. 1:1.

3. A Levite overseer of the time of **Hezekiah** (1) (2 Chr. 31:13).

NAHBI: The spy from Naphtali (Num. 13:14).

NAHOR: 1. Grandfather of Abraham (Gen. 11:22ff.; 1 Chr. 1:26; Lk. 3:24).

   2. Grandson of 1 and brother of Abraham (Gen. 11:26f.; cf. Jos. 24:2). He had eight sons by Milcah (1) and four by Reumah (Gen. 22:20f., 24).

NAHSHON: A Judahite (Num. 1:7, 2:3, 7:12, 10:14; 1 Chr. 2:10) and brother-in-law of Aaron (Exod. 6:23). He was an ancestor of David (Ru. 4:20ff.; 1 Chr. 2:10ff.) and of Jesus (1) (Mt. 1:4; Lk. 3:32).

NAHUM: 1. A Minor Prophet of whom nothing is known beyond what is in his book. He came from Elkosh (Nah. 1:1).

   2. An ancestor of Jesus (1) (Lk. 3:25).

NAIDUS: One who married a foreign wife (1 Esd. 9:31); perhaps the same as Benaiah (9) in Ezr. 10:30.

NANAEA: A goddess whose temple in Persia Antiochus (3) attempted to rob (2 Mac. 1:10ff.), losing his life in consequence (cf. 1 Mac. 6:1ff.).

NAOMI: Wife of Elimelech and mother-in-law of Ruth (Ru. 1:2, 4). She returned from Moab with Ruth and encouraged her daughter-in-law to glean in the field of Boaz (Ru. 2f.), whom Ruth subsequently married (Ru. 4:13).

NAPHISH: Son of Ishmael (1) (Gen. 25:15; 1 Chr. 1:31). His descendants were conquered by the Transjordan tribes (1 Chr. 5:18ff.).

NAPHTALI: Son of Jacob (1) and Bilhah (Gen. 30:7f., 35:25). He gave his name to one of the tribes of Israel.

NARCISSUS: A Roman whose family was greeted by Paul (Rom. 16:11).

NATHAN: 1. Son of David by Bathsheba (2 Sam. 5:13; 1 Chr. 3:5). He was an ancestor of Jesus (1) (Lk. 3:31).

   2. A prophet who dissuaded David from building the Temple and promised him a sure succession (2 Sam. 7:1ff.), and who rebuked him when he sinned with Bathsheba (2 Sam. 12:1ff.). He supported Solomon for the succession (1 Kg. 1:11ff., 38). He wrote a history of the reigns of David (1 Chr. 29:29) and Solomon (2 Chr. 9:29), and helped to organize the Temple music (2 Chr. 29:25). Two of his sons were appointed to office by Solomon (1 Kg. 4:5).

   3. Father of Igal (2) (2 Sam. 23:36). In 1 Chr. 11:38 Igal is called Joel (8) and Nathan is said to be his brother.

   4. One of those sent to Iddo (6) (Ezr. 8:16; 1 Esd. 8:44).

   5. One who married a foreign wife (Ezr. 10:39); called Nethaniah (5) in 1 Esd. 9:34.

   6. A Jerahmeelite (1 Chr. 2:36).

NATHANAEL: 1. A priest who married a foreign wife (1 Esd. 9:22); called Nethanel (8) in Ezr. 10:22.

   2. An ancestor of Judith (2) (Jdt. 8:1).

3. A disciple of Jesus (1) (Jn 1:45ff.). He was present at the Resurrection appearance of Jesus by the Sea of Tiberias (Jn 21:2).

NATHAN-MELECH: A chamberlain who gave his name to a room in the Temple used for idolatrous practices (2 Kg. 23:11).

NEARIAH: 1. A descendant of David (1 Chr. 3:22f.).
2. A Simeonite (1 Chr. 4:42).

NEBAI: One who sealed the covenant (Neh. 10:19).

NEBAIOTH: Son of Ishmael (1) (Gen. 25:13; 1 Chr. 1:29) and brother of Mahalath (1) (Gen. 28:9) or Basemath (2) (Gen. 36:3).

NEBAT: Father of Jeroboam (1) (1 Kg. 11:26 and very frequently).

NEBO: A Babylonian god, mentioned in Isa. 46:1.

NEBUCHADNEZZAR: The less correct form of the name Nebuchadrezzar. The latter is found twenty-nine times in Jeremiah and four times in Ezekiel; the former is found in all other occurrences in the Bible.

NEBUCHADREZZAR: Son and successor of Nabopolassar, the founder of the Neo-Babylonian empire. In 605 B.C., while still Crown Prince, he won the battle of Carchemish (2 Chr. 35:20; Jer. 46:2) against Neco, and this victory brought Palestine under his control (2 Kg. 24:1), though he could not consolidate his position at once as he had to return to Babylon to succeed his father. Jehoiakim (1) submitted for three years and then rebelled (2 Kg. 24:1) and Nebuchadrezzar did not send his own troops against Jerusalem until 597 B.C., when Jehoiakim had died (2 Kg. 24:6, 10) and Jehoiachin had succeeded him (2 Kg. 24:8). Jehoiachin surrendered and was taken prisoner to Babylon (2 Kg. 24:12) and Zedekiah (2) was set on the throne (2 Kg. 24:17). A subsequent rebellion by Zedekiah (2 Kg. 24:20) led to the fall of Jerusalem and the destruction of the Temple (2 Kg. 25:1ff.). Nebuchadrezzar is frequently referred to by the contemporary prophet, Jeremiah (1), and a few times by Ezekiel, who was taken captive in 597 B.C. Nebuchadrezzar figures in several of the stories in the first half of the book of Daniel, where, as frequently also elsewhere, his name is less correctly given as Nebuchadnezzar.

NEBUSHAZBAN: An officer of Nebuchadrezzar (Jer. 39:13).

NEBUZARADAN: Captain of the guard to Nebuchadrezzar (2 Kg. 25:8ff.; Jer. 39:9ff.; 40:1, 41:10, 43:6, 52:12ff.). He carried out the destruction of the Temple and city of Jerusalem (2 Kg. 25:9ff.).

NECO: Pharaoh of Egypt, who marched to the aid of Assyria against the Median and Chaldaean attackers who destroyed Nineveh (2 Kg. 23:29), and who was resisted by Josiah (1) with fatal consequences for himself (2 Kg. 23:29; 2 Chr. 35:20ff.). He removed Jehoahaz (2) from the throne and elevated Jehoiakim (1) (2 Kg. 24:34), and then marched northwards to meet

Nebuchadrezzar, who defeated him at the battle of Carchemish (2 Chr. 35:20; Jer. 46:2).

NEDABIAH: Son of Jehoiachin (1 Chr. 3:18).

NEHEMIAH: 1. One who returned with Zerubbabel (Ezr. 2:2; Neh. 7:7; 1 Esd. 5:8).

2. Cupbearer to Artaxerxes (1) (Neh. 1:11). He was authorized to go to Jerusalem and to rebuild the walls (Neh. 2). Despite the opposition of Sanballat and Tobiah (2) (Neh. 2:10, 4:1ff., 6:1ff.), the work was completed with remarkable speed (Neh. 6:15) and the wall dedicated (Neh. 12:27ff.). Twelve years later Nehemiah returned to court (Neh. 13:6), and then came again to Jerusalem (Neh. 13:7), and found his enemies had secured position and influence in the Temple (Neh. 13:7, 28) and that mixed marriages created problems (Neh. 13:23ff.). He dealt vigorously with the situation.

3. Son of Azbuk (Neh. 3:16). He was one who helped to repair the wall.

NEHUM: One who returned with Zerubbabel (Neh. 7:7); called Rehum (1) in Ezr. 2:2; 1 Esd. 5:8.

NEHUSHTA: Wife of Jehoiakim (1) and mother of Jehoiachin (2 Kg. 24:8).

NEKODA: 1. Ancestor of some Temple servants who returned with Zerubbabel (Ezr. 2:48; Neh. 7:50; 1 Esd. 5:31).

2. Ancestor of some who returned with Zerubbabel, but who were unable to prove their Israelite descent (Ezr. 2:60; Neh. 7:62; 1 Esd. 5:37).

NEMUEL: 1. Son of Simeon (1) (Num. 26:12; 1 Chr. 4:24); called Jemuel in Gen. 46:10; Exod. 6:15.

2. A Reubenite (Num. 26:9).

NEPHEG: 1. A Kohathite Levite (Exod. 6:21).

2. Son of David (2 Sam. 5:15; 1 Chr. 3:7, 14:6).

NEPHISIM: Ancestor of some Temple servants who returned with Zerubbabel (Ezr. 2:50; 1 Esd. 5:31); called Nephushesim in Neh. 7:52.

NEPHUSHESIM: See Nephisim.

NER: Father of Abner (1 Sam. 14:50f., 26:5, 14; 2 Sam. 8:12).

NEREUS: A Roman Christian to whom, with his sister, Paul sent greetings (Rom. 16:15).

NERGAL: God of the city of Cuth (2 Kg. 17:30).

NERGAL-SHAREZER: Officer of Nebuchadrezzar who released Jeremiah (1) from prison (Jer. 39:3, 13f.).

NERI: An ancestor of Jesus (1) (Lk. 3:27).

NERIAH: Father of Baruch (1) (Jer. 32:12, 16, 36:4; Bar. 1:1).

NETHANEL: 1. Representative of Issachar at the census in the wilderness (Num. 1:8) and on other occasions (Num. 2:5, 7:18, 23, 10:15).

    2. Brother of David (1 Chr. 2:14).

    3. A priest in David's time (1 Chr. 15:24).

    4. A Levite (1 Chr. 24:6).

    5. A Levite gatekeeper (1 Chr. 26:4).

    6. One of the princes sent by Jehoshaphat (4) to teach (2 Chr. 17:7).

    7. A Levite chief under Josiah (1) (2 Chr. 35:9; 1 Esd. 1:9).

    8. A priest who married a foreign wife (Ezr. 10:22); called **Nathanael (1)** in 1 Esd. 9:22.

    9. A priest in the days of Joiakim (Neh. 12:21).

    10. A priest who shared in the dedication of the wall (Neh. 12:36).

NETHANIAH: 1. Father of Ishmael (2) (2 Kg. 25:23, 25; Jer. 40:8, 14).

    2. Son of Asaph (2) (1 Chr. 25:2, 12).

    3. A Levite sent by Jehoshaphat (4) to teach (2 Chr. 17:8).

    4. Father of Jehudi (Jer. 36:14).

    5. One who married a foreign wife (1 Esd. 9:34); called **Nathan (5)** in Ezr. 10:39.

NEZIAH: Ancestor of some Temple servants who returned with **Zerubbabel** (Ezr. 2:54; Neh. 7:56; 1 Esd. 5:32).

NIBHAZ: God of the Avvites (2 Kg. 17:31).

NICANOR: 1. A Syrian general sent to fight against **Judas (1)** (1 Mac. 3:38ff.). He tried to deceive Judas (1 Mac. 7:26ff.; 2 Mac. 14:28ff.) and swore to destroy the Temple (1 Mac. 7:35; 2 Mac. 14:33), but was defeated and slain (1 Mac. 7:39ff.; 2 Mac. 15:1ff.). The day of his death was decreed to be kept as a festival in perpetuity (1 Mac. 7:49; 2 Mac. 15:36).

    2. One of the Seven (Ac. 6:5).

NICODEMUS: A Pharisee and a member of the Council (Jn 3:1), who came to **Jesus (1)** by night (Jn 3:2ff.). He spoke for Jesus to the chief priests and Pharisees (Jn 7:45ff.) and brought spices for the burial of Jesus (Jn 19:39f.).

NICOLAUS: A proselyte of Antioch who became one of the Seven (Ac. 6:5).

NIGER: Surname of Symeon (1) (Ac. 13:1).

NIMROD: A descendant of Ham (1 Chr. 1:10) and a mighty hunter (Gen. 10:9). The land of Nimrod is mentioned in Mic. 5:6.

NIMSHI: Father (1 Kg. 19:16; 2 Kg. 9:20; 2 Chr. 22:7) or grandfather (2 Kg. 9:2, 14) of Jehu (2). 'Son' probably stands for 'grandson', as frequently.

NISROCH: An Assyrian god in whose temple **Sennacherib** was assassinated (2 Kg. 19:37; Isa. 37:38).

NOADIAH: 1. A Levite who shared in the care of the Temple treasure (Ezr. 8:33); called **Moeth** in 1 Esd. 8:63.

2. A prophetess who was against Nehemiah (2) (Neh. 6:14).

NOAH: 1. The hero of the Flood story (Gen. 6ff.) and maker of the Ark (Gen. 6:14ff.). He was the son of Lamech (2) (Gen. 5:28; 1 Chr. 1:3f.), and the father of Shem, Ham, and Japheth (Gen. 5:32, 6:10; 1 Chr. 1:4). He is credited with a life of 950 years (Gen. 9:28). After the Flood he offered sacrifice (Gen. 8:20ff.) and God made a covenant with him (Gen. 9:1ff.). He began the cultivation of the vine (Gen. 9:20) and exposed himself when drunk (Gen. 9:21).

2. Daughter of Zelophehad (Num. 26:33, 27:1, 36:11; Jos. 17:3).

NOBAH: A Manassite who conquered Kenath and renamed it after himself (Num. 32:42).

NOGAH: Son of David (1 Chr. 3:7, 14:6).

NOHAH: A Benjaminite (1 Chr. 8:2).

NUMENIUS: An envoy sent to Rome and Sparta by Jonathan (15) (1 Mac. 12:1ff.), and later by Simon (3) to Rome (1 Mac. 14:24, 15:15ff.).

NUN: Father of Joshua (1) (Exod. 33:11; Num. 11:28; Dt. 1:38; Jos. 1:1).

NYMPHA: A Christian lady of Colossae in whose house the church met (Col. 4:15).

O

OBADIAH: 1. Steward of Ahab (1) (1 Kg. 18:3ff.). He protected a hundred prophets from Jezebel (1) (1 Kg. 18:4).
    2. A post-exilic descendant of David (1 Chr. 3:21).
    3. A man of Issachar (1 Chr. 7:3).
    4. A descendant of Saul (1) (1 Chr. 8:38).
    5. A Levite of post-exilic days (1 Chr. 9:16); called Abda (2) in Neh. 11:17.
    6. A Gadite who joined David in the wilderness (1 Chr. 12:9).
    7. Father of Ishmaiah (2) (1 Chr. 27:19).
    8. One of the princes sent by Jehoshaphat (4) to teach (2 Chr. 17:7).
    9. A Levite overseer in the time of Josiah (1) (2 Chr. 34:12).
    10. One who returned with Ezra (1) (Ezr. 8:9; 1 Esd. 8:35).
    11. One who sealed the covenant (Neh. 10:5).
    12. A gatekeeper in the days of Joiakim (Neh. 12:25).
    13. A Minor Prophet, of whom nothing is known outside the short book which records his vision (Ob. 1).

OBAL: Son of Joktan (Gen. 10:28); called Ebal (2) in 1 Chr. 1:22.

OBED: 1. Son of Boaz and Ruth (Ru. 4:17, 21). He was an ancestor of Jesus (1) (Mt. 1:5; Lk. 3:32).
2. A Jerahmeelite (1 Chr. 2:37f.).
3. One of David's heroes (1 Chr. 11:47).
4. A Korahite gatekeeper (1 Chr. 26:7).
5. Father of Azariah (15) (2 Chr. 23:1).
6. One who returned with Ezra (1) (1 Esd. 8:32); called Ebed (2) in Ezr. 8:6.

OBED-EDOM: 1. A man from Gath in whose house near Jerusalem David left the Ark after the death of Uzzah (2 Sam. 6:10f.; 1 Chr. 13:14f., 15:25).
2. A gatekeeper and Levite musician in the time of David (1 Chr. 15:18, 21:24). He took part in the bringing of the Ark to Jerusalem (1 Chr. 16:5, 38). Perhaps the same person is referred to in 1 Chr. 26:4, 8, 15.
3. A gatekeeper, son of Jeduthun (1 Chr. 16:38).
4. One who had care of the sacred vessels of the Temple and who was captured by Jehoash (2) (2 Chr. 25:24).

OBIL: An Ishmaelite in charge of David's camels (1 Chr. 27:30).

OCHIEL: A Levite chief (1 Esd. 1:9); called Jeiel (8) in 2 Chr. 35:9.

OCHRAN: Father of Pagiel (Num. 1:13, 2:27, 7:72, 77, 10:26).

ODED: 1. Father of Azariah (11) (2 Chr. 15:1).
2. A prophet who opposed Pekah when he proposed to make slaves of captured Judahites (2 Chr. 28:9ff.).

ODOMERA: One killed by Jonathan (15) in a raid (1 Mac. 9:66).

OG: King of Bashan, defeated by the Israelites in the time of Moses (Num. 21:33ff.; Dt. 1:4, 3:1ff.). He was of unusual stature (Dt. 3:11) and ruled over sixty cities, including Ashtaroth and Edrei (Jos. 13:30f.). His territory was allotted to the eastern half of Manasseh (Jos. 13:29ff.).

OHAD: Son of Simeon (1) (Gen. 46:10; Exod. 6:15).

OHEL: Son of Zerubbabel (1 Chr. 3:20).

OHOLAH AND OHOLIBAH: Two harlot sisters, whose names are applied to Samaria and Jerusalem (Ezek. 23:4ff.).

OHOLIAB: Assistant of Bezalel (1) (Exod. 31:6, 35:34, 36:1f., 38:23).

OHOLIBAH: See Oholah and Oholibah.

OHOLIBAMAH: 1. Wife of Esau (Gen. 36:2, 5, 14, 18, 25).
2. An Edomite chief (Gen. 36:41; 1 Chr. 1:52).

OLYMPAS: A Roman Christian greeted by Paul (Rom. 16:15).

OMAR: An Edomite (Gen. 36:11, 15; 1 Chr. 1:36).

OMRI: 1. A rival aspirant to the throne of Israel (1 Kg. 16:16) after the assassination of Elah (2) (1 Kg. 16:9f.). He attacked and eliminated Zimri (4), the assassin (1 Kg. 16:17ff.), and then Tibni, another rival (1 Kg. 16:21f.). He reigned for six years (1 Kg. 16:23) and built Samaria to become his capital (1 Kg. 16:24). From the Moabite Stone we learn that he subjugated Moab, and from 2 Kg. 3 we learn of the revolt of Moab in the reign of Jehoram (1). At some point in his reign Omri was forced to cede territory and trading rights to Damascus (1 Kg. 20:34).
2. A Benjaminite (1 Chr. 7:8).
3. A Judahite (1 Chr. 9:4).
4. David's officer over Issachar (1 Chr. 27:18).

ON: A Reubenite (Num. 16:1).

ONAM: 1. A Horite (Gen. 36:23; 1 Chr. 1:40).
2. A Jerahmeelite (1 Chr. 2:26, 28).

ONAN: Son of Judah (1) (Gen. 38:4, 46:12; Num. 26:19; 1 Chr. 2:3). He refused to perform the levirate duty and in consequence died (Gen. 38:8ff.).

ONESIMUS: Philemon's slave, who ran away and became a Christian. Paul sent him back to his master with the request for his emancipation and return to Paul, whom he had already served very acceptably (Phm. 8ff.).

ONESIPHORUS: A Christian whose household is greeted by Paul (2 Tim. 4:19) and who is commended for his kindness to Paul (2 Tim. 1:16ff.).

ONIAS: 1. Onias I, son of Jaddua (2) and High Priest, a contemporary of Arius (1 Mac. 12:7f.).
2. Onias II, grandson of 1 and High Priest (Sir. 50:1).
3. Onias III, son of Simon (2) (Sir. 50:1). He was a man of piety (2 Mac. 3:1), who had a disagreement with Simon (4) (2 Mac. 3:4ff.), who incited the cupidity of Antiochus (4) by a report on the Temple treasure (2 Mac. 3:6). When the king sent Heliodorus to seize it and the envoy was struck dumb by an apparition (2 Mac. 3:22ff.), Onias interceded for him (2 Mac. 3:31ff.). Falsely accused over this by Simon, Onias went to the king to defend himself (2 Mac. 4:1ff.). Later his brother Jason (3) secured the high priesthood by corruption (2 Mac. 4:7ff.), but then lost it to Menelaus (2 Mac. 4:23ff.). When Onias exposed the wickedness of Menelaus, the latter had him murdered (2 Mac. 4:32ff.). His death is referred to in Dan. 9:26.

OPHIR: Son of Joktan (Gen. 10:29; 1 Chr. 1:23), who gave his name to a district of uncertain location, famed for gold.

OPHRAH: Grandson of Othniel (1 Chr. 4:14).

OREB: A Midianite prince captured and killed by Ephraimites after Gideon's victory (Jg. 7:25, 8:3).

OREN: A Jerahmeelite (1 Chr. 2:25).

ORNAN: A Jebusite whose threshing floor David bought (1 Chr. 21:15ff.); called Araunah in 2 Sam. 24:18ff. The threshing floor became the site of Solomon's Temple (2 Chr. 3:2).

ORPAH: Daughter-in-law of Naomi and sister-in-law of Ruth (Ru. 1:3f.). She was a Moabitess and she remained with her people when Naomi returned to Bethlehem (Ru. 1:14).

OSNAPPAR: An Assyrian king who transferred subjects from other places to Samaria (Ezr. 4:10). The name is a corruption of Ashurbanipal, the grandson of Sennacherib and son of Esarhaddon.

OTHNI: A Korahite gatekeeper (1 Chr. 26:7).

OTHNIEL: Nephew of Caleb (Jos. 15:17; Jg. 1:13, 3:9). He married Achsah (Jos. 15:16f.; Jg. 1:12f.) when he captured Kiriath-sepher. He was the first of the Judges as the conqueror of Cushan-rishathaim (Jg. 3:7ff.).

OTHONIAH: One who married a foreign wife (1 Esd. 9:28); called Mattaniah (7) in Ezr. 10:27.

OX: An ancestor of Judith (2) (Jdt. 8:1).

OZEM: 1. Brother of David (1 Chr. 2:15).
2. A Jerahmeelite (1 Chr. 2:25).

OZIEL: An ancestor of Judith (2) (Jdt. 8:1).

OZNI: A Gadite (Num. 26:16); called Ezbon (1) in Gen. 46:16.

P

PAARAI: One of David's heroes (2 Sam. 23:35); called Naarai in 1 Chr. 11:37.

PADON: Ancestor of some Temple servants who returned with Zerubbabel (Ezr. 2:44; Neh. 7:47; 1 Esd. 5:29).

PAGIEL: Representative of Asher at the census in the wilderness (Num. 1:13) and on other occasions (Num. 2:27, 7:72, 77, 10:26).

PAHATH-MOAB: 1. Ancestor of some who returned with Zerubbabel (Ezr. 2:6; Neh. 7:11; 1 Esd. 5:11) and with Ezra (1) (Ezr. 8:4). Some of his descendants married foreign wives (Ezr. 10:30).
2. Father or ancestor of one who helped to repair the wall (Neh. 3:11); perhaps the same as 1.
3. One who sealed the covenant (Neh. 10:14).

PALAL: One who helped to repair the wall (Neh. 3:25).

PALLU: Son of Reuben (Gen. 46:9; Num. 26:5, 8; 1 Chr. 5:3); perhaps the same as Peleth (1) in Num. 16:1.

PALTI: 1. The Benjaminite spy (Num. 13:9).
   2. The husband of Michal (1 Sam. 25:44); called Paltiel (2) in 2 Sam. 3:15.

PALTIEL: 1. Representative of Issachar for the division of the land (Num. 34:26).
   2. See Palti (2).

PARMASHTA: Son of Haman, slain by the Jews (Est. 9:9).

PARMENAS: One of the Seven (Ac. 6:5).

PARNACH: Father of Elizaphan (2) (Num. 34:25).

PAROSH: 1. Ancestor of some who returned with Zerubbabel (Ezr. 2:3; Neh. 7:8; 1 Esd. 5:9) and with Ezra (1) (Ezr. 8:3). Some of his descendants married foreign wives (Ezr. 10:25).
   2. Father or ancestor of one who helped to repair the wall (Neh. 3:25); perhaps the same as 1.
   3. One who sealed the covenant (Neh. 10:14).

PARSHANDATHA: Son of Haman, slain by the Jews (Est. 9:7).

PARUAH: Father of Jehoshaphat (2) (1 Kg. 4:17).

PASACH: An Asherite (1 Chr. 7:33).

PASEAH: 1. An Asherite (1 Chr. 4:12).
   2. Ancestor of some Temple servants who returned with Zerubbabel (Ezr. 2:49; Neh. 7:51; 1 Esd. 5:31).
   3. Father of Joiada (1) (Neh. 3:6).

PASHHUR: 1. Ancestor of some priests who returned with Zerubbabel (Ezr. 2:38; Neh. 7:41; 1 Esd. 5:25) and of some who married foreign wives (Ezr. 10:22).
   2. One who sealed the covenant (Neh. 10:3).
   3. A priest who put Jeremiah (1) in the stocks (Jer. 20:1ff.). Jeremiah predicted that he would die in Babylon.
   4. Father of Gedaliah (4) (Jer. 38:1).
   5. One who urged Zedekiah (2) to put Jeremiah (1) to death (Jer. 38:1ff.). He was one of those sent by Zedekiah to Jeremiah for advice (Jer. 21:1ff.). He is mentioned also in 1 Chr. 9:12; Neh. 11:12.

PATROBAS: A Roman Christian greeted by Paul (Rom. 16:4).

PATROCLUS: Father of Nicanor (1) (2 Mac. 8:9).

PAUL: Name given to Saul (2) (Ac. 13:9) and by which he is principally known in the NT. He was born at Tarsus (Ac. 9:11, 21:39, 22:3) and studied in Jerusalem under Gamaliel (2) (Ac. 22:3). He was a Roman citizen from birth (Ac. 22:28; cf. Ac. 16:37f., 23:27). He was present at the stoning of Stephen (Ac. 7:58, 8:1) and became an ardent persecutor of the Church (Ac. 8:3, 9:1ff.), and was on the way to Damascus on a persecuting mission when he was converted (Ac. 9:2ff., 22:3ff., 26:9ff.) to become Paul the Apostle. He returned to Jerusalem and from there went to Tarsus (Ac. 9:26ff.), whence **Barnabas** brought him to Antioch (Ac. 11:25). The church at Antioch set him apart for missionary work (Ac. 13:2), and from this point the book of Acts is mainly concerned with his three missionary journeys (Ac. 13f., 15:41-21:15), his arrest and trial (Ac. 21:27-26:32) and journey to Rome as a prisoner (Ac. 27f.). He fought for the independence of the Church from the Synagogue and the consequent freedom of Gentile converts from the obligation to be circumcised (Ac. 15), and his many letters to churches and friends form a large part of the NT. His contribution to Christian doctrine, and especially to the elucidation of the significance of the Crucifixion and the Resurrection and to the interpretation of the Person of Christ has been of fundamental importance to the Christian Church.

PAULUS: Sergius Paulus, proconsul of Cyprus (Ac. 13:7), who became a Christian (Ac. 13:12).

PEDAHEL: Representative of Naphtali for the division of the land (Num. 34:28).

PEDAHZUR: Father of Gamaliel (1) (Num. 1:10, 2:20, 7:54, 59, 10:23).

PEDAIAH: 1. Maternal grandfather of Jehoiakim (1) (2 Kg. 23:36).

2. Son of Jehoiachin (1 Chr. 3:18). In 1 Chr. 3:19 he is said to be the father of Zerubbabel, but elsewhere (Ezr. 3:2, 8, 5:2; Neh. 12:1; Hag. 1:1, 12, 14, 2:2, 23; Mt. 1:12; Lk. 3:27) Zerubbabel is said to be the son of Shealtiel (1), the brother of Pedahiah (1 Chr. 3:17).

3. Father of Joel (11) (1 Chr. 27:20).

4. One who helped to repair the wall (Neh. 3:25).

5. One who stood on the left hand of Ezra (1) at the reading of the Law (Neh. 8:4; 1 Esd. 9:44).

6. A Benjaminite (Neh. 11:7).

7. A Levite treasurer in the time of Nehemiah (2) (Neh. 13:13).

PEKAH: Assassin of Pekahiah (2 Kg. 15:25). He made himself king of Israel and is credited with a reign of twenty years (2 Kg. 15:27), but this cannot be reconciled with other evidence. He allied himself with Syria against Ahaz (1) (2 Kg. 16:5f.; Isa. 7:1ff.), and Ahaz appealed to Assyria for help (2 Kg. 16:7ff.). Pekah was assassinated by Hoshea (2) (2 Kg. 15:30).

PEKAHIAH: Son and successor of Menahem, king of Israel (2 Kg. 15:22). He reigned for two years (2 Kg. 15:23) and was assassinated by Pekah (2 Kg. 15:25).

PELAIAH: 1. A descendant of **Solomon** (1 Chr. 3:24).
  2. One who helped to expound the Law (Neh. 8:7; 1 Esd. 9:48).
  3. One who sealed the covenant (Neh. 10:10).

PELALIAH: A priest (Neh. 11:12).

PELATIAH: 1. A descendant of **Zerubbabel** (1 Chr. 3:21).
  2. A Simeonite leader (1 Chr. 4:42).
  3. One who sealed the covenant (Neh. 10:22).
  4. A prince of the people (Ezek. 11:1) against whom **Ezekiel** prophesied, with the result that Pelatiah died (Ezek. 11:13).

PELEG: A descendant of **Shem** (Gen. 10:25; 1 Chr. 1:19; cf. Lk. 3:25).

PELET: 1. A Calebite (1 Chr. 2:47).
  2. A Benjaminite who joined **David** at Ziklag (1 Chr. 12:3).

PELETH: 1. A Reubenite (Num. 16:1); perhaps the same as **Pallu** in Gen. 46:9; Num. 26:5, 8; 1 Chr. 5:3.
  2. A Jerahmeelite (1 Chr. 2:33).

PENINNAH: Wife of **Elkanah** (2) (1 Sam. 1, 2, 4).

PENUEL: 1. A descendant of **Judah** (1) (1 Chr. 4:4).
  2. A Benjaminite (1 Chr. 8:25).

PERESH: A Manassite (1 Chr. 7:16).

PEREZ: Son of **Judah** (1) by **Tamar** (1) (Gen. 38:29; Num. 26:20; Ru. 4:12, 18; 1 Chr. 2:4f.; Mt. 1:3; Lk. 3:33); called **Phares** in 1 Esd. 5:5.

PERIDA: Ancestor of some who returned with **Zerubbabel** (Neh. 7:57); called **Peruda** in Ezr. 2:55; 1 Esd. 5:33.

PERSEUS: King of Kittim (i.e. Macedonia) (1 Mac. 8:5).

PERSIS: A Roman Christian woman greeted by **Paul** (Rom. 16:12).

PERUDA: *See* **Perida.**

PETER: One of the twelve Apostles (Mt. 10:2; Mk 3:16; Lk. 6:14; Ac. 1:13), who belonged to the inner group of three (Mt. 17:1, 26:37; Mk 5:37, 9:2, 14:33; Lk. 8:51, 9:28). His name was really **Simon** (5) (Mt. 4:18, 10:2; Mk 1:16, 29, 36, and often) or **Symeon** (2) (Ac. 15:14), but he was surnamed **Cephas** (Jn 1:42; 1 C. 1:12, 3:22, 9:5, 15:5; Gal. 1:18, 2:9, 11, 14) or its Greek equivalent, Peter. He is also called **Bar-Jona** (Mt. 16:17), or son of **John** (8) (cf. Jn 1:42, 21:15ff.). He was a fisherman before he became a disciple (Mk 1:16) and after the Crucifixion he returned to that occupation (Jn 21:2f.). He was first brought to **Jesus** (1) by his brother **Andrew** (Jn 1:41f.). He figures in many incidents in the Gospels, notably in his recognition that Jesus was the Christ, or Messiah (Mt. 16:16; Mk 8:29; Lk. 9:20), in his denial of Jesus (Mt. 26:69ff.; Mk 14:66ff.; Lk. 22:54ff.; Jn 18:16ff.,

25ff.), and in his visit to the empty tomb (Jn 20:3ff.) and recognition of Jesus by the Sea of Tiberias (Jn 21:7). He played a leading part on the day of Pentecost (Ac. 2:14ff.) and in other incidents in the early Church (Ac. 3:1ff., 4:8ff., 5:1ff., 27ff., 12:1ff.), and especially in the conversion of **Cornelius** (Ac. 10:1ff.). He had a following against **Paul** in the church at Corinth (1 C. 1:12) and Paul complains of his conduct at Antioch (Gal. 2:11ff.). Two NT Letters are attributed to him. His martyrdom at Rome is unrecorded in the NT.

PETHAHIAH: 1. Head of a priestly course (1 Chr. 24:16).
    2. A priest who married a foreign wife (Ezr. 10:23; 1 Esd. 9:23).
    3. A Levite in the time of **Ezra** (1) (Neh. 9:5).
    4. A Levite adviser (Neh. 11:24).

PETHUEL: Father of **Joel** (1) (Jl 1:1).

PEULLETHAI: A Levite gatekeeper (1 Chr. 26:5).

PHALTIEL: A chief of the people (2 Esd. 5:16).

PHANUEL: Father of **Anna** (2) (Lk. 2:36).

PHARAKIM: Ancestor of some Temple servants who returned with **Zerubbabel** (1 Esd. 5:31).

PHARAOH: A title of the rulers of Egypt, to which the personal name of the ruler is sometimes attached. Unnamed Pharaohs are referred to in connexion with **Abraham** (Gen. 12:15ff.), **Joseph** (1) (Gen. 39ff.), the Oppression (Exod. 1f.) and the Exodus (Exod. 2:23f., 3:10ff., and chaps. 4ff.), Solomon' sfather-in-law (1 Kg. 3:1, 9:16, 24, 11:1), the Pharaoh who received **Hadad** (5) (1 Kg. 11:14ff.), the Pharaoh of the time of **Hezekiah** (1) (2 Kg. 18:21; Isa. 36:6), and the father of **Bithiah** (1 Chr. 4:17). For Pharaohs who are named (sometimes without the addition of the word Pharaoh), see **Hophra, Neco, Shishak, Tirhakah.**

PHARES: Form of the name **Perez** found in 1 Esd. 5:5.

PHASIRON: Ancestor of some enemies attacked by **Jonathan** (15) (1 Mac. 9:66).

PHICOL: Captain of **Abimelech** (1) (Gen. 21:22ff., 26:26ff.).

PHILEMON: The person to whom the Letter to Philemon was sent (Phm. 1). Paul sent his runaway slave, **Onesimus**, back to him, with the request that he should be emancipated and sent again to Paul.

PHILETUS: A false teacher condemned by **Paul** (2 Tim. 2:17f.).

PHILIP: 1. Father of **Alexander** (1) (1 Mac. 1:1, 6:2).
    2. A friend of **Antiochus** (4) to whom **Antiochus** (5) was entrusted (1 Mac. 6:14f.). He buried **Antiochus** (4) but then fled to Egypt (2 Mac. 9:29), as **Lysias** (1) had assumed the regency. Later he appeared in Antioch

and sought to secure control of the kingdom (1 Mac. 6:55f.), causing Lysias to raise the siege of Jerusalem (1 Mac. 6:57ff.). Philip was then driven out of Antioch (1 Mac. 6:63).

3. A Phrygian who was left by Antiochus (4) in charge of Jerusalem (2 Mac. 5:22). He was barbarous and cruel (2 Mac. 6:11), but was forced to appeal to Ptolemy (8) (2 Mac. 8:8).

4. Philip V of Macedonia, defeated by Rome in 197 B.C. (1 Mac. 8:5).

5. One of the twelve Apostles (Mt. 10:3; Mk 3:18; Lk. 6:14; Ac. 1:13). He brought Nathanael (3) to Jesus (1) (Jn 1:43ff.). He is mentioned in connexion with the feeding of the five thousand (Jn 6:5, 7) and the visit of the Greeks to Jesus (Jn 12:21f.), and also in Jn 14:8f.

6. One of the Seven (Ac. 6:5). He preached in Samaria (Ac. 8:5ff.), and converted the Ethiopian eunuch (Ac. 8:26ff.). He dwelt at Caesarea, where Paul stayed with him (Ac. 21:8), and he had four unmarried daughters who prophesied (Ac. 21:9).

7. *See* Herod (4).

8. *See* Herod (5).

PHILOLOGUS: A Roman Christian lady greeted by **Paul** (Rom. 16:15).

PHINEHAS: 1. Grandson of **Aaron** (Exod. 6:25; Num. 25:7). His anger was aroused when a Midianite woman was brought into the camp (Num. 25:6ff.), and he accompanied an expedition against the Midianites (Num. 31:6). After the conquest of Canaan he lived at Gibeah (Jos. 24:33), but at the time of the war between Benjamin and the other tribes he ministered at Bethel (Jg. 20:28).

2. Son of Eli; *see* **Hophni and Phinehas**.

3. Father of **Eleazar** (5) (Ezr. 8:33; 1 Esd. 8:63).

PHLEGON: A Roman Christian greeted by **Paul** (Rom. 16:14).

PHOEBE: A deaconess of the church at Cenchreae, whom **Paul** commended to the church at Rome (Rom. 16:1).

PHYGELUS: One who deserted **Paul** (2 Tim. 1:15).

PILATE: Pontius Pilate, governor of Judea at the time of Christ's ministry (Lk. 3:1). He figures only in the account of the trial and Crucifixion of Jesus (1). The Jews delivered Jesus to Pilate (Mt. 27:2; Mk 15:1; Lk. 23:1; Jn 18:28), before whom He was tried (Mt. 27:11ff.; Mk 15:2ff.; Lk. 23:2ff.; Jn 18:29ff.), and who would have released Him (Mt. 27:15ff.; Mk 15:6ff.; Lk. 23:16; Jn 18:39, 19:12), especially in view of his wife's dream (Mt. 27:19f.), had not the crowd demanded His crucifixion (Mt. 27:22; Mk 15:13; Lk. 23:21ff.; Jn 19:6, 15). Pilate delivered Jesus to be crucified and authorized the inscription on the Cross (Jn 19:19) and refused to change it (Jn 19:21f.). He gave permission to **Joseph** (14) to bury the body of Jesus (Mt. 27:58; Mk 15:43f.; Lk. 23:52; Jn 19:38). He was procurator of Judea A.D. 26–36.

PILDASH: Nephew of **Abraham** (Gen. 22:22).

PILHA: One who sealed the covenant (Neh. 10:24).

PILTAI: A priest in the days of Joiakim (Neh. 12:17).

PINON: An Edomite chief (Gen. 36:41; 1 Chr. 1:52).

PIRAM: King of Jarmuth, who joined the alliance against Joshua (1) (Jos. 10:3), and who was put to death when defeated and captured (Jos. 10:26f.).

PISPA: An Asherite (1 Chr. 7:38).

PITHON: A descendant of Saul (1) (1 Chr. 8:35, 9:41).

POCHERETH-HAZZEBAIM: Ancestor of some of Solomon's servants who returned with Zerubbabel (Ezr. 2:57; Neh. 7:59; 1 Esd. 5:34).

PORATHA: Son of Haman, slain by the Jews (Est. 9:8).

PORCIUS FESTUS: *See* Festus

POSIDONIUS: Envoy of Nicanor (1) (2 Mac. 14:19).

POTIPHAR: An officer of Pharaoh to whom Joseph (1) was sold (Gen. 37:36, 39:1). He was captain of the guard, and when Joseph resisted the advances of his mistress (Gen. 39:6ff.), Potiphar cast him into the prison (Gen. 39:19).

POTIPHERA: Priest of On and father-in-law of Joseph (1) (Gen. 41:45).

PRISCA: Wife of Aquila (Rom. 16:3; 1 C. 16:19; 2 Tim. 4:19); also called Priscilla (Ac. 18:2, 18, 26).

PRISCILLA: *See* Prisca.

PROCHORUS: One of the Seven (Ac. 6:5).

PTOLEMY: 1. Ptolemy I, Soter, who founded the Ptolemaic dynasty of Egypt, following the death of Alexander (1). He is alluded to in Dan. 11:5.

2. Ptolemy II, Philadelphus, in whose reign the Septuagint version of the Pentateuch was made. The marriage of his daughter to Antiochus (2) is alluded to in Dan. 11:6.

3. Ptolemy III, Euergetes, who invaded the Syrian kingdom (Dan. 11:7ff.).

4. Ptolemy IV, Philopator, who defeated the army of Antiochus (3) at the battle of Raphia in 217 B.C. (Dan. 11:10f.).

5. Ptolemy V, Epiphanes, who lost Palestine to Antiochus (3) in 198 B.C. (Dan. 11:11ff.). He married Cleopatra (1) (Dan. 11:17).

6. Ptolemy VI, Philometor, who fled before Antiochus (4) (1 Mac. 1:18), who had been represented at his coronation (2 Mac. 4:21). Ptolemy made an alliance with Rome before Antiochus made a second invasion of Egypt (2 Mac. 5:1), with the result that Antiochus was forced by the Roman envoy to withdraw (2 Mac. 5:11). These events are alluded to in Dan. 11:25ff. Ptolemy gave his daughter in marriage to Alexander (2) (1 Mac. 10:57f.) and later to Demetrius (2) (1 Mac. 11:12). His bid for the annexation of

Syria and his death are recorded in 1 Mac. 11:13ff. He is referred to in Ad. Est. 11:1.

7. Son of **Dositheus** (1). He accompanied his father to Egypt (Ad. Est. 11:1).

8. Son of **Dorymenes** (1 Mac. 3:38; 2 Mac. 4:45), surnamed **Macron** (2 Mac. 10:12). He was sent against the Jews (1 Mac. 3:38ff.), but he showed justice to the Jews and was in consequence accused and poisoned himself (2 Mac. 10:12ff.).

9. Son of **Abubus** (1 Mac. 16:11). He was governor of Jericho and son-in-law of **Simon** (3), whom he treacherously murdered (1 Mac. 16:16). He afterwards plotted unsuccessfully to kill **John** (5) (1 Mac. 16:19ff.).

PUAH: 1. One of the Hebrew midwives in Egypt (Exod. 1:15).

2. Son of **Issachar** and brother of **Tola** (1) (1 Chr. 7:1); called **Puvah** in Gen. 46:13; Num. 26:23.

3. Father of **Tola** (2) (Jg. 10:1).

PUBLIUS: Roman official in Malta, whose father was healed by **Paul** (Ac. 28:7f.).

PUDENS: A Christian who sent greetings to **Timothy** (2) (2 Tim. 4:21).

PUL: *See* **Tiglath-pileser.**

PURAH: Servant of **Gideon** (Jg. 7:10f.).

PUT: Son of **Ham** (Gen. 10:6; 1 Chr. 1:8).

PUTIEL: Father-in-law of **Eleazar** (1) (Exod. 6:25).

PUVAH: Son of **Issachar** (Gen. 46:13; Num. 26:23); called **Puah** (2) in 1 Chr. 7:1.

PYRRHUS: Father of **Sopater** (1) (Ac. 20:4).

Q

QUARTUS: A Christian who sent greetings to the Roman church (Rom. 16:23).

QUINTUS MEMMIUS: *See* **Memmius.**

QUIRINIUS: Governor of Syria at the time of the birth of **Jesus** (1) (Lk. 2:2).

R

RAAMA: *See* **Raamah.**

RAAMAH: Grandson of Ham (Gen. 10:7); called **Raama** in 1 Chr. 1:9.

RAAMIAH: One who returned with **Zerubbabel** (Neh. 7:7); called **Reelaiah** in Ezr. 2:2, and **Resaiah** in 1 Esd. 5:8.

RACHEL: Younger daughter of **Laban** (Gen. 29:6, 9ff.), for whom **Jacob** (1) served Laban seven years (Gen. 29:18), only to find himself deceived into marriage with **Leah** (Gen. 29:25) and compelled to serve seven more years before marrying Rachel (Gen. 29:28). She was the mother of two sons (Gen. 30:23f., 35:16ff.), and died in childbirth on the second occasion (Gen. 35:19).

RADDAI: Son of **Jesse** (1 Chr. 2:14).

RAGUEL: Father of **Sarah** (2) (Tob. 3:7, 17f., 14:12).

RAHAB: 1. A harlot of Jericho, who hid the Israelite spies (Jos. 2:1ff.), and whose family was spared when the city was taken (Jos. 6:17ff.).

2. A mythological monster (Job 9:13, 26:12; Ps. 89:10; Isa. 51:9), whose name is used figuratively for Egypt (Ps. 87:4; Isa. 30:7).

3. Mother of **Boaz**, mentioned in the genealogy of **Jesus** (1) (Mt. 1:5).

RAHAM: A Calebite (1 Chr. 2:44).

RAKEM: A Manassite (1 Chr. 7:16).

RAM: 1. An ancestor of David (Ru. 4:19; 1 Chr. 2:9f.) and so of **Jesus** (1) (Mt. 1:3f.); called **Arni** in Lk. 3:33.

2. The family to which **Elihu** (5) belonged (Job 32:2).

RAMIAH: One who married a foreign wife (Ezr. 10:25; 1 Esd. 9:26).

RAPHA: A Benjaminite (1 Chr. 8:2).

RAPHAEL: The angel who assumed the name of **Azarias** (Tob. 5:12) and accompanied **Tobias** (1) (Tob. 5:4ff.). He was sent to heal Tobit's blindness, to effect the marriage of Tobias and **Sarah** (2), and to bind Asmodeus (Tob. 3:17). All of these missions he accomplished.

RAPHAH: A descendant of **Saul** (1) (1 Chr. 8:37); called **Rephaiah** (4) in 1 Chr. 9:43.

RAPHAIM: An ancestor of **Judith** (2) (Jdt. 8:1).

RAPHU: Father of **Palti** (1) (Num. 13:9).

RAZIS: One who preferred death rather than fall into the hands of the enemy (2 Mac. 14:37ff.).

REAIAH: 1. A Judahite (1 Chr. 4:2); called **Haroeh** in 1 Chr. 2:52.
2. A Reubenite (1 Chr. 5:5).
3. Ancestor of some Temple servants who returned with **Zerubbabel** (Ezr. 2:47; Neh. 7:50; 1 Esd. 5:31).

REBA: A Midianite king, slain by Moses (Num. 31:8; Jos. 13:21).

REBECCA: Form of the name **Rebekah** found in Rom. 9:10.

REBEKAH: Daughter of **Bethuel** (Gen. 22:23, 24:15, 25:20, 28:5), and wife of **Isaac** (Gen. 24). Isaac passed her off as his sister in Gerar (Gen. 26:6ff.). She was the mother of **Esau** and **Jacob** (1) (Gen. 25:21ff.), and she incited Jacob to deceive Isaac and so secure the blessing (Gen. 27:1ff.) and afterwards sent him away to escape Esau's wrath (Gen. 27:41ff.). She was buried in the cave of Machpelah (Gen. 49:30).

RECHAB: 1. One of the two who murdered **Ishbosheth** (2 Sam. 4:2, 5, 9).
2. Father of **Jonadab** (2) (2 Kg. 10:15, 23; Jer. 35:6, 8, 14ff.). He gave his name to the Rechabites.

REELAIAH: One who returned with **Zerubbabel** (Ezr. 2:2); called **Raamiah** in Neh. 7:7, and **Resaiah** in 1 Esd. 5:8.

REELIAH: One who returned with **Zerubbabel** (1 Esd. 5:8).

REGEM: A Calebite (1 Chr. 2:47).

REGEM-MELECH: One of those sent to **Zechariah** (31) (Zech. 7:2).

REHABIAH: A Levite (1 Chr. 23:17, 24:21, 26:25).

REHOB: 1. Father of **Hadadezer** (2 Sam. 8:3, 12).
2. One who sealed the covenant (Neh. 10:11).

REHOBOAM: Son and successor of **Solomon** (1 Kg. 11:43; 2 Chr. 9:31). At his accession the kingdom was divided (1 Kg. 12; 2 Chr. 10). He reigned seventeen years (1 Kg. 14:21; 2 Chr. 12:13), and during his reign **Shishak** despoiled Jerusalem (1 Kg. 14:25ff.; 2 Chr. 12:2ff.).

REHUM: 1. One who returned with **Zerubbabel** (Ezr. 2:2; 1 Esd. 5:8); called **Nehum** in Neh. 7:7.
2. Commander in the time of **Artaxerxes** (1) (Ezr. 4:8f., 17:23; 1 Esd. 2:16f., 25).
3. One who helped to repair the wall (Neh. 3:17).
4. One who sealed the covenant (Neh. 10:25).
5. A priest who returned with **Zerubbabel** (Neh. 12:3).

REI: A supporter of **Solomon** at his accession (1 Kg. 1:8).

REKEM: 1. A Midianite king, slain by **Moses** (Num. 31:8; Jos. 13:21).
2. A Calebite (1 Chr. 2:43f.).

REMALIAH: Father of **Pekah** (2 Kg. 15:25, 27, 30; Isa. 7:1, 4f.).

REPHAEL: A Levite gatekeeper (1 Chr. 26:7).

REPHAH: An Ephraimite (1 Chr. 7:25).

REPHAIAH: 1. A Judahite (1 Chr. 3:21).
  2. A Simeonite (1 Chr. 4:42).
  3. A man of Issachar (1 Chr. 7:2).
  4. A descendant of Saul (1) (1 Chr. 9:43); called **Raphah** in 1 Chr. 8:37.
  5. One who helped to repair the wall (Neh. 3:9).

REPHAN: A corruption of **Kaiwan** (Ac. 7:43).

RESAIAH: One who returned with **Zerubbabel** (1 Esd. 5:8); called **Reelaiah** in Ezr. 2:2, and **Raamiah** in Neh. 7:7.

RESHEPH: An Ephraimite (1 Chr. 7:25).

REU: A descendant of **Shem** (Gen. 11:18ff.; 1 Chr. 1:25; Lk. 3:35).

REUBEN: Son of Jacob (1) by **Leah** (Gen. 29:32). He gave his name to one of the tribes of Israel. He tried to save **Joseph** (1) (Gen. 37:21ff.; cf. 42:22) and offered to guarantee the return of **Benjamin** (1) (Gen. 42:37).

REUEL: 1. Son of Esau by **Basemath** (1) (Gen. 36:4, 10, 13).
  2. Father-in-law of **Moses** (Exod. 2:18); called **Jethro** in Exod. 3:1, 4:18, 18:1ff. and **Hobab** in Num. 10:29; Jg. 4:11. In Num. 10:29 Reuel is the father of Hobab.
  3. Father of **Eliasaph** (1) (Num. 2:14); called **Deuel** in Num. 1:14, 7:42, 47, 10:20.
  4. A Benjaminite (1 Chr. 9:8).

REUMAH: The concubine of **Nahor** (2) (Gen. 22:24).

REZIN: 1. King of Damascus and ally of **Pekah** against Judah (2 Kg. 15:37, 16:5; Isa. 7:1ff.). The king of Assyria conquered Damascus and deported its people and killed Rezin (2 Kg. 16:9).
  2. Ancestor of some Temple servants who returned with **Zerubbabel** (Ezr. 2:48; Neh. 7:50; 1 Esd. 5:31).

REZON: A Syrian leader who gave **Solomon** trouble (1 Kg. 11:23ff.).

RHESA: An ancestor of Jesus (1) (Lk. 3:27).

RHODA: Maid-servant in the house of **Mary** (5) (Ac. 12:13).

RHODOCUS: A Jewish traitor (2 Mac. 13:21).

RIBAI: Father of **Ittai** (2) (2 Sam. 23:29; 1 Chr. 11:31).

RIMMON: 1. Syrian god worshipped by the king of Damascus (2 Kg. 5:18). He is to be identified with **Hadad** (1).
  2. A Benjaminite (2 Sam. 4:2, 5, 9).

RINNAH: A Judahite (1 Chr. 4:20).

RIPHATH: Son of Gomer (1) (Gen. 10:3); called Diphath in 1 Chr. 1:6.

RIZIA: An Asherite (1 Chr. 7:39).

RIZPAH: Daughter of Aiah (2) and concubine of Saul (1) (2 Sam. 3:7). She was taken by Abner after Saul's death and this caused a quarrel with Ishbosheth (2 Sam. 3:7ff.). When David gave seven of Saul's descendants to be hanged, Rizpah guarded the bodies (2 Sam. 21:10).

ROHGAH: An Asherite (1 Chr. 7:34).

ROMAMTI-EZER: A Levite musician (1 Chr. 25:4, 31).

ROSH: Son of Benjamin (Gen. 46:21).

RUFUS: 1. Son of Simon (11) and brother of Alexander (3) (Mk 15:21).
2. Roman Christian greeted by Paul (Rom. 16:13); possibly the same as 1.

RUTH: A Moabitess, wife of Mahlon (Ru. 4:10) and daughter-in-law of Naomi (Ru. 1:2). She accompanied Naomi when she returned to Bethlehem (Ru. 1:16ff.) and gleaned in the field of Boaz (Ru. 2:2ff.) and subsequently married him (Ru. 4:13) and became the ancestress of David (Ru. 4:17, 21f.) and of Jesus (1) (Mt 1:5).

S

SABBAIAS: One who married a foreign wife (1 Esd. 9:32); possibly the same as Shemaiah (17) (Ezr. 10:31).

SABTA: Son of Cush (1) (1 Chr. 1:9); called Sabtah in Gen. 10:7.

SABTAH: See Sabta.

SABTECA: Son of Cush (1) (Gen. 10:7; 1 Chr. 1:9).

SACHAR: 1. Father of Ahiam (1 Chr. 11:35); called Sharar in 2 Sam. 23:33.
2. A Levite gatekeeper (1 Chr. 26:4).

SACHIA: A Benjaminite (1 Chr. 8:10).

SAKKUTH: A god (Am. 5:26), also known as Ninurta, god of the planet Saturn. Hence Kaiwan and Sakkuth are synonymous. For 'Sakkuth your king' Ac. 7:43 has 'in the tent of Moloch'.

SALA: An ancestor of Jesus (1) (Lk. 3:32); called Salmon in Ru. 4:20f.; Mt. 1:4f., and Salma (1) in 1 Chr. 2:11.

SALAMIEL: An ancestor of Judith (2) (Jdt. 8:1).

SALLAI: 1. A Benjaminite (Neh. 11:8).
2. A priest (Neh. 12:20); called **Sallu** (2) in Neh. 12:7.

SALLU: 1. A Benjaminite (1 Chr. 9:7; Neh. 11:7).
2. *See* Sallai (2).

SALMA: 1. Father of **Boaz** (1 Chr. 2:11); called **Salmon** in Ru. 4:20f.; Mt. 1:4f., and **Sala** in Lk. 3:32.
2. A Calebite and 'father' or founder of Bethlehem (1 Chr. 2:51, 54).

SALMON: *See* Salma (1).

SALOME: 1. Daughter of **Herodias** who danced before **Herod** (3) and caused **John** (6) the Baptist to be beheaded. She is referred to, but not named, in Mt. 14:6ff.; Mk 6:22ff.
2. One of the women present at the Crucifixion (Mt. 15:40) and at the empty tomb (Mk 16:1).

SALU: Father of **Zimri** (1) (Num. 25:14; 1 Mac. 2:26).

SAMGAR-NEBO: Officer of **Nebuchadrezzar** at the taking of Jerusalem (Jer. 39:3). But the word may be the corruption of a title.

SAMLAH: An Edomite king (Gen. 36:36f.; 1 Chr. 1:47f.).

SAMSON: One of the Judges (Jg. 13ff.). His birth was announced by an angel (Jg. 13:1ff.) and he was a Nazirite from his birth (Jg. 13:7). He had extraordinary strength, which he used against the Philistines. But he had a weakness for Philistine women, who betrayed him (Jg. 14:1ff., 16:1ff., 4ff.). His betrayal by **Delilah** made him a prisoner of the Philistines, who blinded him (Jg. 16:21), but at Gaza, where they were making sport of him, he brought the house upon them and upon himself (Jg. 16:23ff.).

SAMUEL: Son of **Elkanah** (2) and **Hannah** (1 Sam. 1:19f.). He was born in answer to prayer (1 Sam. 1:11) and was dedicated to God at Shiloh, where he ministered to **Eli** (1 Sam. 2:11). There he received a message from God for Eli (1 Sam. 3). When grown up he became a Judge (1 Sam. 7:15) and a seer or prophet (1 Sam. 9:9). He was instrumental in establishing the monarchy (1 Sam. 9ff.) and he anointed **Saul** (1) (1 Sam. 10:1) and later **David** (1 Sam. 16:13). He soon broke with Saul (1 Sam. 13:8ff., 15:35) and saw no more of him. He died and was buried at Ramah (1 Sam. 25:1; 28:3), but Saul consulted him through a necromancer before the battle of Gilboa (1 Sam. 28:8ff.).

SANBALLAT: Governor of Samaria in the time of **Nehemiah** (2) and his bitterest opponent (Neh. 2:10), using derision (Neh. 2:19, 4:1ff.) and threats (Neh. 4:7ff.) and wiles (Neh. 6:1ff.) against him in vain. While Nehemiah was absent at court the High Priest's son married Sanballat's daughter and Nehemiah drove him out of the Temple (Neh. 13:28) on his return.

SAPH: A Philistine giant slain at Gob (2 Sam. 21:18); called **Sippai** in 1 Chr. 20:4.

SAPPHIRA: Wife of **Ananias** (1) who lied to the Apostles and fell down dead (Ac. 5:1ff.).

SARAH: 1. Wife of **Abraham** (Gen. 11:29). She was at first called **Sarai**, but her name was changed to Sarah (Gen. 17:15). She was the half-sister of Abraham (Gen. 20:12), and he passed her off as his sister in Egypt (Gen. 12:10ff.) and in Gerar (Gen. 20:1ff.). She bore **Isaac** when she was already of an advanced age (Gen. 21:1ff.). Before this, on her initiative Abraham had a son, **Ishmael** (1), by **Hagar** (Gen. 16:15), but Sarah's harshness caused Hagar to flee before the birth of her child (Gen. 16:6), and though she returned Sarah caused her to be driven out with her son after the birth of Isaac (Gen. 21:8ff.). She died at Hebron at the age of 127 and was buried in the cave of Machpelah (Gen. 23:1f., 19).

2. Daughter of **Raguel** (Tob. 3:7, 17) and wife of **Tobias** (1) (Tob. 7:13). Previously she had had seven husbands, each of whom had been killed by **Asmodeus** on her bridal night (Tob. 3:8).

SARAI: *See* **Sarah** (1).

SARAPH: A Judahite (1 Chr. 4:22).

SARASADAI: An ancestor of **Judith** (2) (Jdt. 8:1).

SAREA: One of the scribes of **Ezra** (1) (2 Esd. 14:24).

SARGON: An Assyrian king mentioned in the Bible only in Isa. 20:1 in connexion with the attack on Ashdod. He seized the throne at the death of **Shalmaneser,** who had begun the siege of Samaria (2 Kg. 17:3ff.), but it was to Sargon that the city fell (2 Kg. 17:6), though his name is unmentioned in this connexion.

SAROTHIE: Ancestor of some of Solomon's servants who returned with **Zerubbabel** (1 Esd. 5:34).

SARSECHIM: An officer of **Nebuchadrezzar** (Jer. 39:3).

SATAN: The word means 'adversary', and it is frequently so translated in the OT. In Job 1:6ff., 2:1ff. it refers to one who stands in the court of God and who appears to be an angel charged with the task of accusing men before God. Similarly in Zech. 3:2f. it signifies the accuser. In both of these cases the Hebrew says 'the Satan'. In 1 Chr. 21:1 it is a proper name and it signifies the Tempter. In the NT he is the Tempter (Mk 1:13; cf. Mt. 16:23), and he is identified with the beguiler of Eve (Rev. 20:2). Elsewhere he is the prince of the Demons (Mt. 12:26; Mk 3:23, 26; Lk. 10:18; Ac. 26:18).

SATHRABUZANES: Form of the name **Shethar-bozenai** found in 1 Esd. 6:3, 7, 27, 7:1.

SAUL: 1. A Benjaminite (1 Sam. 9:1f.), who went to **Samuel** for help in finding his father's lost asses (1 Sam. 9:3ff.) and was anointed by him and encouraged to take the lead against the Philistines (1 Sam. 10:1ff.). He delivered Jabesh-gilead from the Ammonites (1 Sam. 11:1ff.), and was confirmed as king (1 Sam. 11:14) and then turned his arms against the Philistines. By the battle of Michmash (1 Sam. 14:1ff.) he cleared them out of the centre of the country and by the battle of Ephes-dammim (1 Sam. 17:1ff.) he stopped them penetrating up the defiles into Judah. At the end of his reign they marched up the coast and into the Valley of Esdraelon to attack from the north, and Saul was defeated and died at the battle of Gilboa (1 Sam. 31; 2 Sam. 1). Before this he had lost the support of Samuel (1 Sam. 13:8ff., 15:35), whom he consulted through a necromancer before the battle of Gilboa (1 Sam. 28:8ff.). He was subject to moods of depression and **David** was brought to court to soothe him (1 Sam. 16:14ff.), but he became jealous of David and sought to kill him (1 Sam. 18:10ff.), and when David fled and became an outlaw (1 Sam. 19:18ff., 21:1ff.), Saul frequently tried to capture him (1 Sam. 22:6ff., 23:6ff., 24:1ff., 26:1ff.). When Saul died David wrote an elegy on Saul and **Jonathan** (1) (2 Sam. 1:19ff.).

2. Saul of Tarsus (Ac. 9:11); *see* **Paul**.

SCEVA: A Jewish exorcist in Ephesus, whose sons vainly tried to exorcise evil spirits in the name of 'the Jesus whom Paul preaches' (Ac. 19:13ff.).

SEBA: Son of **Cush** (1) (Gen. 10:7; 1 Chr. 1:9). He gave his name to the Sabaeans.

SECUNDUS: A Thessalonian companion of **Paul** (Ac. 20:4).

SEGUB: 1. Son of **Hiel**, who lost his life when Jericho was rebuilt (1 Kg. 16:34).

2. A Judahite (1 Chr. 2:21f.).

SEIR: A Horite (Gen. 36:20f.; 1 Chr. 1:38).

SELED: A Jerahmeelite (1 Chr. 2:30).

SELEMIA: One of the scribes of **Ezra** (1) (2 Esd. 14:24).

SELEUCUS: 1. Seleucus I, Nicator, an officer of **Alexander** (1), who established himself as ruler of Syria and much of the eastern part of Alexander's empire after the conqueror's death. He is alluded to, but not by name, in Dan. 8:8, 11:4f.; 1 Mac. 1:8f. The dynasty he founded is called the Seleucid dynasty.

2. Seleucus II, Callinicus, son of **Antiochus** (2) and great-grandson of 1. His war with **Ptolemy** (3) is alluded to in Dan. 11:7ff.

3. Seleucus III, Ceraunus, son of 2. He was one of the sons referred to in Dan. 11:10, **Antiochus** (3) being the other.

4. Seleucus IV, Philopator, son of **Antiochus** (3). He is the exactor of tribute mentioned in Dan. 11:20. He dispatched **Heliodorus** to plunder the Temple (2 Mac. 3:7ff.), and was afterwards murdered by Heliodorus (cf. Dan. 11:20).

SEMACHIAH: A Korahite gatekeeper (1 Chr. 26:7).

SEMEIN: An ancestor of Jesus (1) (Lk. 3:26).

SENAAH: Ancestor of some who returned with **Zerubbabel** (Ezr. 2:35; Neh. 7:38; 1 Esd. 5:23); perhaps the same as **Hassenaah** in Neh. 3:3.

SENNACHERIB: Son of **Sargon** and king of Assyria, contemporary with Hezekiah (1) (2 Kg. 18:13). **Merodach-baladan** revolted against him and established himself in Babylon, and his ambassage to Hezekiah (2 Kg. 20:12ff.; Isa. 39:1ff.) was doubtless to foster trouble for Assyria in the west also. Hezekiah rebelled against him (2 Kg. 18:7) and Sennacherib overran the country (2 Kg. 18:13; Isa. 36:1), and Hezekiah submitted and paid an indemnity (2 Kg. 18:14ff.). Later Sennacherib sent an army to occupy Jerusalem and **Isaiah** encouraged Hezekiah to refuse it entry (2 Kg. 19:1ff.; 2 Chr. 32:9ff.; Isa. 37:1ff.) and Jerusalem was miraculously delivered (2 Kg. 19:35; Isa. 37:36). Some years later Sennacherib was murdered (2 Kg. 19:37; Isa. 37:38).

SEORIM: Head of a priestly course (1 Chr. 24:8).

SERAH: Daughter of **Asher** (Gen. 46:17; Num. 26:46; 1 Chr. 7:30).

SERAIAH: 1. David's secretary (2 Sam. 8:17); called **Shavsha** in 1 Chr. 18:16, **Sheva** (2) in 2 Sam. 20:25. He is probably the same as **Shisha** in 1 Kg. 4:3.
    2. Chief priest at the time of the fall of Jerusalem, who was put to death at Riblah by **Nebuchadrezzar** (2 Kg. 25:18, 21; Jer. 52:24, 27). He was an ancestor of **Ezra** (1) (Ezr. 7:1; 1 Esd. 8:1; 2 Esd. 1:1). He is mentioned in 1 Chr. 6:14; 1 Esd. 5:5.
    3. One who joined **Gedaliah** (1) at Mizpah (2 Kg. 25:23; Jer. 40:8).
    4. A Judahite (1 Chr. 4:13f.).
    5. A Simeonite (1 Chr. 4:35).
    6. One who returned with **Zerubbabel** (Ezr. 2:2; 1 Esd. 5:8); called **Azariah** (22) in Neh. 7:7. He is mentioned also in Neh. 12:1, 12.
    7. One who sealed the covenant (Neh. 10:2).
    8. A post-exilic priest (Neh. 11:11); called **Azariah** (10) in 1 Chr. 9:11.
    9. One of those sent to arrest **Jeremiah** (1) (Jer. 36:26).
    10. Quartermaster under **Zedekiah** (2) to whom **Jeremiah** (1) delivered an oracle (Jer. 51:59ff.).

SERED: Son of **Zebulun** (Gen. 46:14; Num. 26:26).

SERGIUS PAULUS: *See* **Paulus.**

SERON: Syrian general defeated by **Judas** (1) (1 Mac. 3:13, 23f.).

SERUG: A descendant of **Shem** (Gen. 11:20ff.; 1 Chr. 1:26; Lk. 3:35).

SESTHEL: One who married a foreign wife (1 Esd. 9:31); called **Bezalel** (2) in Ezr. 10:30.

SETH: Son of **Adam** (Gen. 4:25f., 5:3ff.; 1 Chr. 1:1; Lk. 3:38). He is declared 'honoured among men' in Sir. 49:16.

SETHUR: The Asherite spy (Num. 13:13).

SHAAPH: 1. A Calebite (1 Chr. 2:47).
2. Another Calebite (1 Chr. 2:49).

SHAASHGAZ: Eunuch of **Ahasuerus** (1) (Est. 2:14).

SHABBETHAI: 1. A Levite who opposed **Ezra** (1) on mixed marriages (Ezr. 10:15; cf. 1 Esd. 9:14). He helped to expound the Law (Neh. 8:7; 1 Esd. 9:48).
2. A Levite chief in Jerusalem (Neh. 11:16); possibly the same as 1.

SHADRACH: One of the companions of **Daniel** (5) (Dan. 1:7). His Hebrew name was **Hananiah** (15) (Dan. 1:6f., 11, 19). He was cast into the fire for refusing to worship the image of **Nebuchadnezzar** (Dan. 3:20ff.), and praised God (S 3 Ch. 28ff.).

SHAGEE: Father of **Jonathan** (6) (1 Chr. 11:34).

SHAHARAIM: A Benjaminite (1 Chr. 8:8).

SHALLUM: 1. Assassin of **Zechariah** (1) (2 Kg. 15:10). He reigned over Israel for one month (2 Kg. 15:13).
2. Name of **Jehoahaz** (2) in Jer. 22:10ff.; 1 Chr. 3:15.
3. Husband of **Huldah** (2 Kg. 22:14; 2 Chr. 34:22).
4. A Jerahmeelite (1 Chr. 2:40f.).
5. A Simeonite (1 Chr. 4:25).
6. A priest, ancestor of **Ezra** (1) (1 Chr. 6:12f.; Ezr. 7:2; 1 Esd. 8:1; 2 Esd. 1:1; Bar. 1:7).
7. Son of **Naphtali** (1 Chr. 7:13); called **Shillem** in Gen. 46:24; Num. 26:49.
8. A gatekeeper who returned with **Zerubbabel** (Ezr. 2:42; Neh. 7:45; 1 Esd. 5:28).
9. A Korahite gatekeeper (1 Chr. 9:17, 19, 31); perhaps the same as **Meshelemiah** in 1 Chr. 9:21, 26:1f., 9, and **Shelemiah** (1) in 1 Chr. 26:14.
10. Father of **Jehizkiah** (2 Chr. 28:12).
11. A gatekeeper who married a foreign wife (Ezr. 10:24; 1 Esd. 9:25).
12. A layman who married a foreign wife (Ezr. 10:42); perhaps the same as **Shemaiah** (28) in 1 Esd. 9:34.
13. One who helped to repair the wall (Neh. 3:12).
14. Another who helped to repair the wall (Neh. 3:15).
15. Uncle of **Jeremiah** (1) (Jer. 32:7).
16. Father of **Maaseiah** (20) (Jer. 35:4).

SHALMAI: Ancestor of some Temple servants who returned with **Zerubbabel** (Neh. 7:48); called **Shamlai** in Ezr. 2:46; 1 Esd. 5:30.

SHALMAN: An unknown king (Hos. 10:14); sometimes thought to be Shalmaneser.

SHALMANESER: Shalmaneser V, king of Assyria, son of Tiglath-pileser. Hoshea (2) rebelled against him and he besieged Samaria (2 Kg. 17:3f., 18:9), but died before the city fell. *See* Sargon.

SHAMA: One of David's heroes (1 Chr. 11:44).

SHAMGAR: One who killed six hundred Philistines (Jg. 3:31), and in whose days lawlessness made travel dangerous (Jg. 5:6).

SHAMHUTH: One of David's monthly officers (1 Chr. 27:8); probably the same as Shammah (4) in 2 Sam. 23:25, and Shammoth in 1 Chr. 11:27.

SHAMIR: A Levite (1 Chr. 24:24).

SHAMLAI: Ancestor of some Temple servants who returned with Zerubbabel (Ezr. 2:46; 1 Esd. 5:30); called Shalmai in Neh. 7:48.

SHAMMA: An Asherite (1 Chr. 7:37).

SHAMMAH: 1. An Edomite (Gen. 36:13; 1 Chr. 1:37).
2. Brother of David (1 Sam. 16:9, 17:13); called Shimeah (1) in 2 Sam. 13:3, Shimea (1) in 1 Chr. 2:13, 20:7, and Shimei (3) in 2 Sam. 21:21.
3. One of David's heroes (2 Sam. 23:11f.). He fought heroically against the Philistines, but this feat is attributed to Eleazar (3) in 1 Chr. 11:13f.
4. Another of David's heroes (2 Sam. 23:25); called Shammoth in 1 Chr. 11:27, and probably the same as Shamhuth in 1 Chr. 27:8.

SHAMMAI: 1. A Jerahmeelite (1 Chr. 2:28, 32).
2. A Calebite (1 Chr. 2:44f.).
3. A Judahite (1 Chr. 4:17).

SHAMMOTH: One of David's heroes (1 Chr. 11:27); called Shammah (4) in 2 Sam. 23:25, and probably the same as Shamhuth in 1 Chr. 27:8.

SHAMMUA: 1. The Reubenite spy (Num. 13:4).
2. Son of David (2 Sam. 5:14); called Shimea (2) in 1 Chr. 3:5.
3. A Levite (Neh. 11:17); called Shemaiah (6) in 1 Chr. 9:16.
4. A priestly head (Neh. 12:18).

SHAMSHERAI: A Benjaminite (1 Chr. 8:26).

SHAPHAM: A Gadite (1 Chr. 5:12).

SHAPHAN: 1. Secretary of Josiah (1) who was sent to Hilkiah (2) (2 Kg. 22:3ff.; 2 Chr. 34:8ff.). His sons were Ahikam, Elasah (2) and Gemariah (1), and his grandsons Gedaliah (1) and Micaiah (7).
2. Father of Jaazaniah (3) (Ezek. 8:11).

SHAPHAT: 1. The Simeonite spy (Num. 13:5).
2. Father of Elisha (1 Kg. 19:16, 19; 2 Kg. 3:11, 6:31).
3. A descendant of David (1 Chr. 3:22).
4. A Gadite (1 Chr. 5:12).
5. A herdsman of David (1 Chr. 27:29).
6. Ancestor of some of Solomon's servants who returned with Zerubbabel (1 Esd. 5:34).

SHARAI: One who married a foreign wife (Ezr. 10:40).

SHARAR: Father of Ahiam (2 Sam. 23:33); called Sachar (1) in 1 Chr. 11:35.

SHAREZER: 1. Son of Sennacherib who with his brother murdered their father (2 Kg. 19:17; Isa. 37:38).
2. One sent from Bethel to inquire of the Lord (Zech. 7:2).

SHASHAI: One who married a foreign wife (Ezr. 10:40; 1 Esd. 9:34).

SHASHAK: A Benjaminite (1 Chr. 8:14, 25).

SHAUL: 1. An Edomite king (Gen. 36:37f.; 1 Chr. 1:48f.).
2. Son of Simeon (1) (Gen. 46:10; Exod. 6:15; Num. 26:13; 1 Chr. 4:24).
3. An ancestor of Samuel (1 Chr. 6:24); called Joel (6) in 1 Chr. 6:36.

SHAVSHA: David's secretary (1 Chr. 18:16); called Seraiah (1) in 2 Sam. 8:17, and Sheva (2) in 2 Sam. 20:25. He is probably the same as Shisha in 1 Kg. 4:3.

SHEAL: One who married a foreign wife (Ezr. 10:29; 1 Esd. 9:30).

SHEALTIEL: 1. Father of Zerubbabel (Ezr. 3:2, 8, 5:2; Neh. 12:1; Hag. 1:1ff.; Mt. 1:12; Lk. 3:27). See Pedaiah (2).
2. Another name for Ezra (1) (2 Esd. 3:1).

SHEARIAH: A descendant of Saul (1) (1 Chr. 8:38, 9:44).

SHEAR-JASHUB: A symbolic name given by Isaiah to his son (Isa. 7:3).

SHEBA: 1. A rebel against David (2 Sam. 20:1ff.). Amasa (1) dealt feebly with the rising and was treacherously slain by Joab (1) (2 Sam. 20:8ff.), who speedily suppressed the rebellion (2 Sam. 20:10ff.). Sheba was beheaded in Abel of Beth-maacah and his head thrown over the wall (2 Sam. 20:22).
2. A Gadite (1 Chr. 5:13).
3. Queen of Sheba, an unnamed queen who visited Solomon (1 Kg. 10:1ff.), probably on a trading mission.
4. Son of Joktan (Gen. 10:28; 1 Chr. 1:22) or Jokshan (Gen. 25:3; 1 Chr. 1:32) and eponymous ancestor of an Arabian tribe.

SHEBANIAH: 1. A priest of the time of David (1 Chr. 15:24).
2. A Levite who was present at the reading of the Law (Neh. 9:4f.).
3. A priest who sealed the covenant (Neh. 10:4); perhaps the same as in Neh. 12:14.

4. A Levite who sealed the covenant (Neh. 10:10).

5. Another Levite who sealed the covenant (Neh. 10:12).

SHEBER: A Calebite (1 Chr. 2:48).

SHEBNA: Steward of Hezekiah (1), denounced by Isaiah (Isa. 22:15ff.); called Shebnah in 2 Kg. 18:26, but Shebna in 2 Kg. 18:37 and elsewhere. He is described as secretary in 2 Kg. 18:18, 26, 37, 19:2; Isa. 36:3, 11, 22, 37:2.

SHEBNAH: *See* Shebna.

SHEBUEL: 1. Son of Gershom (1) (1 Chr. 23:16, 26:24); called Shubael (1) in 1 Chr. 24:20.

2. A Levite musician (1 Chr. 25:4); called Shubael (2) in 1 Chr. 25:20.

SHECANIAH: 1. A descendant of Zerubbabel (1 Chr. 3:21f.; cf. Ezr. 8:3; 1 Esd. 8:29) and father of Shemaiah (18) (Neh. 3:29).

2. Head of a priestly course (1 Chr. 24:11).

3. A priest in the time of Hezekiah (1) (2 Chr. 31:15).

4. One who returned with Ezra (1) (Ezr. 8:5; 1 Esd. 8:32).

5. Father-in-law of Tobiah (2) (Neh. 6:18).

6. One who married a foreign wife (Ezr. 10:2; 1 Esd. 8:92).

7. A priest who returned with Zerubbabel (Neh. 12:3).

SHECHEM: 1. Son of Hamor (Gen. 33:19, 34:2, 4, 13; Jos. 24:32; Jg. 9:28).

2. A Manassite head, parallel to Shemida (Num. 26:31; Jos. 17:2) or the son of Shemida (1 Chr. 7:19).

SHEDEUR: Father of Elizur (Num. 1:5, 2:10, 7:30, 35, 10:18).

SHEERAH: Daughter of Ephraim (1 Chr. 7:24).

SHEHARIAH: A Benjaminite (1 Chr. 8:26).

SHELAH: 1. A descendant of Shem (Gen. 10:24, 11:13ff.; 1 Chr. 1:18, 24; Lk. 3:35).

2. Son of Judah (1) (Gen. 38:5, 11, 46:12; Num. 26:20; 1 Chr. 2:3, 4:21). He was withheld from Tamar (1) (Gen. 38:14, 26).

SHELEMAIAH: 1. Father of Zechariah (9) (1 Chr. 26:14); called Meshelemiah in 1 Chr. 9:21, 26:1f., 9. He is perhaps the same as Shallum (9) in 1 Chr. 9:17, 19, 31.

2. One who married a foreign wife (Ezr. 10:39; 1 Esd. 9:34).

3. Another who married a foreign wife (Ezr. 10:41).

4. Father of Hananiah (7) (Neh. 3:30).

5. A priest appointed treasurer by Nehemiah (2) (Neh. 13:13).

6. Ancestor of Jehudi (Jer. 36:14).

7. One of those sent to arrest Jeremiah (1) (Jer. 36:26).

8. Father of Jehucal (Jer. 37:3).

9. Father of Irijah (Jer. 37:13).

SHELEPH: Son of Joktan (Gen. 10:26; 1 Chr. 1:20).

SHELESH: An Asherite (1 Chr. 7:35).

SHELOMI: Father of Ahihud (1) (Num. 34:27).

SHELOMITH: 1. Mother of one who blasphemed and was stoned (Lev. 24:11).
   2. Daughter of Zerubbabel (1 Chr. 3:19).
   3. A Levite (1 Chr. 23:18); called Shelomoth (2) in 1 Chr. 24:22.
   4. Son or daughter of Rehoboam (2 Chr. 11:20).
   5. One who returned with Ezra (1) (Ezr. 8:10; 1 Esd. 8:36).

SHELOMOTH: 1. A Levite of the time of David (1 Chr. 23:9).
   2. A Levite (1 Chr. 24:22); called Shelomith (3) in 1 Chr. 23:18.
   3. A descendant of Moses (1 Chr. 26:25f., 28).

SHELUMIEL: Representative of Simeon (1) at the census in the wilderness (Num. 1:6) and on other occasions (Num. 2:12, 7:36, 41, 10:19).

SHEM: Son of Noah (1) (Gen. 5:32, 6:10, 7:13; 1 Chr. 1:4; Lk. 3:36). He showed modesty when his father was drunk (Gen. 9:23).

SHEMA: 1. A Calebite (1 Chr. 2:43f.).
   2. A Reubenite (1 Chr. 5:8).
   3. A Benjaminite, one of those who routed the Gittites (1 Chr. 8:13); called Shimei (10) in 1 Chr. 8:21.
   4. One who stood on the right of Ezra (1) at the reading of the Law (Neh. 8:4; 1 Esd. 9:43).

SHEMAAH: A Benjaminite (1 Chr. 12:3).

SHEMAIAH: 1. A prophet who warned Rehoboam not to attempt to suppress the revolt of the northern tribes (1 Kg. 12:22ff.; 2 Chr. 11:2ff.). He delivered a further message to Rehoboam in 2 Chr. 12:5ff., and wrote a history of Rehoboam's reign (2 Chr. 12:15).
   2. A descendant of Zerubbabel (1 Chr. 3:21f.).
   3. A Simeonite (1 Chr. 4:37).
   4. A Reubenite (1 Chr. 5:4).
   5. A Levite in post-exilic times (1 Chr. 9:14; Neh. 11:15).
   6. Father of Obadiah (5) (1 Chr. 9:16); called Shammua in Neh. 11:17.
   7. A Levite in the time of David (1 Chr. 15:8, 11).
   8. A Levite scribe in the time of David (1 Chr. 24:6). He was the son of Nethanel (4).
   9. A Levite gatekeeper (1 Chr. 26:4, 6f.).
   10. One who taught the Law in the time of Jehoshaphat (4) (2 Chr. 17:8).
   11. A Levite in the time of Hezekiah (1) (2 Chr. 29:14).
   12. A Levite who distributed the freewill offerings in the time of Hezekiah (1) (2 Chr. 31:15).
   13. A Levite chief in the time of Josiah (1) (2 Chr. 35:9; 1 Esd. 1:9).

14. One who returned with **Ezra** (1) (Ezr. 8:13; 1 Esd. 8:39).

15. One sent for by **Ezra** (1) (Ezr. 8:16; 1 Esd. 8:44).

16. A priest who married a foreign wife (Ezr. 10:21; 1 Esd. 9:21).

17. A layman who married a foreign wife (Ezr. 10:31); perhaps the same as **Sabbaias** in 1 Esd. 9:32.

18. One who helped to repair the wall (Neh. 3:29).

19. A prophet hired by **Sanballat** to frighten **Nehemiah** (2) (Neh. 6:10ff.).

20. A priest who sealed the covenant (Neh. 10:8).

21. A priest who returned with **Zerubbabel** (Neh. 12:6, 18); perhaps also mentioned in Neh. 12:35.

22. A prince of Judah who shared in the dedication of the wall (Neh. 12:34).

23. A musician who shared in the dedication of the wall (Neh. 12:36).

24. Another who did the same (Neh. 12:42).

25. Father of **Uriah** (5) (Jer. 26:20).

26. A prophet in Babylon who opposed **Jeremiah** (1) (Jer. 29:24ff.).

27. Father of **Delaiah** (5) (Jer. 36:12).

28. One who married a foreign wife (1 Esd. 9:34); perhaps the same as **Shallum** (12) in Ezr. 10:42.

29. A relative of **Tobias** (1) (Tob. 5:13).

SHEMARIAH: 1. A Benjaminite who joined **David** at Ziklag (1 Chr. 12:5).

2. Son of **Rehoboam** (2 Chr. 11:19).

3. One who married a foreign wife (Ezr. 10:32).

4. Another who married a foreign wife (Ezr. 10:41).

SHEMEBER: King of Zeboiim, defeated by **Chedorlaomer** and his allies (Gen. 14:2ff.).

SHEMED: A Benjaminite (1 Chr. 8:12).

SHEMER: 1. Owner of the site of Samaria (1 Kg. 16:24).

2. A Levite (1 Chr. 6:46).

3. An Asherite (1 Chr. 7:34); called **Shomer** (2) in 1 Chr. 7:32.

SHEMIDA: A Manassite (Num. 26:32; Jos. 17:2; 1 Chr. 7:19).

SHEMIRAMOTH: 1. A Levite musician in the time of **David** (1 Chr. 15:18, 20, 16:5).

2. A Levite who taught the Law in the time of **Jehoshaphat** (4) (2 Chr. 17:8).

SHEMUEL: 1. The representative of Simeon for the division of the land (Num. 34:20).

2. A man of Issachar (1 Chr. 7:2).

SHENAZZAR: Son of **Jehoiachin** (1 Chr. 3:18); perhaps the same as **Sheshbazzar**.

SHEPHATIAH: 1. Son of David (2 Sam. 3:4; 1 Chr. 3:3).
2. A Benjaminite (1 Chr. 9:8).
3. A Benjaminite who joined David at Ziklag (1 Chr. 12:5).
4. A Simeonite (1 Chr. 27:16).
5. Son of Jehoshaphat (4) (2 Chr. 21:2).
6. Ancestor of some who returned with Zerubbabel (Ezr. 2:4; Neh. 7:9; 1 Esd. 5:9) and with Ezra (1) (Ezr. 8:8; 1 Esd. 8:34).
7. Ancestor of some of Solomon's servants who returned with Zerubbabel (Ezr. 2:57; Neh. 7:59; 1 Esd. 5:33).
8. A Judahite (Neh. 11:4).
9. One who urged Zedekiah (2) to put Jeremiah (1) to death (Jer. 38:1ff.).

SHEPHI: A Horite (1 Chr. 1:40); called Shepho in Gen. 36:23.

SHEPHO: *See* Shephi.

SHEPHUPHAM: Son of Benjamin (1) (Num. 26:39); called Muppim in Gen. 46:21, Shuppim (1) in 1 Chr. 7:12, 15, and Shephuphan in 1 Chr. 8:5.

SHEPHUPHAN: *See* Shephupham.

SHEREBIAH: 1. A Levite who joined Ezra (1) (Ezr. 8:18; 1 Esd. 8:47) and to whom the sacred vessels were entrusted (Ezr. 8:24f.; 1 Esd. 8:54f.). He expounded the Law (Neh. 8:7; 1 Esd. 9:48) and was present when it was read (Neh. 9:4f.).
2. One who sealed the covenant (Neh. 10:12).
3. A Levite who returned with Zerubbabel (Neh. 12:8).
4. A Levite in the days of Joiakim (Neh. 12:24).

SHERESH: A Manassite (1 Chr. 7:16).

SHESHAI: A descendant of Anak at Hebron (Num. 13:22), driven out by Caleb (Jos. 15:14; Jg. 1:10).

SHESHAN: A Jerahmeelite (1 Chr. 2:31, 34f.).

SHESHBAZZAR: A prince of Judah (Ezr. 1:8) who was appointed governor (Ezr. 5:14; 1 Esd. 2:12, 6:18). Cyrus delivered the sacred vessels to him (Ezr. 1:8; 1 Esd. 2:12ff., 6:18) and he brought them to Jerusalem (Ezr. 1:11; 1 Esd. 2:15). He also laid the foundations of the Temple (Ezr. 5:16; 1 Esd. 6:20). He is perhaps to be identified with Shenazzar (1 Chr. 3:18), in which case he was the son of Jehoiachin. Zerubbabel would then be his nephew. In Ezr. 3:8 Zerubbabel is said to have made a beginning with the rebuilding of the Temple (cf. Ezr. 5:2), but it is probable that Zerubbabel succeeded Sheshbazzar as governor and belonged to the reign of Darius (1) and that little progress had been made in the reign of Cyrus.

SHETH: An else unknown name used parallel to Moab in Num. 24:17.

SHETHAR: One of the seven princes of **Ahasuerus (1)** (Est. 1:14).

SHETHAR-BOZENAI: One of those who wrote to **Darius (1)** about the rebuilding of the Temple (Ezr. 5:3, 6, 6:6, 13); called **Sathrabuzanes** in 1 Esd. 6:3, 7, 27, 7:1.

SHEVA: 1. A Calebite (1 Chr. 2:49).
  2. David's secretary (2 Sam. 20:25); called **Seraiah (1)** in 2 Sam. 8:17, and **Shavsha** in 1 Chr. 18:16. He is probably the same as **Shisha** in 1 Kg. 4:3.

SHILHI: Father-in-law of Asa (1) (1 Kg. 22:42; 2 Chr. 20:31).

SHILLEM: Son of **Naphtali** (Gen. 46:24; Num. 26:49); called **Shallum (7)** in 1 Chr. 7:13.

SHILSHAH: An Aaronite (1 Chr. 7:37).

SHIMEA: 1. Brother of **David** (1 Chr. 2:13, 20:7); called **Shammah (2)** in 1 Sam. 16:9, 17:3, **Shimeah (1)** in 2 Sam. 13:3, and **Shimei (3)** in 2 Sam. 21:21.
  2. Son of **David** (1 Chr. 3:5); called **Shammua (2)** in 2 Sam. 5:14.
  3. A Levite (1 Chr. 6:30).
  4. Another Levite (1 Chr. 6:39).

SHIMEAH: 1. *See* **Shimea (1)**.
  2. A Benjaminite (1 Chr. 8:32); called **Shimeam** in 1 Chr. 9:38.

SHIMEAM: *See* **Shimeah (2)**.

SHIMEATH: Father of **Jozacar** (2 Kg. 12:21) or **Zabad (4)** (2 Chr. 24:26).

SHIMEI: 1. Grandson of **Levi (1)** (Exod. 6:17; Num. 3:18; 1 Chr. 6:17, 23:7, 9f.).
  2. A Benjaminite of the family of **Saul (1)** who cursed **David** when he fled before **Absalom (1)** (2 Sam. 16:5ff.) and begged forgiveness when **David** returned (2 Sam. 19:16ff.). At his death **David** advised **Solomon** to take vengeance on **Shimei** (1 Kg. 2:8ff.), which he did (1 Kg. 2:36ff.).
  3. Brother of **David** (2 Sam. 21:21); *see* **Shimea (1)**.
  4. A supporter of **Solomon** at his accession (1 Kg. 1:8). He became **Solomon's** officer in Benjamin (1 Kg. 4:18).
  5. Brother of **Zerubbabel** (1 Chr. 3:19).
  6. A Simeonite (1 Chr. 4:26f.).
  7. A Reubenite (1 Chr. 5:4).
  8. A Merarite Levite (1 Chr. 6:29).
  9. Great-grandson of **Levi (1)** (1 Chr. 6:42).
  10. One of the Benjaminites who routed the Gittites (1 Chr. 8:21); called **Shema (3)** in 1 Chr. 8:13.
  11. Head of a division of Levites (1 Chr. 25:17).
  12. One who had charge of **David's** vineyards (1 Chr. 27:27).

13. A Levite of the time of Hezekiah (1) (2 Chr. 29:14), probably the one who had charge of the tithes (2 Chr. 31:12f.).
14. A Levite who married a foreign wife (Ezr. 10:23; 1 Esd. 9:23).
15. A layman who married a foreign wife (Ezr. 10:33; 1 Esd. 9:33).
16. Another layman who married a foreign wife (Ezr. 10:38; 1 Esd. 9:34).
17. An ancestor of Mordecai (2) (Est. 2:5; Ad. Est. 11:2).

SHIMEON: One who married a foreign wife (Ezr. 10:31); called Simon (1) Chosamaeus in 1 Esd. 9:32.

SHIMON: A Judahite (1 Chr. 4:20).

SHIMRATH: A Benjaminite (1 Chr. 8:21).

SHIMRI: 1. A Simeonite (1 Chr. 4:37).
2. Father of Jediael (2) (1 Chr. 11:45).
3. A Levite gatekeeper (1 Chr. 26:10).
4. A Levite of the time of Hezekiah (1) (2 Chr. 29:13).

SHIMRITH: Parent of Jehozabad (1) (2 Chr. 24:26); called Shomer (1) in 2 Kg. 12:21.

SHIMRON: Son of Issachar (Gen. 46:13; Num. 26:24; 1 Chr. 7:1).

SHIMSHAI: The scribe of Rehum (2) (Ezr. 4:8f., 17, 23; 1 Esd. 2:16f., 25).

SHINAB: King of Admah, defeated by Chedorlaomer and his allies (Gen. 14:2ff.).

SHIPHI: A Simeonite (1 Chr. 4:37).

SHIPHRAH: One of the Hebrew midwives in Egypt (Exod. 1:15).

SHIPHTAN: Father of Kemuel (2) (Num. 34:24).

SHISHA: Solomon's secretary (1 Kg. 4:3); probably the same as Seraiah (1) (1 Sam. 8:17), Sheva (2) (2 Sam. 20:25), and Shavsha (1 Chr. 18:16).

SHISHAK: The Pharaoh of Egypt to whom Jeroboam (1) fled (1 Kg. 11:40) and who attacked and despoiled Jerusalem in the reign of Rehoboam (1 Kg. 14:25ff.; 2 Chr. 12:2ff.). From his own monuments it is known that he also raided districts of northern Israel.

SHITRAI: A herdsman of David (1 Chr. 27:29).

SHIZA: Father of Adina (1 Chr. 11:42).

SHOBAB: 1. Son of David (2 Sam. 5:14; 1 Chr. 3:5, 14:4).
2. A son of Caleb (1 Chr. 2:18).

SHOBACH: Commander of the army of Hadadezer, who was wounded in battle against David and died (2 Sam. 10:16ff.); called Shophach in 1 Chr. 19:16, 18.

SHOBAI: Ancestor of some gatekeepers who returned with **Zerubbabel** (Ezr. 2:42; Neh. 7:45; 1 Esd. 5:28).

SHOBAL: 1. A Horite (Gen. 36:20, 23, 29; 1 Chr. 1:38, 40).
   2. A Calebite (1 Chr. 2:50, 52, 4:1f.).

SHOBEK: One who sealed the covenant (Neh. 10:24).

SHOBI: One who met **David** with supplies when he fled before **Absalom** (1) (2 Sam. 17:27ff.). He was the son of **Nahash** (1) and brother of **Hanun** (1) (2 Sam. 10:1; 1 Chr. 19:1f.).

SHOHAM: A Levite in the time of **David** (1 Chr. 24:27).

SHOMER: 1. Parent of **Jehozabad** (1) (2 Kg. 12:21); called **Shimrith** in 2 Chr. 24:26.
   2. An Asherite (1 Chr. 7:32); called **Shemer** (3) in 1 Chr. 7:34.

SHOPHACH: Commander of the army of **Hadadezer** (1 Chr. 19:16, 18); called **Shobach** in 2 Sam. 10:16, 18.

SHUA: 1. Father of the Canaanite wife of **Judah** (1) (Gen. 38:2, 12). She is called **Bathshua** (1) in 1 Chr. 2:3.
   2. An Asherite woman (1 Chr. 7:32).

SHUAH: Son of **Abraham** and **Keturah** (Gen. 25:2; 1 Chr. 1:32).

SHUAL: An Asherite (1 Chr. 7:36).

SHUBAEL: 1. Son of **Gershom** (1) (1 Chr. 24:20); called **Shebuel** (1) in 1 Chr. 23:16, 26:24.
   2. A Levite musician (1 Chr. 25:20); called **Shebuel** (2) in 1 Chr. 25:4.

SHUHAH: A Judahite (1 Chr. 4:11).

SHUHAM: Son of **Dan** (Num. 26:42); called **Hushim** (1) in Gen. 46:23.

SHUNI: Son of **Gad** (Gen. 46:16; Num. 26:15).

SHUPPIM: 1. A Benjaminite (1 Chr. 7:12, 15); called **Muppim** in Gen. 46:21, **Shephupham** in Num. 26:39, and **Shephuphan** in 1 Chr. 8:5.
   2. A Levite gatekeeper (1 Chr. 26:16).

SHUTHELAH: 1. An Ephraimite (Num. 26:35f.; 1 Chr. 7:20).
   2. An Ephraimite descendant of 1 (1 Chr. 7:21).

SIA: Ancestor of some Temple servants who returned with **Zerubbabel** (Neh. 7:47); called **Siaha** in Ezr. 2:44; 1 Esd. 5:29.

SIAHA: *See* **Sia**.

SIBBECAI: One of David's heroes (2 Sam. 21:18; 1 Chr. 11:29, 20:4, 27:11); called **Mebunnai** in 2 Sam. 23:27.

SIDON: A descendant of **Ham** through **Canaan** (Gen. 10:15), who gave his name to the city of Sidon.

SIHON: King of the Amorites in Transjordan, who refused to let the Israelites pass through his land and who was defeated and conquered by them (Num. 21:21ff.; Dt. 2:26ff.; Jg. 11:19ff.). His territory was included in that settled by the eastern two and a half tribes (Num. 32:33f.; Dt. 29:7; Jos. 13:8ff.).

SILAS: A Jerusalem Christian sent with **Paul** to Antioch (Ac. 15:22ff.), and then Paul's companion on his second missionary journey (Ac. 15:40). He was imprisoned with Paul at Philippi (Ac. 16:19ff.) and accompanied him to Thessalonica (Ac. 17:4) and Beroea (Ac. 17:10), but remained at Beroea (Ac. 17:14) and later joined Paul in Corinth (Ac. 18:5). In his letters Paul refers to him as **Silvanus** (2 C. 1:19; 1 Th. 1:1; 2 Th. 1:1), and this form of his name is used in 1 Peter (1 Pet. 5:12).

SILVANUS: *See* **Silas.**

SIMEON: 1. Son of **Jacob** (1) by **Leah** (Gen. 29:33). He gave his name to one of the tribes of Israel. He joined **Levi** (1) in avenging the dishonour of **Dinah** (Gen. 34:25ff.) and was cursed by Jacob (Gen. 49:5ff.). He remained in Egypt with **Joseph** (1) as a hostage (Gen. 42:24).
   2. Grandfather of **Mattathias** (1) (1 Mac. 2:1).
   3. The righteous and devout man who blessed **Jesus** (1) in the Temple when He was an infant (Lk. 2:25ff.).
   4. An ancestor of **Jesus** (1) (Lk. 3:30).

SIMON: 1. Simon Chosamaeus, one who married a foreign wife (1 Esd. 9:32); called **Shimeon** in Ezr. 10:31.
   2. High Priest, son of **Onias** (2), praised in Sir. 50:1ff.
   3. Son of **Mattathias** (1) and surnamed Thassi (1 Mac. 2:3). He succeeded **Jonathan** (15) in the high priesthood and the leadership of the Jews (1 Mac. 13:8, 14:41ff.). He furthered the fortunes of the Jews by diplomacy and by arms (1 Mac. 13ff.) until he was treacherously murdered by his son-in-law, **Ptolemy** (9) (1 Mac. 16:19ff.).
   4. A Benjaminite, who reported to **Apollonius** (1) on the Temple treasures (2 Mac. 3:4ff.).
   5. *See* **Peter.**
   6. One of the twelve Apostles (Mt. 10:4; Mk 3:18; Lk. 6:15; Ac. 1:13). Before becoming a disciple of **Jesus** (1), he was a member of the extreme nationalist group of Jews known as the Zealots (Lk. 6:15; Ac. 1:13) or Cananaeans (Mt. 10:4; Mk 3:18). The two terms are identical in meaning.
   7. Brother of **Jesus** (1) (Mt. 13:55; Mk 6:3).
   8. Simon the Leper, the host of **Jesus** (1) at Bethany (Mt. 26:6; Mk 14:3), apparently in the house of **Martha** and **Mary** (3) (cf. Jn 12:2). He may have been the husband of Martha or Mary, or the father of Martha, Mary, and **Lazarus** (1).
   9. A Pharisee who entertained **Jesus** (1) (Lk. 7:40). In his home the penitent woman anointed His feet (Lk. 7:37ff.).

10. Father of Judas (5) Iscariot (Jn 13:2; cf. 6:71, 13:26).

11. A man of Cyrene, who carried the Cross of Jesus (1) (Mt. 27:32; Mk 15:21; Lk. 23:26). He was the father of Alexander (3) and Rufus (1) (Mk 15:21).

12. Simon Magus, a Samaritan magician who sought to buy the power to confer the Holy Spirit (Ac. 8:9ff.).

13. A tanner of Joppa, with whom Peter stayed (Ac. 9:43).

SIPPAI: A Philistine giant slain by Sibbecai (1 Chr. 20:4); called Saph in 2 Sam. 21:18.

SIRACH: *See* Jesus (2).

SISERA: 1. Captain of Jabin (Jg. 4:2) defeated by Deborah (2) and Barak (Jg. 4:4ff.) and killed by Jael (Jg. 4:17ff., 5:24ff.). In the Song of Deborah celebrating the victory (Jg. 5) Jabin is unmentioned and Sisera would appear to be an independent prince.

2. Ancestor of some Temple servants who returned with Zerubbabel (Ezr. 2:53; Neh. 7:55; 1 Esd. 5:32).

SISINNES: Governor of Syria and Phoenicia in the time of Darius (1) (1 Esd. 6:3, 7, 27, 7:1); called Tattenai in Ezr. 5:3, 6, 6:6, 13.

SISMAI: A Jerahmeelite (1 Chr. 2:40).

SITHRI: A Levite (Exod. 6:22).

SO: An Egyptian with whom Hoshea (2) conspired before rebelling against Assyria (2 Kg. 17:4). He is called 'king of Egypt', but it is probable that he was an Egyptian commander-in-chief.

SODI: Father of Gaddiel (Num. 13:10).

SOLOMON: Son and successor of David (1 Kg. 1:39). He was the son of Bathsheba (2 Sam. 12:24), and his elevation to the throne destroyed the expectation of Adonijah (1) that he would succeed (1 Kg. 1:5ff.). He removed Adonijah and Joab (1) (1 Kg. 2:13ff.) and also Shimei (2) (1 Kg. 2:36ff.), and achieved a reputation for wisdom (1 Kg. 4:29ff.; cf. 3:16ff.). He built the Temple and the palace (1 Kg. 5ff.; 2 Chr. 2ff.) and organized the kingdom (1 Kg. 4:7ff.). He made extensive use of forced labour (1 Kg. 9:15ff.) and developed state trading enterprises (1 Kg. 9:26ff., 10:14ff.; 2 Chr. 8:17f., 9:13ff.). The Queen of Sheba (3) visited him on a trading mission (1 Kg. 10:1ff.; 2 Chr. 9). He lost much of the empire David had built up (1 Kg. 11:14ff.) and aroused discontent within Israel (1 Kg. 11:26ff.). He is traditionally credited with the authorship of Proverbs, Ecclesiastes and the Song of Solomon.

SOPATER: A Beroean who accompanied Paul on his final journey to Jerusalem (Ac. 20:4). *See also* Sosipater.

SOPHERETH: Ancestor of some of Solomon's servants who returned with Zerubbabel (Neh. 7:57); called Hassophereth in Ezr. 2:55; 1 Esd. 5:33.

SOSIPATER: One who sent greetings to the church at Rome (Rom. 16:21); perhaps the same as **Sopater** (another form of the same name).

SOSTHENES: 1. Ruler of the synagogue at Corinth, who was beaten when the case against **Paul** was dismissed by **Gallio** (Ac. 18:17).
2. One associated with **Paul** in the first Letter to the Corinthians (1 C. 1:1).

SOSTRATUS: Captain of the citadel in Jerusalem under **Antiochus (4)** (2 Mac. 4:28f.).

SOTAI: Ancestor of some of Solomon's servants who returned with **Zerubbabel** (Ezr. 2:55; Neh. 7:57).

STACHYS: A Roman Christian greeted by **Paul** (Rom. 16:9).

STEPHANAS: A Corinthian, members of whose household were baptized by **Paul** (1 C. 1:16). They were the first converts in Achaia (1 C. 16:15). Stephanas was with Paul when he wrote (1 C. 16:17f.).

STEPHEN: One of the Seven (Ac. 6:5). He was a formidable debater (Ac. 6:9ff.) and was brought before the Council (Ac. 6:12). His speech (Ac. 7:2ff.) angered the Council (Ac. 7:54) and he was forthwith stoned (Ac. 7:58). He was the first martyr for Christ, and, like his Master, he prayed for those who killed him (Ac. 7:60).

SUAH: An Asherite (1 Chr. 7:34).

SUBAS: Ancestor of some of Solomon's servants who returned with **Zerubbabel** (1 Esd. 5:34).

SUDIAS: Ancestor of some Levites who returned with **Zerubbabel** (1 Esd. 5:26); called **Hodaviah (4)** in Ezr. 2:40, **Judah (2)** in Ezr. 3:9, **Hodevah** in Neh. 7:43, and **Joda (1)** in 1 Esd. 5:58.

SUSANNA: 1. A Jewess who was falsely accused of adultery by two elders when she refused their advances (Sus. 15ff.) and condemned to death (Sus. 41), but was delivered by **Daniel** (Sus. 47ff.).
2. One of the women who ministered to **Jesus (1)** of their means (Lk. 8:3).

SUSI: A Manassite (Num. 13:12).

SYMEON: 1. A Christian of Antioch, called **Niger** (Ac. 13:1).
2. Name of Simon **Peter** in Ac. 15:14.

SYNTYCHE: A Christian woman of Philippi, whom **Paul** urges to be reconciled to **Euodia** (Phil. 4:2f.).

T

TABBAOTH: Ancestor of some Temple servants who returned with Zerubbabel (Ezr. 2:43; Neh. 7:46; 1 Esd. 5:29).

TABEEL: 1. An official of Artaxerxes (1) (Ezr. 4:7; 1 Esd. 2:16).
  2. Father of the person Rezin (1) and Pekah proposed to make king in Jerusalem (Isa. 7:6).

TABITHA: A Christian woman of Joppa, also called Dorcas, who was raised from the dead by Peter (Ac. 9:36ff.).

TABRIMMON: Father of Benhadad (1) (1 Kg. 15:18).

TAHAN: 1. An Ephraimite (Num. 26:35).
  2. Another Ephraimite who lived much later (1 Chr. 7:25).

TAHASH: Son of Nahor (2) by Reumah (Gen. 22:24).

TAHATH: 1. A Levite (1 Chr. 6:24, 37).
  2. An Ephraimite (1 Chr. 7:20).
  3. Grandson of 2 (1 Chr. 7:20).

TAHPENES: Queen of Egypt, whose sister married Hadad (5) (1 Kg. 11:19f.).

TAHREA: Grandson of Mephibosheth (1) (1 Chr. 9:41); called Tarea in 1 Chr. 8:35.

TALMAI: 1. Descendant of Anak at Hebron (Num. 13:22), driven out by Caleb (Jos. 15:14; Jg. 1:10).
  2. King of Geshur, whose daughter Maacah (2) married David (2 Sam. 3:3, 13:37; 1 Chr. 3:2).

TALMON: 1. A gatekeeper (1 Chr. 9:17), some of whose descendants returned with Zerubbabel (Ezr. 2:42; Neh. 7:45; 1 Esd. 5:28).
  2. A gatekeeper in the time of Nehemiah (2) (Neh. 11:19, 12:25).

TAMAR: 1. A Canaanite woman who married Er (1) (Gen. 38:6) and then Onan (Gen. 38:8f.). Subsequently she bore Perez and Zerah (3) to her father-in-law, Judah (1) (Gen. 38:12ff.; Ru. 4:12; 1 Chr. 2:4; Mt. 1:3).
  2. Sister of Absalom (1), violated by Amnon (1) (2 Sam. 13:1ff.).
  3. Daughter of Absalom (1) (2 Sam. 14:27).

TAMMUZ: A Babylonian vegetation god of the fertility cult, whose death was cultically celebrated annually with mourning rites (Ezek. 8:14).

TANHUMETH: Father of Seraiah (3) (2 Kg. 25:23; Jer. 40:8).

TAPHATH: Daughter of Solomon (1 Kg. 4:11). She married Ben-abinadab.

TAPPUAH: A Calebite, son of Hebron (2) (1 Chr. 2:43).

TAREA: Grandson of Mephibosheth (1) (1 Chr. 8:35); called **Tahrea** in 1 Chr. 9:41.

TARSHISH: 1. A Benjaminite (1 Chr. 7:10).
2. One of the seven eunuchs of **Ahasuerus** (1) (Est. 1:14).

TARTAK: An else unknown god of the Avvites (2 Kg. 17:31).

TATTENAI: Governor of the province Beyond the River under **Darius** (1) (Ezr. 5:3, 6, 6:6, 13); called **Sisinnes** in 1 Esd. 6:3, 7, 27, 7:1.

TEBAH: Son of Nahor (2) by **Reumah** (Gen. 22:24).

TEBALIAH: A Temple gatekeeper (1 Chr. 26:11).

TEHINNAH: A Judahite (1 Chr. 4:12).

TELAH: An Ephraimite (1 Chr. 7:25).

TELEM: A gatekeeper who married a foreign wife (Ezr. 10:24; 1 Esd. 9:25).

TEMA: Son of Ishmael (1) (Gen. 25:15; 1 Chr. 1:30). He gave his name to an Arabian oasis.

TEMAH: Ancestor of some Temple servants who returned with **Zerubbabel** (Ezr. 2:53; Neh. 7:55; 1 Esd. 5:32).

TEMAN: Grandson of Esau (Gen. 36:11; 1 Chr. 1:36) and an Edomite chief (Gen. 36:15; 1 Chr. 1:53).

TEMENI: A Judahite (1 Chr. 4:6).

TERAH: Father of Abraham (Gen. 11:26; 1 Chr. 1:26f.; Lk. 3:34). He migrated with Abraham and Lot from Ur to Haran, where he died at the age of 205 (Gen. 11:31f.). He is said to have served other gods (Jos. 24:2).

TERESH: A eunuch of Ahasuerus (1) who plotted against the king (Est. 2:21); called **Tharra** in Ad. Est. 12:1.

TERTIUS: The scribe who wrote the Letter to the Romans and who sent his personal greeting (Rom. 16:22).

TERTULLUS: The spokesman for the Jews against **Paul** before Felix (Ac. 24:1ff.).

THADDAEUS: One of the twelve Apostles of Jesus (1) (Mt. 10:3; Mk 3:8); called **Judas** (6) in Lk. 6:16; Ac. 1:13.

THARRA: A eunuch of Ahasuerus (1) (Ad. Est. 12:1); called **Teresh** in Est. 2:21.

THASSI: Surname of Simon (3) (1 Mac. 2:3).

THEODOTUS: One of the envoys sent by **Nicanor** (1) to **Judas** (1) (2 Mac. 14:19).

THEOPHILUS: The person to whom the Gospel according to Luke and the Acts of the Apostles are addressed (Lk. 1:3; Ac. 1:1).

THEUDAS: A Jewish nationalist leader who raised a rebellion against the Romans before **Judas** (8), mentioned by **Gamaliel** (2) in Ac. 5:36. Nothing is known of this rising from any other source, but there were many abortive risings. A rising by Theudas some ten years after the speech of Gamaliel is known. The rising of Judas was about thirty years before the speech of Gamaliel.

THOMAS: One of the twelve Apostles of **Jesus** (1) (Mt. 10:3; Mk 3:18; Lk. 6:15; Ac. 1:13). His name probably means 'twin' and he is called the Twin in Jn 11:16, 20:24, 21:2. He speaks to the other disciples before Jesus goes to raise **Lazarus** (1) (Jn 11:16) and to Jesus at the Last Supper (Jn 14:5). He was not present when Jesus appeared to the other disciples and was sceptical (Jn 20:24ff.), but his doubts were later resolved (Jn 20:26ff.). He was present by the Sea of Tiberias when Jesus appeared (Jn 21:2). Tradition attributes to him the preaching of the Gospel in India.

TIBERIUS: Roman emperor, successor of **Augustus**. He reigned A.D. 14–37. The beginning of the ministry of **John** (6) the Baptist is dated in the fifteenth year of his reign (Lk. 3:1). The references to **Caesar** in the Gospels, with the exception of Lk. 2:1, are to him.

TIBNI: A rival aspirant to the throne of Israel who was eliminated by **Omri** (1) after four years of conflict (1 Kg. 16:21ff.).

TIDAL: King of Goiim (Gen. 14:1), one of the kings defeated by **Abraham** (Gen. 14:15, 17).

TIGLATH-PILESER: King of Assyria who exacted tribute from **Mena-hem** (2 Kg. 15:19) and took the northern part of the kingdom of Israel in the reign of **Pekah** and deported the inhabitants (2 Kg. 15:29ff.), and to whom **Ahaz** (1) appealed when he was attacked by Syria and Israel (2 Kg. 16:7ff.; 2 Chr. 28:16ff.). Ahaz went to submit to him in Damascus and on his return made changes in the Temple worship (2 Kg. 16:10ff.), doubtless to conform to Assyrian patterns. He was also called **Pul** (2 Kg. 15:19; 1 Chr. 5:26), and the Chronicler corrupts his name to **Tilgath-pilneser** (1 Chr. 5:6, 26; 2 Chr. 28:20).

TIKVAH: 1. Father-in-law of **Huldah** (2 Kg. 22:14); called **Tokhath** in 2 Chr. 34:22.
    2. Father of **Jahzeiah** (Ezr. 10:15; 1 Esd. 9:14).

TILGATH-PILNESER: *See* **Tiglath-pileser**.

TILON: A Judahite (1 Chr. 4:20).

TIMAEUS: Father of **Bartimaeus** (Mk 10:46).

TIMNA: 1. A concubine of **Eliphaz** (1) (Gen. 36:12).

2. A Horite woman (Gen. 36:22; 1 Chr. 1:39).

3. An Edomite chief (Gen. 36:40; 1 Chr. 1:51).

4. Grandson of Esau (1 Chr. 1:36).

TIMON: One of the Seven (Ac. 6:5).

TIMOTHY: 1. An Ammonite enemy of Judas (1) (1 Mac. 5:6ff., 34ff.; 2 Mac. 8:30ff., 9:3, 10:24ff., 12:2ff.).

2. A native of Lystra, the son of a Gentile father and a Jewish mother (Ac. 16:1), who had been taught the Scriptures by his mother **Eunice** and his grandmother **Lois** (2 Tim. 1:5, 3:15). **Paul** circumcised him and took him as his companion (Ac. 16:3ff.). He was left in Beroea (Ac. 17:14) and joined Paul in Corinth (Ac. 18:5). He was sent from Ephesus to Macedonia (Ac. 19:22). Paul refers to his being sent to Corinth (1 C. 4:17, 16:10) and to his preaching there (2 C. 1:19), and he sent greetings to the Roman church (Rom. 16:21). Several of Paul's letters are sent in Timothy's name as well as his own (2 C. 1:1; 1 Th. 1:1; 2 Th. 1:1; Phm. 1) and two letters to him are included in the NT.

TIRAS: Son of **Japheth** (Gen. 10:2; 1 Chr. 1:5).

TIRHAKAH: King of Ethiopia (2 Kg. 19:9; Isa. 37:9), who later became the ruler of Egypt. He is mentioned in connexion with **Sennacherib's** campaign against **Hezekiah** (1). In 701 B.C., when Sennacherib is known to have attacked Jerusalem, Tirhakah was not yet on the throne, and hence it is possible that his name has been anachronistically used for that of an earlier king of the same dynasty, or that the title 'king' is proleptically applied to him. Many scholars think Sennacherib may have mounted two campaigns, but of the second there is no evidence.

TIRHANAH: Son of **Caleb** by **Maacah** (5) (1 Chr. 2:48).

TIRIA: A Judahite (1 Chr. 4:16).

TIRZAH: Daughter of **Zelophehad** (Num. 26:33, 27:1, 36:11; Josh. 17:3).

TITIUS JUSTUS: *See* **Justus** (2).

TITUS: A Greek convert (Gal. 2:3), whom **Paul** calls his true child in the faith (Tit. 1:4). He accompanied Paul and **Barnabas** to Jerusalem (Gal. 2:1), but was not compelled to be circumcised (Gal. 2:3). He is associated especially with the Corinthian church, of which he brought news to Paul (2 C. 7:6) and in which he had worked (2 C. 8:6, 23, 12:18). Paul speaks of his earnest care for the church there (2 C. 8:16) and of his joy at its state (2 C. 7:13f.). He paid a visit to Dalmatia (2 Tim. 4:10), and one of the Pastoral Letters was addressed to him (Tit. 1:4).

TITUS MANIUS: *See* **Manius**.

TOAH: A Levite (1 Chr. 6:34); perhaps the same as **Tohu in 1 Sam.** 1:1, and **Nahath** (2) in 1 Chr. 6:26.

TOB-ADONIJAH: A Levite who taught the Law in the time of Jehoshaphat (4) (2 Chr. 17:8).

TOBIAH: 1. Ancestor of some who could not prove their Israelite descent (Ezr. 2:60; Neh. 7:62; 1 Esd. 5:37).
2. An Ammonite who with **Sanballat** opposed Nehemiah (2) (Neh. 2:10, 19, 4:3, 7, 6:1, 12, 14, 17). When Nehemiah returned to Jerusalem he found Tobiah installed in a large chamber in the Temple (Neh. 13:4ff.) and forcibly ejected him (Neh. 13:8).

TOBIAS: 1. The son of **Tobit** (Tob. 1:9), who was sent to Rages to collect a debt (Tob. 4:1ff.). Accompanied by the angel **Raphael**, disguised as **Azarias** (Tob. 5:12), Tobias fulfils his mission and marries **Sarah** (2) (Tob. 6ff.).
2. Father of **Hyrcanus** (2 Mac. 3:11).

TOBIEL: Father of **Tobit** (Tob. 1:1).

TOBIJAH: 1. A Levite who taught the Law in the time of Jehoshaphat (4) (2 Chr. 17:8).
2. One who brought gifts for the Temple (Zech. 6:10, 14).

TOBIT: A pious Naphtalite Jew (Tob. 1:1ff.), who became blind (Tob. 2:10) and who had left money in trust at Rages (Tob. 4:1). He sent his son **Tobias** (1) to reclaim it (Tob. 4:2ff.), and with the help of the angel **Raphael** he not merely fulfilled his mission but cured Tobit's blindness (Tob. 11:7ff.).

TOGARMAH: Son of **Gomer** (1) (Gen. 10:3; 1 Chr. 1:6).

TOHU: An Ephraimite (1 Sam. 1:1); perhaps the same as **Nahath** (2) in 1 Chr. 6:26, and **Toah** in 1 Chr. 6:34.

TOI: King of Hamath, who congratulated **David** on his defeat of **Hadadezer** (2 Sam. 8:9f.); called **Tou** in 1 Chr. 18:9f.

TOKHATH: Father-in-law of **Huldah** (2 Chr. 34:22); called **Tikvah** (1) in 2 Kg. 22:14.

TOLA: 1. Son of **Issachar** (Gen. 46:13; Num. 26:23; 1 Chr. 7:1f.).
2. A man of Issachar and a Minor Judge (Jg. 10:1f.).

TOU: *See* **Toi**.

TROPHIMUS: A Christian from Ephesus (Ac. 21:29), who accompanied **Paul** to Jerusalem (Ac. 20:4). When Paul was seen in the city with Trophimus, the Jews thought he had taken him into the Temple and this occasioned the riot that led to Paul's arrest (Ac. 21:29ff.). In 2 Tim. 4:20 there is a reference to his being ill at Miletus.

TRYPHAENA: A Roman Christian woman greeted by **Paul** (Rom. 16:12).

TRYPHO: An officer of **Alexander** (2) who supported **Antiochus** (6) against **Demetrius** (2) (1 Mac. 11:39). He caused **Jonathan** (15) (1 Mac.

12:39ff.) and **Antiochus (6)** (1 Mac. 13:31) to be murdered and then made himself king (1 Mac. 13:32). He was driven out by **Antiochus (7)** (1 Mac. 15:10ff., 37ff.). From non-biblical sources we learn that he committed suicide.

TRYPHOSA: A Roman Christian woman greeted by **Paul** (Rom. 16:12).

TUBAL: Son of **Japheth** (Gen. 10:2; 1 Chr. 1:5).

TUBAL-CAIN: A descendant of **Cain** who forged instruments of bronze and iron (Gen. 4:22).

TYCHICUS: A man of Asia who accompanied **Paul** on his journey to Jerusalem (Ac. 20:4). He was the bearer of two of Paul's letters (Eph. 6:21f.; Col. 4:7f.) and he is described by Paul as a beloved brother and faithful minister (Eph. 6:21). He was sent to Crete (2 Tim. 4:12), and Paul planned to send him or **Artemas** to Crete (Tit. 3:12).

TYRANNUS: A person whose name was borne by the hall in which **Paul** preached in Ephesus (Ac. 19:9).

U

UCAL: One of two persons to whom **Agur's** words were addressed (Prov. 30:1).

UEL: One who married a foreign wife (Ezr. 10:34); called **Joel (15)** in 1 Esd. 9:34.

ULAM: 1. A Manassite (1 Chr. 7:16f.).
2. A Benjaminite whose sons were famous bowmen (1 Chr. 8:39f.).

ULLA: An Asherite (1 Chr. 7:39).

UNNI: A Levite musician in **David's** time (1 Chr. 15:18, 20).

UNNO: A Levite who returned with **Zerubbabel** (Neh. 12:9).

UR: Father of **Eliphal** (1 Chr. 11:35); corresponding to **Ahasbai** in 2 Sam. 23:34.

URBANUS: A Roman Christian greeted by **Paul** (Rom. 16:9).

URI: 1. Father of **Bezalel (1)** (Exod. 31:2, 35:30, 38:22; 1 Chr. 2:20; 2 Chr. 1:5).
2. Father of **Geber** (1 Kg. 4:19).
3. A gatekeeper who married a foreign wife (Ezr. 10:24).

URIAH: 1. A Hittite, husband of **Bathsheba** (2 Sam. 11:3). After **David's** adultery with Bathsheba the king sought to use Uriah to cover his sin (2 Sam. 11:6ff.), and when this failed he arranged for Uriah to be killed (1 Sam. 11:14ff.). For this he was condemned by **Nathan** (2) (1 Sam. 12:9). Uriah was one of David's heroes (2 Sam. 23:39; 1 Chr. 11:41).

2. Priest in the time of **Ahaz** (1) (2 Kg. 16:10ff.; Isa. 8:2).

3. Father of **Meremoth** (1) (Ezr. 8:33; 1 Esd. 8:62; Neh. 3:4, 21).

4. One who stood on the right of **Ezra** (1) at the reading of the Law (Neh. 8:4; 1 Esd. 9:43).

5. A prophet in the reign of **Jehoiakim** (1) whom the king sought to kill. He escaped to Egypt, but was extradited and slain (Jer. 26:20ff.).

URIEL: 1. A Levite (1 Chr. 6:24, 15:5, 11).

2. Father of **Micaiah** (3) (2 Chr. 13:2).

3. An angel sent to enlighten **Ezra** (1) (2 Esd. 4:1ff., 5:20, 10:28ff.).

UTHAI: 1. A Judahite of post-exilic days (1 Chr. 9:4).

2. One who returned with **Ezra** (1) (Ezr. 8:14; 1 Esd. 8:40).

3. Ancestor of some who returned with **Zerubbabel** (1 Esd. 5:30).

UZ: 1. Grandson of **Shem** (Gen. 10:22f.; cf. 1 Chr. 1:17).

2. Son of **Nahor** (2) and **Milcah** (1) (Gen. 22:21).

3. A Horite (Gen. 36:28).

UZAI: Father of **Palal** (Neh. 3:25).

UZAL: Son of **Joktan** (Gen. 10:27; 1 Chr. 1:21).

UZZA: 1. One whose name was given to the garden in which **Manasseh** (2) and **Amon** (1) were buried (2 Kg. 21:18, 26).

2. A Levite (1 Chr. 6:29).

3. A Benjaminite (1 Chr. 8:7).

4. Ancestor of some Temple servants who returned with **Zerubbabel** (Ezr. 2:49; Neh. 7:51; 1 Esd. 5:31).

UZZAH: One who brought the Ark from Kiriath-jearim and who fell down dead when he steadied the Ark on the cart (2 Sam. 6:3ff.; 1 Chr. 13:7ff.).

UZZI: 1. A descendant of **Aaron** (1 Chr. 6:5f., 51; Ezr. 7:4; 1 Esd. 8:2).

2. A grandson of **Issachar** (1 Chr. 7:2f.).

3. A grandson of **Benjamin** (1) (1 Chr. 7:7).

4. A Benjaminite (1 Chr. 9:8).

5. A Levite overseer (Neh. 11:22).

6. A priest in the days of **Joiakim** (Neh. 12:19, 42).

7. An ancestor of **Ezra** (1) (2 Esd. 1:2).

UZZIA: One of **David's** heroes (1 Chr. 11:44).

UZZIAH: 1. Son and successor of **Amaziah** (1), king of Judah (2 Kg. 14:21; 2 Chr. 26:1). He is also called **Azariah** (1) (2 Kg. 14:21, 15:1; cf. 15:13).

He reigned for fifty-two years (2 Kg. 15:2; 2 Chr. 26:2). He became a leper and his son, Jotham (2), was regent (2 Kg. 15:5). The Chronicler attributes his leprosy to his assumption of the priestly office (2 Chr. 26:16ff.). He also records the expansion of the power of Judah in Uzziah's reign (2 Chr. 26:6ff.). Isaiah was called to the prophetic office in the year that Uzziah died (Isa. 6:1).

2. A Levite (1 Chr. 6:24); called Azariah (9) in 1 Chr. 6:36.

3. Father of Jonathan (8) (1 Chr. 27:25).

4. A priest who married a foreign wife (Ezr. 10:21); called Azariah (26) in 1 Esd. 9:21.

5. Father of Athaiah (Neh. 11:4).

6. A magistrate of Bethulia (Jdt. 6:15, 7:23, 8:10, 28, 35, 10:6, 13:18, 14:6, 15:4).

UZZIEL: 1. Son of Kohath (Exod. 6:18, 22; Lev. 10:4; Num. 3:19, 30; 1 Chr. 6:2,18, 15:10, 23:12, 20).

2. A Simeonite leader (1 Chr. 4:42).

3. Grandson of Benjamin (1) (1 Chr. 7:7).

4. A musician, son of Heman (4) (1 Chr. 25:4); called Azarel (2) in 1 Chr. 25:18.

5. A Levite in the time of Hezekiah (1) (2 Chr. 29:14).

6. A goldsmith who helped to repair the wall (Neh. 3:8).

V

VAIZATHA: Son of Haman, slain by the Jews (Est. 9:9).

VANIAH: One who married a foreign wife (Ezr. 10:36; 1 Esd. 9:34).

VASHTI: Queen of Ahasuerus (1) who disobeyed his command and was divorced (Est. 1:9ff.).

VOPHSI: Father of Nahbi (Num. 13:14).

Z

ZAAVAN: A Horite (Gen. 36:27; 1 Chr. 1:42).

ZABAD: 1. A Jerahmeelite (1 Chr. 2:36f.).
2. An Ephraimite (1 Chr. 7:21).
3. One of David's heroes (1 Chr. 11:41).
4. One of the assassins of Jehoash (1) (2 Chr. 24:26); called Jozacar in 2 Kg. 12:21.
5. One who married a foreign wife (Ezr. 10:27; 1 Esd. 9:28).
6. Another who married a foreign wife (Ezr. 10:33; 1 Esd. 9:33).
7. A third who married a foreign wife (Ezr. 10:43; 1 Esd. 9:35).

ZABBAI: 1. One who married a foreign wife (Ezr. 10:28; 1 Esd. 9:29).
2. Father of Baruch (2) (Neh. 3:20).

ZABDI: 1. Grandfather of Achan (Jos. 7:1, 17f.); called Zimri (2) in 1 Chr. 2:6.
2. A Benjaminite (1 Chr. 8:19).
3. David's officer over the vineyards (1 Chr. 27:27).
4. A Levite (Neh. 11:17); called Zichri (5) in 1 Chr. 9:15.

ZABDIEL: 1. Father to Jashobeam (1 Chr. 27:2).
2. A priestly overseer in the time of Nehemiah (2) (Neh. 11:14).
3. An Arab who beheaded Alexander (2) (1 Mac. 11:17).

ZABUD: Son of Nathan (2) (1 Kg. 4:5).

ZACCAI: Ancestor of some who returned with Zerubbabel (Ezr. 2:9; Neh. 7:14); called Chorbe in 1 Esd. 5:12.

ZACCHAEUS: 1. A Jewish traitor slain by Judas (1) (2 Mac. 10:18ff.).
2. A tax collector who entertained Jesus (1) (Lk. 19:1ff.).

ZACCUR: 1. Father of Shammua (1) (Num. 13:4).
2. A Simeonite (1 Chr. 4:26).
3. A Merarite (1 Chr. 24:27).
4. An Asaphite (1 Chr. 25:2, 10; Neh. 12:35).
5. Ancestor of some who returned with Ezra (1) (Ezr. 8:14); called Istalcurus in 1 Esd. 8:40, where he is said to be the son of Uthai (2).
6. One who helped to repair the wall (Neh. 3:2).
7. One who sealed the covenant (Neh. 10:12).
8. Father of Hanan (9) (Neh. 13:13).
9. A Temple singer who married a foreign wife (1 Esd. 9:24).

ZADOK: 1. A priest who first appears beside Abiathar after David conquered Jerusalem (2 Sam. 8:17). He was accompanying David with the Ark when the king fled before Absalom (1), but was sent back (2 Sam.

15:24ff.). His son **Ahimaaz (2)** (2 Kg. 15:36) carried news to David (2 Sam. 17:17ff.). Zadok supported **Solomon** for the succession (1 Kg. 1:8, 32ff.), and when Abiathar was dismissed (1 Kg. 2:26ff.) he became the sole head of the Jerusalem priesthood (1 Kg. 2:35). The Chronicler traces his genealogy to **Eleazar (1)** (1 Chr. 6:4ff.).

2. Father of **Jerusha** (2 Kg. 15:33; 2 Chr. 27:1).
3. A descendant of 1 (1 Chr. 6:12).
4. A warrior who joined **David** at Hebron (1 Chr. 12:28).
5. One who helped to repair the wall (Neh. 3:4).
6. Another who helped to repair the wall (Neh. 3:29).
7. One who sealed the covenant (Neh. 10:21).
8. A scribe appointed treasurer by **Nehemiah (2)** (Neh. 13:13).
9. An ancestor of **Jesus (1)** (Mt. 1:14).

ZAHAM: Son of **Rehoboam** (2 Chr. 11:19).

ZALAPH: Father of **Hanun (3)** (Neh. 3:30).

ZALMON: One of **David's** heroes (2 Sam. 23:28); called **Ilai** in 1 Chr. 11:29.

ZALMUNNA: A Midianite king, pursued and slain by **Gideon** (Jg. 8:5ff.).

ZAPHENATH-PANEAH: Name given to **Joseph (1)** by **Pharaoh** (Gen. 41:45).

ZARIUS: Brother of **Jehoiakim (1)** (1 Esd. 1:38), said to have been brought out of Egypt. The parallel passage (2 Chr. 36:4) says the king of Egypt took **Jehoahaz (2)**, the brother of Jehoiakim, down to Egypt.

ZATTU: 1. Ancestor of some who returned with **Zerubbabel** (Ezr. 2:8; Neh. 7:13; 1 Esd. 5:12) and with **Ezra (1)** (Ezra. 8:5; 1 Esd. 8:32). Some members of the family married foreign wives (Ezr. 10:27; 1 Esd. 9:28).

2. One who sealed the covenant (Neh. 10:14).

ZAZA: A Jerahmeelite (1 Chr. 2:33).

ZEBADIAH: 1. A Benjaminite (1 Chr. 8:15).
2. Another Benjaminite (1 Chr. 8:17).
3. One who joined **David** at Ziklag (1 Chr. 12:7).
4. A Korahite gatekeeper (1 Chr. 26:2).
5. One of **David's** monthly officers (1 Chr. 27:7).
6. A Levite sent by **Jehoshaphat (4)** to teach the Law (2 Chr. 17:8).
7. Governor of the house of Judah under **Jehoshaphat (4)** (2 Chr. 19:11).
8. One who returned with **Ezra (1)** (Ezr. 8:8); called **Zeraiah** in 1 Esd. 8:34.
9. A priest who married a foreign wife (Ezr. 10:20; 1 Esd. 9:21).

ZEBAH: A Midianite king, pursued and slain by **Gideon** (Jg. 8:5ff.).

ZEBEDEE: Father of James (1) and John (7) (Mt. 4:21, 10:2; Mk 1:19f., 3:17; Lk. 5:10).

ZEBIDAH: Mother of Jehoiakim (1) (2 Kg. 23:26).

ZEBINA: One who married a foreign wife (Ezr. 10:43).

ZEBUL: Governor of Shechem under Abimelech (2) (Jg. 9:30). He helped to overthrow the plot of Gaal (Jg. 9:26ff.).

ZEBULUN: Son of Jacob (1) and Leah (Gen. 30:20, 35:23, 46:14f.). He gave his name to one of the tribes of Israel.

ZECHARIAH: 1. Son and successor of Jeroboam (2) (2 Kg. 14:29). After reigning six months he was assassinated by Shallum (1) (2 Kg. 15:10).

2. Maternal grandfather of Hezekiah (1) (2 Kg. 18:2; 2 Chr. 29:1).

3. A Reubenite (1 Chr. 5:7).

4. A gatekeeper (1 Chr. 9:21, 26:2).

5. Great-uncle of Saul (1) (1 Chr. 9:37, 39); called Zecher in 1 Chr. 8:31.

6. A Levite musician (1 Chr. 15:18, 20, 16:5).

7. A priest who took part in bringing the Ark to Jerusalem (1 Chr. 15:24).

8. A Levite (1 Chr. 24:25).

9. A Levite gatekeeper (1 Chr. 26:11).

10. Father of Iddo (3) (1 Chr. 27:21).

11. One of those sent to teach the Law by Jehoshaphat (4) (2 Chr. 17:7).

12. Father of Jahaziel (4) (2 Chr. 20:14).

13. Son of Jehoshaphat (4) (2 Chr. 21:2).

14. Son of Jehoiada (3) (2 Chr. 24:20). He prophesied against idolatry and was stoned in the court of the Temple by command of Jehoash (1) (2 Chr. 24:20ff.).

15. One who instructed Uzziah (1) in the fear of God (2 Chr. 26:5).

16. A Levite who helped to cleanse the Temple in the days of Hezekiah (1) (2 Chr. 29:13).

17. An overseer of the repair of the Temple in the days of Josiah (1) (2 Chr. 34:12).

18. A chief officer of the Temple in the days of Josiah (1) (2 Chr. 35:8; 1 Esd. 1:8).

19. A reliable witness used by Isaiah (Isa. 8:30).

20. One who returned with Ezra (1) (Ezr. 8:3; 1 Esd. 8:30).

21. Another who returned with Ezra (1) (Ezr. 8:11; 1 Esd. 8:37).

22. One of those sent to Iddo (6) (Ezr. 8:16; 1 Esd. 8:44).

23. One who married a foreign wife (Ezr. 10:26; 1 Esd. 9:27).

24. One who stood at the left hand of Ezra (1) at the reading of the Law (Neh. 8:4; 1 Esd. 9:44).

25. A Judahite (Neh. 11:4).

26. Another Judahite (Neh. 11:5).

27. A priest (Neh. 11:12).

28. A priest in the days of Joiakim (Neh. 12:16).

29. A Levite who shared in dedicating the wall (Neh. 12:35).

30. A priest who shared in dedicating the wall (Neh. 12:41).

31. A Minor Prophet, who prophesied in the days of Darius (1) (Ezr. 5:1, 6:14; Zech. 1:1). He shared with Haggai in stimulating the people to rebuild the Temple (Ezr. 6:14f.).

32. A Temple singer (1 Esd. 1:15). The name replaces Heman (4) of the parallel 2 Chr. 35:15.

33. Father of Joseph (7) (1 Mac. 5:18, 56).

34. Husband of Elizabeth and father of John (6) the Baptist (Lk. 1:5ff.). The birth of John was announced to him by Gabriel, and owing to his disbelief he became dumb until the child was named (Lk. 1:64). He then uttered the Benedictus (Lk. 1:67ff.).

35. A martyr mentioned by Jesus (1) (Mt. 23:35; Lk. 11:51). In Matthew he is said to be the son of Barachiah, and this would suggest identification with 31 above, since he is described as the son of Berechiah (Zech. 1:1). But no tradition of his martyrdom is known. It is more probable that the reference is to 14 above, and that 'son of Barachiah' (absent from Luke) is a mistaken addition in Matthew. As 2 Chronicles, which records this martyrdom, is the last book in the Hebrew Bible, it would seem that when Jesus (1) spoke of the blood shed from Abel to Zechariah He meant all the innocent blood of which the OT records the shedding.

ZECHER: Great-uncle of Saul (1) (1 Chr. 8:31, 33); called Zechariah (5) in 1 Chr. 9:37.

ZEDEKIAH: 1. A prophet in the time of Ahab (1) who urged the king to fight at Ramoth-gilead and who was opposed by Micaiah (1) (1 Kg. 22:11ff.; 2 Chr. 18:10ff.).

2. The last king of Judah. He was the uncle (2 Chr. 36:10 wrongly says brother) and successor of Jehoiachin, and his name originally was Mattaniah (1) (2 Kg. 24:17). He reigned eleven years (2 Kg. 24:18; 2 Chr. 36:11). He rebelled against Nebuchadrezzar (2 Kg. 24:20; 2 Chr. 36:13), and the Babylonian army besieged Jerusalem for a year and a half and then took it and destroyed the Temple (2 Kg. 25:1ff.; 2 Chr. 36:17ff.). He sought advice and prayer from Jeremiah (1) (Jer. 21:1ff., 37:3ff., 17ff., 38:14) and was repeatedly warned by the prophet of the consequences of his policy (Jer. 21:3ff., 24:8ff., 27:1ff., 28:1ff., 34:2ff., 37:6ff., 38:15), but the king was too weak to resist his courtiers. He imprisoned Jeremiah (Jer. 32:3), and later consented to his imprisonment (Jer. 38:5), but authorized Ebed-melech to deliver him from the cistern in which he had been placed (Jer. 38:9ff.). When Jerusalem fell, Zedekiah was taken to Riblah and his sons were slain before his eyes and then his eyes were put out and he was taken to Babylon (2 Kg. 25:6ff.; Jer. 39:5ff.).

3. One who sealed the covenant (Neh. 10:1).

4. A false prophet (Jer. 29:21ff.).

5. One of the princes of 2 who heard Baruch (1) read the scroll of Jeremiah (1) (Jer. 36:12).

6. An ancestor of Baruch (1) (Bar. 1:1).

ZEEB: A Midianite prince captured and killed by Ephraimites after Gideon's victory (Jg. 7:25, 8:3).

ZELEK: One of David's heroes (2 Sam. 23:37; 1 Chr. 11:39).

ZELOPHEHAD: A Manassite who died without male heir. His five daughters were given an inheritance (Num. 26:33, 27:1ff., 36:2ff.; Jos. 17:3; 1 Chr. 7:15).

ZEMIRAH: A Benjaminite (1 Chr. 7:8).

ZENAS: A lawyer whom Paul asks Titus to send to him from Crete (Tit. 3:13).

ZEPHANIAH: 1. A Kohathite Levite (1 Chr. 6:36).

2. A priest in the time of Zedekiah (2) (Jer. 21:1, 29:25, 29, 37:3). He was a member of a group sent by the king to Jeremiah (1) (Jer. 21:1, 37:3). He is called the second priest (2 Kg. 25:18), Seraiah (2) being the chief priest. When Jerusalem fell, he was taken to Riblah and killed (Jer. 52:24ff.).

3. A Minor Prophet, who prophesied in the days of Josiah (1) (Zeph. 1:1).

4. Father of Josiah (2) (Zech. 6:10, 14).

ZEPHI: Grandson of Esau (1 Chr. 1:36); called Zepho in Gen. 36:11, 15.

ZEPHO: See Zephi.

ZEPHON: A Gadite (Num. 26:15); called Ziphion in Gen. 46:16.

ZERAH: 1. Son of Reuel (1) (Gen. 36:13, 17; 1 Chr. 1:37).

2. Father of Jobab (2) (Gen. 36:33; 1 Chr. 1:44).

3. Son of Judah (1) by Tamar (1) and twin brother of Perez (Gen. 38:30). He was an ancestor of Achan (Jos. 7:1).

4. A Simeonite (Num. 26:13; 1 Chr. 4:24); called Zohar (2) in Gen. 46:10; Exod. 6:15.

5. A Gershonite Levite (1 Chr. 6:21, 41).

6. An Ethiopian who invaded Judah in the reign of Asa (1) (2 Chr. 14:9ff.).

ZERAHIAH: 1. An ancestor of Ezra (1) (Ezr. 7:4; cf. 1 Chr. 6:6); called Arna in 2 Esd. 1:2.

2. Father of Eliehoenai (2) (Ezr. 8:4; 1 Esd. 8:31).

ZERAIAH: One who returned with Ezra (1) (1 Esd. 8:34); called Zebadiah (8) in Ezr. 8:8.

ZERDAIAH: One who married a foreign wife (1 Esd. 9:28); called Aziza in Ezr. 10:27.

ZERESH: Wife of Haman (Est. 5:10ff., 6:13).

ZERETH: A Judahite (1 Chr. 4:7).

ZERI: A Levite musician (1 Chr. 25:3); perhaps the same as **Izri** in 1 Chr. 25:11.

ZEROR: An ancestor of **Saul** (1) (1 Sam. 9:1).

ZERUAH: Mother of **Jeroboam** (1) (1 Kg. 11:26).

ZERUBBABEL: Grandson of **Jehoiachin** (1 Chr. 3:19; Mt. 1:12) who returned from Babylon (Ezr. 2:2; Neh. 7:7; 1 Esd. 5:8) and became governor (Hag. 1:1). In 1 Esd. 3ff. he is said to have won in a trial of wits at the court of the king. In Jerusalem he was urged by **Haggai** and **Zechariah** (31) to rebuild the Temple (Hag. 1:2ff., 2:1ff.; Zech. 4:6ff.; cf. Ezr. 6:14), and he began to do so (Ezr. 5:2). He seems to have disappeared from the scene before the work was finished (Ezr. 6:14f.).

ZERUIAH: Mother of **Joab** (1), **Abishai**, and **Asahel** (1) (2 Sam. 2:18). Their father is never mentioned. Zeruiah was a sister of **David** (1 Chr. 2:16), but her sister **Abigail** (2) (1 Chr. 2:16) is elsewhere said to be a daughter of **Nahash** (2) (2 Sam. 17:25). It is possible that the mother of Zeruiah and Abigail had been married to Nahash before marrying **Jesse**, and that they were half-sisters of David.

ZETHAM: A Gershonite Levite (1 Chr. 23:8, 26:22).

ZETHAN: A Benjaminite (1 Chr. 7:10).

ZETHAR: One of the seven eunuchs of **Ahasuerus** (1) (Est. 1:10).

ZEUS: A Greek god, who was head of the pantheon. **Antiochus** (4) polluted the Temple and made it a shrine of Olympian Zeus (2 Mac. 6:2) and made the Samaritan temple a shrine of Zeus the Friend of Strangers. The people of Lystra called **Barnabas** Zeus (Ac. 14:12).

ZIA: A Gadite (1 Chr. 5:13).

ZIBA: A servant of **Saul** (1) whom **David** consulted about Saul's family (2 Sam. 9:1ff.), and who was made steward for **Mephibosheth** (1) (2 Sam. 9:9ff.). When David fled before **Absalom** (1), Ziba accused Mephibosheth of disloyalty and was given his estate (2 Sam. 16:1ff.). When David returned Mephibosheth protested his loyalty and the estate was divided between him and Ziba (2 Sam. 19:24ff.).

ZIBEON: A Horite, father of **Anah** (1) (Gen. 36:2, 14, 20, 24, 29; 1 Chr. 1:38, 40).

ZIBIA: A Benjaminite (1 Chr. 8:9).

ZIBIAH: Mother of **Jehoash** (1) (2 Kg. 12:1; 2 Chr. 24:1).

ZICHRI: 1. Grandson of **Kohath** (Exod. 6:21).
2. A Benjaminite (1 Chr. 8:19).

3. Another Benjaminite (1 Chr. 8:23).
4. A third Benjaminite (1 Chr. 8:27).
5. A Levite (1 Chr. 9. 15); called **Zabdi** (4) in Neh. 11:17.
6. A Levite, descendant of **Eliezer** (5) (1 Chr. 26:25).
7. A Reubenite, father of **Eliezer** (6) (1 Chr. 27:16).
8. A Judahite, father of **Amasiah** (2 Chr. 17:16).
9. Father of **Elishaphat** (2 Kg. 23:1).
10. An Ephraimite who slew **Maaseiah** (4) and others (2 Chr. 28:7).
11. Father of **Joel** (14) (Neh. 11:9).
12. A priest in the days of **Joiakim** (Neh. 12:17).

ZIHA: Ancestor of some Temple servants who returned with **Zerubbabel** (Ezr. 2:43; Neh. 7:46, 11:21; 1 Esd. 5:29).

ZILLAH: One of the wives of **Lamech** (1) (Gen. 4:19f.).

ZILLETHAI: 1. A Benjaminite (1 Chr. 8:20).
2. A Manassite who joined **David** at Ziklag (1 Chr. 12:20).

ZILPAH: Leah's slave girl (Gen. 29:24), who became the concubine of **Jacob** (1) (Gen. 30:9). She was the mother of **Gad** and **Asher** (Gen. 30:10ff.).

ZIMMAH: 1. A Gershonite Levite (1 Chr. 6:20; 2 Chr. 29:12).
2. Another Gershonite Levite (1 Chr. 6:42).

ZIMRAN: Son of **Abraham** by Keturah (Gen. 25:2; 1 Chr. 1:32).

ZIMRI: 1. A Simeonite slain by **Phinehas** (1) for bringing a Midianite woman into the camp (Num. 25:6ff.; 1 Mac. 2:26).
2. Grandfather of **Achan** (1 Chr. 2:6; cf. Jos. 7:1); called **Zabdi** (1) in Jos. 7:1, 17f.
3. A Benjaminite (1 Chr. 8:36, 9:42).
4. An assassin who slew **Elah** (2) (1 Kg. 16:8ff.) and who ended his own life seven days later (1 Kg. 16:15ff.). Jezebel hailed **Jehu** (2) as a Zimri (2 Kg. 9:31).

ZINA: A Gershonite Levite (1 Chr. 23:10); called **Zizah** in 1 Chr. 23:11.

ZIPH: 1. A Calebite (1 Chr. 2:42).
2. A Judahite, brother of **Ziphah** (1 Chr. 4:16).

ZIPHAH: A Judahite, brother of **Ziph** (2) (1 Chr. 4:16).

ZIPHION: A Gadite (Gen. 46:16); called **Zephon** in Num. 26:15.

ZIPPOR: Father of **Balak** (Num. 22:2, 4, 10, 16; Jos. 24:9; Jg. 11:25).

ZIPPORAH: Daughter of **Reuel** (2) or **Jethro** and wife of **Moses** (Exod. 2:21). She was the mother of **Gershom** (Exod. 2:22). She circumcised her son when the Lord sought to kill Moses (Exod. 4:24ff.). Her second son (Exod. 18:3) is not named in the Bible.

ZIZA: 1. A Simeonite (1 Chr. 4:37).
  2. Son of **Rehoboam** (2 Chr. 11:20).

ZIZAH: A Gershonite Levite (1 Chr. 23:11); called **Zina** in 1 Chr. 23:10.

ZOBEBAH: A Judahite (1 Chr. 4:8).

ZOHAR: 1. Father of **Ephron** (Gen. 23:8, 25:9).
  2. Son of **Simeon** (1) (Gen. 46:10; Exod. 6:15); called **Zerah** (4) in Num. 26:13; 1 Chr. 4:24.

ZOHETH: A Judahite (1 Chr. 4:20).

ZOPHAH: An Asherite (1 Chr. 7:35f.).

ZOPHAI: An ancestor of **Samuel** (1 Chr. 6:26); called **Zuph** in 1 Sam. 1:1; 1 Chr. 6:35.

ZOPHAR: One of the three friends of **Job** (Job 2:11), whose speeches stand in Job 11 and 20. He is condemned in Job 42:7, and Job interceded for him (Job 42:9). He is described as a Naamathite.

ZUAR: Father of **Nethanel** (1) (Num. 1:8, 2:5, 7:18, 23, 10:15).

ZUPH: Ancestor of **Samuel** (1 Sam. 1:1; 1 Chr. 6:35); called **Zophar** in 1 Chr. 6:26.

ZUR: 1. A Midianite chief whose daughter was slain by **Phinehas** (1) (Num. 25:15). Zur was himself also killed (Num. 31:8; Jos. 13:21).
  2. A Benjaminite (1 Chr. 8:30, 9:36).

ZURIEL: A Merarite Levite (Num. 3:35).

ZURISHADDAI: Father of **Shelumiel** (Num. 1:6, 2:12, 7:36, 41, 10:19).